Trials and Tribulations in the Implementation of Pre-Commercial Procurement in Europe

Ramona Apostol

Trials and Tribulations in the Implementation of Pre-Commercial Procurement in Europe

ASSER PRESS

Springer

Ramona Apostol
Corvers Procurement Services BV
's-Hertogenbosch
The Netherlands

ISBN 978-94-6265-155-5 ISBN 978-94-6265-156-2 (eBook)
DOI 10.1007/978-94-6265-156-2

Library of Congress Control Number: 2016954619

Published by T.M.C. ASSER PRESS, The Hague, The Netherlands www.asserpress.nl
Produced and distributed for T.M.C. ASSER PRESS by Springer-Verlag Berlin Heidelberg

Printed on acid-free paper

This Springer imprint is published by Springer Nature
The registered company is Springer Science+Business Media B.V.
The registered company address is: Van Godewijckstraat 30, 3311 GX Dordrecht, The Netherlands

Preface

Pre-commercial procurement (PCP) is a specific approach to the procurement of research and development (R&D) services outside the remit of the European Public Procurement Directives.

The European Commission brought this approach to the front of the innovation European policy agenda since 2007. In a Communication from 2007, the Commission explained what economic benefits the wide deployment of PCP may generate and clarified the applicable legal framework.

The European Commission's initiative was partly motivated by the desire to emulate the perceived success of the United States (US) Small Business Innovation Research (SBIR) program and partly by the desire to prevent that similar national initiatives in the United Kingdom (UK) and the Netherlands would be deployed as illegal state aid schemes. Since its 2007 Communication, the European Commission has undertaken additional efforts to encourage procurers in the European Union (EU) to engage in PCPs; It has commissioned studies with the purpose to understand the barriers to implementation and to promote good practices; it has co-funded cross-border collaborative PCPs; it has financed the drafting of a practical Toolkit which explains the steps in the deployment of a PCP and it has endorsed a team of experts to advise procurers on various aspects of implementation.

The Commission has had several attempts to assess the economic and social impacts of PCP in Europe, with mixed outcomes. This was particularly due to the limited number of projects that qualify as PCP and that have been finalized. The national R&D procurement programs (e.g. in the UK, the Netherlands and Belgium) have also come under internal scrutiny in 2014–2015, prior to deciding their continuation.

PCP in particular and R&D procurement in general are not yet established approaches in the EU. PCP is not widely implemented and the successful examples are still very few. However, partly due to the European Commission efforts, the level of interest and the level of understanding of this procedure by procurers throughout Europe are increasing.

Due to the unfolding debate on the topic, there have been so far no attempts in literature to tackle PCP from a general perspective. Only several articles have been written on PCP, mainly concerning legal aspects or its place within the innovation policy framework.

This book aims to advance the understanding of PCP as innovation policy instrument. First of all, it seeks to place PCP within its political and economic context. It elucidates its origins and its economic rationale. It provides a list of minimum requirements for the appropriate implementation of PCP policy and the appropriate deployment of PCP projects. Second, it assesses the value and achievements of similar policy programs, in the US, the UK, the Netherlands and Belgium and draws additional lessons for the effective implementation of PCP. Third, it suggests a clear conceptualization of PCP and a clear delineation from other innovation policy instruments. In this context, it highlights the gaps in the legislative framework. Fourth, it raises awareness of the remaining obstacles to its wide and effective implementation. It examines various solutions ranging from coordination measures by the European Commission to law interpretation and legislative reform.

This book can be useful to all actors involved in the setting up, coordination and assessment of PCP programs and in the implementation of PCP projects. It is also useful for teaching and training purposes.

This book makes use of illustrative practical examples of policy-making and projects implementation in various countries. Particularly the approaches and performances of the US SBIR program, the UK SBRI program, of the Dutch SBIR program and of the Flemish Procurement of Innovation (PoI) program are discussed. The analysis of these programs is used to assess the appropriateness of EU's effort to promote its own variant of R&D procurement, the PCP. But the book goes beyond presenting cases and policy or legislative frameworks. It outlines the author's own analysis and interpretation of the PCP legal frameworks and cases.

The material in the book is up to date as of July 2016.

's-Hertogenbosch, The Netherlands Ramona Apostol

Contents

Chapter 1
Introduction

Contents

1.1 Pre-Commercial Procurement ('PCP')—Definition and Background

Pre-commercial procurement ('PCP') is the model recommended by the European Commission in its 2007 PCP Communication and the afferent Staff Working Document ('SWD') for the public procurement of research and development services where the contracting authority or contracting entity shares the results and benefits of the contract with the providers under market conditions and where the purchase of commercial volumes of products or services is the object of a separate contract.[1]

PCP is part of the response to the re-evaluation of EU innovation policy that started in 2000. European policy-makers agreed that innovation leads to increased productivity and to sustained economic growth. They moreover believed that innovation can solve critical challenges for Europe's future welfare (e.g. climate change, increased and aged population, shortage of natural resources, global food security, increasing competition from developing countries etc.).[2]

However, they concluded that EU's innovation policy did not target solutions to the above mentioned challenges, but stimulated economic competitiveness in general. The employed innovation policy instruments (supply-side measures such as subsidies, tax measures etc.), which identified broad areas of interest and left

---

[1] PCP Communication 2007, p. 1.

[2] Innovation is not a goal in itself, but broadly accepted by economists as one of the key potential inputs/driving forces for sustainable economic growth. See for example Hadfield 2011; Spence 2011, p. 36.

R. Apostol, *Trials and Tribulations in the Implementation of Pre-Commercial Procurement in Europe*, DOI 10.1007/978-94-6265-156-2_1

the selection of specific research topics to the innovator, did not sufficiently incentivize the private market to upscale research and development ('R&D') investments in desired projects.[3]

In this context, demand-side instruments were assessed.[4] Public procurement of R&D services emerged as a suitable mechanism to achieve the following objectives:

- steer private innovators' efforts towards publicly desirable solutions;
- improve public services;
- eventually enhance the global competitiveness of European companies.[5]

Due to its limited competences in the area of innovation policy, the Commission used a soft-law instrument, a communication, to recommend European public procurers a specific approach to the procurement of R&D services.

The purpose of the PCP Communication was twofold. Firstly, the Commission wanted to draw attention to this untapped opportunity. Although the EU procurement rules allowed more flexibility in the conduct of R&D procurement, European public procurers had not consistently engaged in such practices.

Secondly, the Commission wanted to clarify the applicable legal framework, in order to prevent distortive implementations of R&D procurement. National programs launched in the UK in 2001 and in the Netherlands in 2004 strongly resembled subsidy schemes with little or no involvement of the public end-customer and with participation restricted to national companies.

Prior to the drafting of the PCP Communication, the Commission hired experts to investigate the potential benefits of PCP. The experts pointed out that other competing economies such as the United States ('US') succeed relatively better in 'pulling' R&D into the commercialization phase and in enhancing the international competitiveness of their domestic suppliers.[6] The experts partly attributed this success to the use of public procurement of R&D, which was a strategic part of the US Small Business Innovation Research ('SBIR') program. According to the experts, high-risk R&D procurements performed by the US Department of Defense ('DoD') led to the creation of new industries (e.g. the semiconductors industry, the Internet etc.) in which US companies became world market leaders. In their opinion, the US had used procurement of R&D strategically, '*to provide a strong home market for their domestic supplier base in well-defined areas of desired international competitiveness*'.[7] The study also confirmed that European procurers did not engage sufficiently in R&D procurement, and considerably less than their US peers.[8]

---

[3] Edler and Georghiou 2007, p. 958.

[4] Edler et al. 2012.

[5] For a more detailed discussion on this topic, see Chap. 2, Sect. 2.2.

[6] National IST Research Directors Forum Working Group on Public Procurement in support of ICT Research and Innovation [PCP Expert Group 2006].

[7] PCP Expert Group 2006.

[8] PCP Expert Group 2006.

The European Commission 'used' the success of the SBIR policies, as perceived by the experts, to justify its support for PCP deployment, without questioning whether government intervention through the SBIR-type of action would be effective in the European context.[9] Although meant to emulate the perceived success of the US SBIR, PCP was adapted by the European Commission to EU realities, made of:

- EU rules meant to maximize EU-wide competition in public contracts;
- EU rules meant to minimize public aid to national businesses;
- Limited EU competences in the area of innovation policy.

As a consequence, the resulting EU instrument embodies major differences when compared to its US counterprogram. Some of the more important differences include:

- the non-binding implementation of PCP;
- the obligation to pay a market price that reflects the pre-defined division of risks and benefits;[10]
- the prohibition to purchase the PCP innovative results without conducting a separate competitive procedure in compliance with the Procurement Directives.[11]
- the application to both technological and services sectors;[12]

The European Commission did not analyze what impact these differences may have on the potential of PCP to achieve its envisaged policy objectives.

Arguably, in the absence of extended competences to mandate or coordinate the innovation policies of its Member States, the Commission focused primarily on safeguarding open competition under market conditions, such as to prevent innovation agencies in EU Member States from granting unwarranted state funding to national companies under the label of 'R&D procurement'. Further judgments related to economic grounds or operational prerequisites for effective implementation of PCP were left to the implementing authorities.

1.2 The Reality of PCP Implementation

The Commission hoped that increased clarity on the legal conditions for implementation would be sufficient to encourage those European public procurers, who need advanced solutions to perform their operational tasks, to deploy PCPs.

---

9 European Commission [PCP Communication 2007].

10 Article 16(f) of Directive 2004/18/EC (Public Sector Directive) and Article 24(e) of Directive 2004/17/EC (Utilities Directive).

11 Commission 2007, p. 9–10.

12 Commission 2007, 3.

Despite these expectations, and despite additional efforts undertaken by the European Commission,[13] the uptake of PCP has been slow and inconsistent.[14]

Mostly PCP-'like' initiatives have so far been implemented consistently in the EU. These PCP-'like' initiatives are mainly the specialty of centralized innovation agencies.[15] They are run in a national environment, with marginal EU-wide competition and often with limited involvement of end-customers. Following internal or external evaluations throughout 2014 and 2015, the 3 most established PCP-'like' initiatives in the UK, Netherlands and Flanders are undergoing major adjustments, particularly related to minimizing the role of the coordinating innovation agency and to delegating the main responsibilities to the deploying procurers.[16] The national programs are discussed in more detail in Chap. 6 below.

Where PCP is (or has been) applied, no confirmation of its economic benefits in practice has become available. The few cases of deployed PCP-like initiatives have not yet proven that they are triggering the benefits envisaged by EU policy-makers.[17] The European Innovation Scoreboard 2016 shows that the EU has been unable in the past 8 years to close the gap with its major competitors, the US, Japan and South Korea in R&D expenditures in the business sector.[18] Apparently, the overall EU innovation policy, which includes PCP, is not inducing private businesses to scale up their investments in R&D.

Among the national PCP-'like' initiatives, only the UK SBRI has demonstrated positive impacts, in terms of incentivizing firms to conduct R&D that would otherwise not materialize and in terms of increased firm sales.[19]

In conclusion, PCP as envisaged by the European Commission, has so far not achieved the desired results in practice. Barriers to the wide implementation of PCPs persist and positive impacts are still to be proven.

---

[13] Since 2009, the European Commission funded networks of procurers to facilitate collaboration and exchange of knowledge. Since 2011, Framework Program 7 (FP7) funded the costs incurred by procuring authorities during the organisation of cross-border collaborative PCP procedures. This is carried on by the Horizon 2020 funding program.

[14] European Commission 2011; Izsak and Edler 2011, p. 22–3; Camerer and van Eijl 2011, p. 177–86. T33, Spark and Deloitte 2014, 3. Bedin et al. 2015.

[15] This book only analyses the 3 most established PCP-'like' initiatives in the UK, the Netherlands and Flanders.

[16] This is most clear in the case of the UK SBRI.

[17] Bedin et al. 2015. The study concluded that PCP has positive impacts, mainly based on estimations and interviews with involved public procurers. The Study highlighted the difficulty in finding a consistent amount of analytical data (in other words proper PCP cases).

[18] The Innovation Scoreboard 2010 does not evaluate the impact of the PCP instrument, but it is considered by the EU as a reliable indication of the impact achieved by its innovation policy. UNU-MERIT 2016, 30.

[19] SBRI Review 2012, 11.

Assuming that government action to spur innovation is needed and that the PCP-type of innovation policy measure is one of the best available measures, questions related to the most appropriate regulatory conditions are motivating my writing of this book.

1.3 Outline of the Book

The book is structured as follows.

Chapter 2 (Political background to PCP adoption—an institutional approach) presents the context in which the PCP has been embraced by EU policy makers. This is based on a compilation of policy documents emanating from the main actors involved in setting the EU innovation agenda: the European Council, the European Commission and the European Parliament. The analysis goes back to 2000, the year that marked the revival of the EU policy-makers' interest in demand-side policies in support of innovation.

Based on this documentary analysis, this chapter provides a general view on how the political interest in demand-side innovation policy instruments amounted to the adoption and support of PCP.

Chapter 3 (The economic rationale for PCP) aims to identify in how far the policy expectations and the policy choices related to PCP resonate with economic theories on the public intervention(s) embraced by the EU. To this end, I compare the economic assumptions underlying policy-makers' expectations from PCP, against authoritative economic theories and empirical studies. Based on this analysis, I will also conclude on the economic prerequisites for PCP to achieve its objectives and I will clarify under which circumstances PCP cannot be economically effective and should therefore not be applied.

Chapter 4 (The US model of R&D procurement—lessons for PCP) analyzes the features and the outcomes of the US SBIR programme based on a documentary analysis of relevant US legislation, policy guidelines and evaluation studies.

Based on this analysis, I will identify the features of the US SBIR that relate to its perceived efficacy and I will conclude whether these strengths are reflected into the PCP. Moreover, by reference to the economic prerequisites identified in Chap. 2, I will conclude whether the main differences between PCP and the US SBIR weaken the potential of the PCP to achieve its objectives.

Chapter 5 (Placing PCP within the legislative framework) presents a broad overview of PCP's objectives and features, as envisaged by the European Commission in its 2007 PCP Communication and the accompanying Staff Working Document. This chapter points out the gaps and ambiguities in the conceptual design of the PCP and seeks complementary guidance on the interpretation of relevant concepts in documents endorsed by the European Commission (e.g. the Frascati Manual, the Expert Group report preceding the PCP Communication) and in other legislative areas of the EU (e.g. State aid).

Finally, this chapter places PCP within the broader framework of EU innovation policy approaches. It outlines the differences between PCP and related (and potentially complementary) innovation policy instruments (e.g. subsidies, forward commitment procurement etc.).

Chapter 6 (The realities of public R&D procurement implementation in the EU—trials and tribulations) provides an overview of the main PCP-like national schemes, that have been implemented so far in the EU. It also outlines the European Commission's efforts to trigger a generalized practice of transnational implementation of PCP.

More specifically, this chapter assesses three of the most established national PCP-'like' initiatives in the UK, the Netherlands and Belgium, against the economic prerequisites identified in Chap. 2. To this end, a documentary analysis of the guidelines and conditions for implementation of the 3 initiatives is performed. The assessment is also based on a study of the calls for proposals published within the framework of these initiatives. This is complemented by interviews conducted with functionaries involved in deploying these initiatives.

Based on this analysis, I comment on the success of the current implementation of the PCP policy. I also highlight the reasons for the limited appeal of the PCP or PCP-'like' initiatives as mentioned by individual public authorities themselves.

Chapter 7 (Legal barriers and paradoxes) analyzes the main legal barriers that are frequently invoked by public procurers for not getting (regularly) engaged in the deployment of PCPs. Based on the analysis of the laws that underlie these barriers, Chap. 7 suggests suitable ways of interpretation or legal amendments. This chapter also concludes on the suitability of the current regulatory framework to advance EU's interests in the area of R&D and innovation and points out possible solutions to the problems thus identified.

Chapter 8 (Concluding remarks—the case for a EU coordinated deployment of PCP) draws general conclusions and makes the case for EU coordination and supervision of PCP deployment.

What Does This Book Not Aim to Achieve?

This book does not aim to evaluate the quantitative impacts of the PCP instrument on leveraging private R&D investments, on increasing the commercialization rate of R&D projects or on improving public service efficiency. Such measurements are outside the scope of this book.

This book will neither strive to find alternatives to the use of PCP or to indicate a combination of innovation policy instruments which can best enhance the innovative capability and capacity of private actors. It provides a broad outline of one instrument from the innovation policy repository, namely pre-commercial procurement. It acknowledges though that the proper functioning of pre-commercial procurement cannot be seen in isolation from other systemic conditions (such as availability of qualified researchers, availability of technological opportunities, entrepreneurial culture etc.).

Moreover, this book focuses on the efficacy of legal instruments, not on the quality or the correctness of the economic theories that they implement. Consequently, this research is based on the conclusions of existing economic theories that have provided justification for EU intervention through PCP. By analyzing the current economic paradigm embraced by the EU-institutions, the research identifies under which economic conditions PCP can be effective and in which cases PCP might do more harm than good.

References

Bedin S, Decarolis F, Iossa E (2015) Quantifying the impact of Pre-Commercial Procurement (PCP) in Europe based on evidence from the ICT sector (SMART: 2014/0009)

Camerer E, van Eijl H (2011) Demand-side innovation policies in the European Union. In: Demand-side innovation policies (OECD)

Commission (2007) Pre-commercial Procurement: Driving innovation to ensure sustainable high quality public services in Europe. COM 799 final

Commission (2011) Compilation of Results of the EC Survey on the Status of Implementation of Pre-Commercial procurement Across Europe. http://cordis.europa.eu/fp7/ict/pcp/pcp-survey.pdf. Accessed 12 Nov 2012

Directive 2004/17/EC (Utilities Directive) of the European Parliament and of the Council of 31 March 2004 coordinating the procurement procedures of entities operating in the water, energy, transport and postal services sectors [2004] OJ L134/1

Directive 2004/18/EC (Public Sector Directive) of the European Parliament and of the Council of 31 March 2004 on the coordination of procedures for the award of public works contracts, public supply contracts and public service contracts [2004] OJ L134/114

Edler J, Georghiou L (2007) Public Procurement and innovation—Resurrecting the demand side. Research Policy 36

Edler J et al (2012) Evaluating the demand side: new challenges for evaluation. Research Evaluation 21:33

Hadfield G (2011) Producing Law and Innovation. In: Litan RE (ed) (Task Force organizer), Rules for growth: promoting innovation and growth through legal reform (Ewing Marion Kauffman Foundation)

Izsak K, Edler E (2011) Trends and Challenges in Demand-Side Innovation Policies in Europe Thematic Report 2011 under Specific Contract for the Integration of INNO Policy Trend Chart with ERAWATCH (2011–2012). http://ec.europa.eu/enterprise/newsroom/cf/_getdocument.cfm?doc_id=7011. Accessed 2 Feb 2013

MERIT (2016) European Innovation Scoreboard 2016. http://ec.europa.eu/DocsRoom/documents/17822. Accessed 24 July 2016

National IST Research Directors Forum on Public Procurement in support of ICT Research and Innovation, (PCP Expert Group) (2006) Pre-commercial Procurement of Innovation: A Missing Link in the European Innovation Cycle. ftp.cordis.europa.eu/pub/fp7/ict/docs/pcp/precommercial-procurement-of-innovation_en.pdf. Accessed 12 Nov 2012

Spence M (2011) The next convergence—the future of economic growth in a multispeed world (Farrar, Straus and Giroux)

T33, Spark & Deloitte (2014) Quantifying public procurement of R&D of ICT solutions in Europe. https://ec.europa.eu/digital-single-market/en/news/quantifying-amount-public-procurement-ict-and-rd-across-europe. Accessed 22 July 2016

The EU Economy Yearly Review (2012) http://ec.europa.eu/economy_finance/publications/publ_page8701_en.htm. Accessed 12 Dec 2012

Chapter 2
Political Background to PCP Adoption—An Institutional Approach

Contents

2.1 Introduction

Before the 1980s, Europe's R&D policy took place at national level and was focused on supporting 'national champions' (also called 'flagship companies'). In the face of rising international competition in technological sectors in the 1980s and 1990s, increased coordination at EU level was set in motion.[1]

Since 2000, EU policy-makers searched for improved policy instruments to catalyze the development of innovative solutions to serious threats to EU's advancement (e.g. increasing competitive pressure from emerging economies, climate change, shortage of natural resources, ageing etc.). In this context, they re-discovered demand-side policy instruments. Particularly public procurement was brought to the fore. In 2005, the Commission decided to exploit the potential of public procurement as source of investment in desirable R&D projects.[2] This eventually led to the adoption of the PCP Communication in 2007.

[1] Gulbrandsen 1999, 230.

[2] Commission 2005, 8.

R. Apostol, *Trials and Tribulations in the Implementation of Pre-Commercial Procurement in Europe*, DOI 10.1007/978-94-6265-156-2_2

This chapter describes the policy processes that preceded the adoption of the PCP and the policy actions that were subsequently undertaken, in order to boost its implementation in practice. The Chapter focuses on the political support and the relevant policy measures adopted in this context by the different EU institutions which have a say in the innovation policy arena. Section 2.2 describes the political support offered by the European Council (which gives the political impetus and support for certain action to stimulate innovation). Section 2.3 describes the actions undertaken by the European Commission (which translates the European Council´s guidance into concrete activities) to design and subsequently encourage the deployment of PCP. Section 2.4 outlines the endorsement provided by the European Parliament (which has a say as co-legislator, in case legislation needs to be adopted). Section 2.5 outlines concluding remarks.

2.2 European Council's Guidance

In 2000, the European Council[3] adopted the 'Lisbon Strategy', the EU coordinated innovation policy framework. The 'Lisbon Strategy' provided the necessary political impetus for renewing EU's objectives in the face of challenges brought by economic globalization (e.g. increased competition from developing countries, climate change, ageing, scarcity of natural resources etc.). The European Council set the ambitious goal for Europe to become the most competitive and dynamic economy in the world within a decade.

To reach this goal, Europe needed to increase research and technology intensive production and to improve the innovative capabilities of European businesses. This could be achieved by ensuring (i) coordination of research efforts at EU level and (ii) uptake of the resulting innovations; (iii) diversion of public expenditure towards R&D, innovation and information technologies.[4]

In Lisbon, the European Council concurrently decided to introduce the concept of 'open method of coordination' (OMC). OMC is a decentralized approach by which the European Council defines annual political goals related to the Lisbon areas (employment, innovation, economic reform and social cohesion). The European Commission defines specific actions that are needed to achieve these goals, with related timetables. However, the implementation of these actions is left to the Member States.

Yet, the European Commission monitors the implementation by each Member State against quantitative and qualitative indicators and benchmarks. It draws up annual reports on the progress made in each area. For the comparative assessment of the research and innovation performance of the 27 Member States and

[3] The European Council is the organ which gives the political impetus to the Union's economic, social and environmental action. It is formed of the heads of the Member States.

[4] Expert Group 2006.

the relative strengths and weaknesses of their research and innovation systems, the Commission uses the innovation indicators of the Innovation Union Scoreboard. These outcomes of these assessments are subsequently used as justification for policy choices.

The OMC approach leaves the European Commission with no direct enforcement mechanisms, yet it allows for evidence-based arguments to persuade and leverage peer pressure.

Since 2000, the European Council re-endorsed and fine-tuned the Lisbon Strategy on innovation during each of its annual meetings. Different measures meant to create favourable conditions for businesses to invest in R&D and innovation were proposed. Hereafter, I will highlight European Council's most important decisions for spurring investments in R&D and innovation and for using procurement as a policy instrument to this end.

In 2001 in Göteborg, the European Council underlined the need to consider the environmental effects of all policies (including innovation policy). Setting policy objectives for sustainable development, next to the economic and social objectives, would unleash much needed technological innovation, particularly in sectors such as energy and transport.[5]

An important step was taken during the 2002 European Council in Barcelona, when it was agreed that investment in R&D and innovation in the Union should increase to 3 % of the GDP by 2010, of which two-thirds should come from the private sector.[6] The Council underlined the need to ensure '*better access to risk capital*', networking and improved technology diffusion as part of an integrated strategy. The Council laid a particular emphasis on priority areas in frontier technologies such as biotechnology and energy, considered instrumental for closing the gap between the EU and its major competitors.[7]

During its 2003 Spring meeting, the European Council[8] stressed the need to improve access to public finance in order to incentivize businesses to increase their R&D investments. It also recognized the important role defence R&D procurement had in promoting leading-edge technologies[9] and re-stated that environmental innovations must be treated as a priority in EU's public research and innovation strategy.[10]

In 2004, the European Council remarked that the EU had not booked sufficient progress towards reaching the 3 % investment target, but reiterated its political commitment therefore. Among others, it called upon Member States to use targeted public R&D investments in order to catalyze greater private investments in R&D.[11]

---

[5] Council 2001, paras 19–21.

[6] Council 2002, paras 47–48.

[7] Council 2002, paras 12, 29.

[8] Council 2003, 14.

[9] Council 2003, 4.

[10] Council 2003, 25.

[11] Council 2004, 2.

In 2005, faced with a negative mid-term evaluation of the Lisbon Strategy targets,[12] the European Council explicitly added public procurement to the array of innovation policy instruments.[13] This addition was prompted by the French, German and UK governments' request to upscale the use of public procurement in support of innovation.[14] Investments in eco-technologies in the energy and transport sectors were considered particularly suitable to be stimulated through public procurement.[15]

In the following years, the European Council continued to back the commitments made in Lisbon specified areas of European strategic interest: ICT, eco-innovations, and the energy sector (energy efficiency, sustainable energies and low emission technologies),[16] eco-innovations to combat climate change (sustainable safe low carbon technologies, renewable energies, energy and resource efficient technologies).[17]

In 2008, in the face of the unraveling economic crisis, the Spring European Council reinforced its support for a coordinated innovation policy deployment. The Council concluded that innovation was more than ever needed to deal with growing long-term challenges, in the context of restricted financial resources.[18] The Council underscored the need to support innovative SMEs by creating a EU-wide market for venture capital and by enabling their participation in public procurement.[19]

Based on the 2007 Innovation Union Scoreboard, which concluded that EU performs significantly weaker than competing economies in areas such as availability of early stage venture capital and public R&D expenditure,[20] the European Council strengthened its commitment to invest more, but also more effectively, in research, such as to achieve the 3 % R&D investment target. Public procurement was again mentioned as one of the instruments capable to contribute to deployment of desired innovations.[21]

In 2010, the European Council endorsed the new Europe 2020 Strategy and reconfirmed its political commitment to the Lisbon 3 % target,[22] while in 2011 it

[12] Commission 2005b.

[13] Council 2005, paras 13, 19.

[14] French, German, UK Governments 2004.

[15] Ibid., 6.

[16] Council 2006a, paras 22, 34.

[17] Council 2007, 11–2.

[18] Council 2008.

[19] Ibid., paras 7, 11.

[20] The EU-US gap in public R&D expenditure was reportedly increasing and the GDP share of early-stage venture capital in the US was still more than 50 % higher as compared to the EU. See European Innovation Scoreboard 2007, p. 17; Pro Inno Europe 2007.

[21] Council 2008.

[22] Council 2010, 11.

invited the Commission to explore the feasibility of a Small Business Innovation Research Scheme, with the purpose of lifting remaining obstacles to the cross-border operation of venture capital.[23]

The European Council of March 2012 acknowledged for the first time the need to put demand-led innovation at the core of Europe's R&D policy and expressly mentioned the need to make more efficient use of pre-commercial procurement.[24] A year later, in its October 2013 meeting, the Council highlighted the need to support commercialization of valuable research projects and suggested to this end a '*better-coordinated use of tools such as grants, pre-commercial public procurement and venture capital, and an integrated approach from research and innovation to market deployment.*'[25] In the defense sector, the Council invited Member States to focus on dual-use technologies (e.g. key enabling technologies and energy efficiency technologies) and to ensure uptake through pooled procurement.[26] Increased participation of SMEs in the defense supply chain was singled out as a significant source of innovation, and the Commission was requested to facilitate SMEs access to defense and security markets.[27]

In the followings years, pressing issues such as the Greek economic crisis, migration and security against terrorism and most recently Great Britain's decision to exit the EU captured policy-makers' attention, and innovation received less emphasis. However, the Council mentioned in 2015 again the importance of innovation in addressing energy and climate-related challenges and singled out renewables, electricity storage and carbon capture and storage, energy efficiency in the housing sector and sustainable transport[28] as well as digital technologies.[29]

In conclusion, the European Council provided since 2000 broad guidance on the policy action needed to improve EU's innovative capabilities and transform Europe into the most competitive and dynamic economy in the world. It underlined the need for an integrated and coordinated approach between EU's and Member States' actions in support of research and innovation. Among the various conditions needed to leverage private investments in research and innovation, the European Council mentioned the need to increase not only the amount but also the efficiency of public R&D investments. In this context, it explicitly pointed at the need for public authorities to purchase those innovations which present social benefits.

Following the lead of competing economies such as the US, the European Council proposed to increase public R&D and innovation investments up to 1 % of the GDP. The European Commission was asked to guide Member States and

---

[23] Council 2011, 8.

[24] Council 2012, para 18.

[25] Council 2013a, para 16.

[26] Council 2013b, 8.

[27] Council 2013b, 9.

[28] Council 2015a.

[29] Council 2015b, para 12.

monitor the amount and impact of their investments. The aim was to deploy public R&D investments in such a way as to leverage increased private R&D and innovation investments up to an additional 2 % of GDP. The Innovation Union Scoreboard was initially designated to comparatively assess the achievement of these targets by the EU Member States. Recently, the Commission has developed the Innovation Output Indicator, a complementary tool to the Innovation Union Scoreboard, aiming to measure the innovation performance of a country in terms of output.[30] These assessment tools do not distinguish between the impact of various types of policies, but look at their concurrent effect. Another recently adopted instrument, the Research and Innovation Observatory assesses each member state research and innovation policy and provides specific recommendations for improvement.[31]

PCP was not mentioned as a distinct policy instrument before 2012. However, the guidance offered before 2012 left sufficient leeway for the European Commission to promote and finance PCP. The express reference to PCP in 2012 seems to indicate increased political support for its deployment as distinct innovation policy instrument.

2.3 European Commission's Actions

2.3.1 Actions to Promote Public Procurement as Innovation Policy Instrument

Since 2000, the European Commission gave concrete form to the political guidance offered by the European Council. In 2002, it started to pay attention to the potential of public procurement as an important instrument to stimulate private actors to invest in R&D and innovation. The Commission underlined in a number of communications the importance of public procurement as funding source particularly for some industries (such as transport, communications and defence) as well as the need to overcome fragmentation of EU procurement markets in areas where scale is necessary to incentivize innovators to invest in high-risk R&D.[32] In 2003, the Commission included public demand in its Research Investment Action Plan, as an instrument to raise R&D expenditure to the 3 % Barcelona target.[33]

Besides explicitly identifying public procurement as a suitable policy instrument to leverage private R&D investments, the Commission introduced new possibilities to procure innovative products into the 2004 Procurement Directives, by creating an equal footing for formal standards and functional specifications, and

---

30 Commission 2013.

31 See https://rio.jrc.ec.europa.eu/en.

32 Commission 2002, 14.

33 Commission 2003.

by introducing the competitive dialogue.[34] Subsequently, the European Commission provided clarity regarding the possibilities to procure innovative solutions in compliance with the legal framework.[35]

The Commission concluded that public procurement may incentivize private investment in R&D, based on a number of funded studies (outlined below). The commissioned studies underlined the importance of customers 'needs and risk-taking attitudes in influencing private firms' decisions to invest in R&D and innovation, and warned that the lack of focus on public technology procurement constituted a missed opportunity towards achieving the 3 % target.

Experts advised the European Commission, among others, to set targets for Member States regarding public procurement of R&D and to stimulate the establishment of analogues to the US SBIR.[36] The same conclusions were validated by yearly EU surveys among private actors. These surveys repeatedly reported that businesses who had the opportunity to offer innovations in publicly tendered contracts, were the most likely to increase their innovation budgets. At the same time, public procurement tenders reportedly did not offer sufficient opportunities to bid innovative solutions, while in the few cases where they did, large companies had a higher chance to win the award.[37]

Some of the most representative studies contracted by the Commission on this topic were the Kok Report which pointed out the possibility to use public procurement to offer lead markets to innovative products[38] and the Wilkinson Report which re-confirmed the need for demand-side innovation policy.[39] But the Aho Group Report, which was commissioned by the EU leaders in the aftermath of their Spring Summit in 2006[40] provided the most important input for the EU broad-based innovation strategy formulated by the European Commission in the same year.[41] The Aho Group underlined that the demand-side was concomitantly the most promising and the most under-represented approach in the EU innovation policy. The Group argued for 4 priority actions: creating innovation friendly markets, strengthening R&D resources, increasing structural mobility and fostering a culture that celebrates innovation. The EU Council endorsed the conclusions of the Aho Group and the possibility of using public procurement to stimulate demand for innovation was reiterated at the Ministerial Meeting organized during the Finnish Presidency in 2006.[42]

---

[34] Arts 23 and 29 Directive 2004/18/EC.

[35] Wilkinson et al. 2005.

[36] Gheorghiou et al. 2003, Business Decisions Limited 2003.

[37] Gallup Organization 2009, 59.

[38] Kok et al. 2004.

[39] Wilkinson et al. 2005.

[40] Aho et al. 2006.

[41] The 2006 innovation strategy is the predecessor to the current EU innovation policy (Innovation Union Flagship).

[42] Edler and Georghiou 2007, 958.

The EU broad-based innovation strategy adopted by the European Commission in September 2006, proposed to improve access to finance in support of innovation, to create an innovation friendly regulatory environment and to create demand for innovation as well as to reinforce the activities of institutions relevant for innovation, including the links between research institutions and industry.[43] Amongst the instruments to achieve these goals, public procurement was mentioned. By purchasing innovation, the public sector may stimulate the dissemination of innovations onto the private market through the power of example, while at the same time improving the quality and productivity of the public services. The Commission considered that, in order to achieve a significant impact, the focus should lie on the purchase of innovative products that have the potential to improve public service and for which the public sector is an important customer (such as ICT). Moreover, the need to stimulate all forms of innovation (technological, organizational and innovation in services) was underscored.[44]

In 2006, the Commission also contracted a broad study to assess the practical uptake of innovation in public procurement in EU countries. On the basis of this study, the Commission drafted in the spring of 2007 the Handbook on Public Procurement for Innovation, to provide legal certainty on the possibilities offered by the procurement directives to procure innovative products.[45]

By 2006, the Commission had mainly focused on the procurement of commercially available innovative products and not on the procurement of R&D services. Its measures had mainly focused on guidance and improvement of the legislative framework. In 2006, the Commission added pre-commercial procurement to its agenda and started to explore its potential. The concrete steps are described in the next Sect. 2.3.2.

In 2007, the Commission adopted a more hands-on approach and brought policy-makers from different Member States together in the Lead Market Initiative ('LMI'), with the purpose of deploying demand-side measures (e.g. public procurement, standardization and regulation) in a coordinated manner. LMI would be deployed in several sectors (eHealth, protective textiles, sustainable construction, recycling, bio-based products and renewable energies) which were already supported by means of supply-side measures. In addition, LMI envisaged support for Member States in the development of innovation-oriented procurement policies.[46]

Following the adoption of demand-side instruments by several Member States in their innovation policies, the Commission contracted in 2011 a study to investigate the trends and challenges in demand-side innovation policies in Europe. The study concluded that there was a tendency in the EU Member State to focus on public procurement and pre-commercial procurement in their innovation policies, but that it was '*still too early to say whether demand-side type of activities meet*

---

[43] Council 2006b, 2.

[44] Commission 2006, 11.

[45] Commission 2007c.

[46] Commission 2007a.

the expectations'.[47] The study signalled the importance of 'intelligent learning' as compared to 'policy copying' as well as the importance of experimentation with demand-side policies, before assessing their positive effects.

Another study commissioned in 2011, warned that Europe needs to significantly improve the *quality* of R&D and innovation expenditure in order to close the innovation gap with its major competitors (South Korea, Japan and the US). The study argued that a successful innovation policy requires supranational coordination and governance.[48] Among other solutions, the Report pleads for '*the use of pre-commercial and early-commercialization procurement*' and for extended competences of the European Commission, beyond sharing practices and granting funds.[49]

The new Public Procurement Directives represent the most recent legislative initiative of the Commission to simplify the deployment of innovation procurement (including pre-commercial procurement, procurement of innovative solutions and innovation partnerships).[50] The most important changes supposed to encourage the innovation supportive practices are: the simplification of the grounds for application of the competitive dialogue procedure and the competitive procedure with negotiation; and the legal guidance on the applicable rules in case of cross-border procurements. The new directives also introduce the procedure of Innovation Partnerships, which is meant to stimulate contracting authorities to engage in procurements of R&D. For a critical analysis of the legislative choices concerning this instrument and its relation to PCP, see Chap. 7.

2.3.2 Actions to Promote PCP Within the EU Innovation Policy

Until 2006, the European Commission had mainly focused on the use of commercial public procurement to encoura-ge private actors to invest more in R&D. The procurement of innovative products (whether new to the market or to the public purchaser) was expected to give private actors the trust that follow-up innovations would find a market in the public sector. This would potentially nudge them towards assuming more risks and investing more in R&D.

The European Commission decided though to add a new dimension to the use of public procurement as innovation policy instrument. Already in a Communication of 2005 the Commission announced its intention '*to raise awareness of the benefits of re-orienting public procurement towards stimulating*

[47] Technopolis 2011.

[48] Ernst & Young and CEP 2011, 14.

[49] Ernst & Young and CEP 2011, 17.

[50] Directive 2014/24/EU and Directive 2014/25/EU.

research'.[51] In 2006, the European Commission put together a group of experts to investigate the need to stimulate R&D activities in the ICT sector through demand-side policies.[52]

The ICT sector was singled out as a dynamic and innovative sector that is responsive to public demand, that is of common European interest and that can generate spill-over effects and enable innovative capabilities into other sectors of the economy.[53] It was also considered that increasing R&D investments (both public and private) to levels comparable to those of competing economies such as the US, could leverage the competitive advantages Europe held in certain ICT markets.[54] Although the scope of PCP was later broadened beyond its initial focus, ICT continues to be suitable focus area. On the one side, the ICT sector holds the potential to provide revolutionary solutions for the sustainable economy of the future[55] and on the other side, needs public steering towards environmentally friendly choices.[56] In the context of the economic slowdown after 2008, innovative ICT solutions were also seen as a source of potential efficiency gains and spending cuts in the public sector.[57]

The expert group reported that PCP is a suitable instrument to pull innovative solutions from the R&D phase into the commercialization phase in the ICT sector as well as elsewhere.[58] The conclusion reached by the experts motivated the Commission to support the implementation of PCP as innovation policy instrument.[59]

The PCP Expert Group mentioned several reasons why use of public procurement of R&D was considered necessary.

[51] Commission 2005c, 8.

[52] PCP Expert Group 2006.

[53] ISTAG 2006, Aho et al. 2006.

[54] Commission 2009, 3. The Commission underlines the world leadership Europe holds in ICT application markets such as telemedicine and medical equipment, in automotive and aerospace electronics, and in embedded ICT. See also Joint Research Centre 2008.

[55] The ICT sector generates more than a fifth of all patents in Europe. See Joint Research Center 2008.

[56] In 2009, the ICT sector and ICT products were considered responsible for about 2 % of global GHG emissions and this harmful contribution was expected to grow quickly. See also OECD 2009.

[57] For example, by making significant savings in energy possible, in sectors such as transport, buildings and in manufacturing, ICT technologies are expected to help reduce 20 % of the CO_2 emissions in Europe by 2020. See Commission, 'A European Economic Recovery Plan' COM 2008 800 final. See also COM 2009, 116.

[58] PCP Expert Group 4.

[59] These reasons could also be valid for the deployment of PCP in other sectors.

1. Firstly, Europe's major competitor, the United States (US) succeeded more often to pull technological R&D into the commercialisation phase and to strengthen the competitive capabilities of its domestic suppliers on the global market,[60] by:
   a. strategically using various R&D procurement procedures in well-defined areas in which they aspired to gain international competitiveness (e.g. design contests with considerable prizes, the SBIR competitions for high-tech solutions, value engineering, risk and IPR sharing in R&D procurement etc.) and
   b. restricting R&D procurement to domestic suppliers. The US succeeded thus to offer a strong home market to their domestic suppliers.
2. Secondly, the US federal government spent 20 times more (49 Bn euro) compared to the EU (2.5 Bn dollar)[61] on demand of R&D. This investment gap was most obvious in public procurement of R&D (and not in other financial instruments such as R&D subsidies, loans or fiscal measures).
3. Thirdly, due to the increasing opening of the Internal Market, the practice in the EU Member States to share the risks of R&D between state monopolies and private suppliers had disappeared and European companies were left without an important source of funding for risky R&D projects.[62]
4. Fourthly, the private market in the EU had not stepped into fill the funding gap. In the case of projects focused on the public market, this was due to the limited upside commercialisation potential.[63] This situation was mainly observed in the case of products destined to meet intrinsic needs of the public organisation, but it was also present in cooperative procurement (when the innovative product addresses needs of both the public sector and the private customer) and in catalytic procurement (when the innovative product is destined to meet extrinsic needs to the procuring organization). Consequently, the experts concluded that the private market failed to fund risky R&D in general and R&D oriented towards solutions to public needs, in particular. Such market failures justified, according to the experts, government intervention.[64]
5. Fifthly, the supply-side instruments such as subsidies, were considered insufficient to stimulate the creation of ICT solutions for the public sector. Unlike subsidies, procurement of R&D did not co-finance firms to carry out R&D in line with company plans, but directed R&D towards public needs.[65]

---

[60] PCP Expert Group 9.

[61] PCP Expert Group 10.

[62] PCP Expert Group 5.

[63] According to the PCP Expert Group 24, before deciding to invest in R&D projects, companies calculate the value of the different investment options as a function of time of the upside commercialisation potential and the downside risk that the project will not be well received in the market. Products destined to the public market have a limited upside commercialisation potential due to the smaller size of the public market and to the risk aversion of public procurers.

[64] PCP Expert Group 24.

[65] PCP Expert Group18.

The experts concluded that, in the context of increased global competition, the underutilization of pre-commercial procurement, as well as the fragmented national public policy objectives were Europe's most important weaknesses compared to its competitors.[66]

The PCP Expert Group recommended a concerted European approach to the procurement of R&D which involved pooling together resources, demand and competencies and which encouraged GPA-wide competition, provided that the majority of the R&D is performed in the EU. According to the experts, this approach minimized organisational and financial risks for each participating contracting authority and ensured more efficient spending of public money. From an EU perspective, this approach would increase interoperability and coherence of implemented solutions.[67]

The experts' conclusion that procurement of R&D in the EU was desirable was based on a comparison with the set of instruments in the US innovation policy. The experts did not question the effectiveness of government intervention in support of innovation. Moreover, no evaluation methodology of the impact of PCP was suggested[68] and no need was signalled to check on a case-by-case basis whether PCP is a suitable instrument and is capable of bringing more benefits than harm in the context of competitive markets. The policy recommendation to implement PCPs was in concert with the desire of both the policy-makers and the expert group to explore whether PCP could reproduce the success of the US SBIR and '*bring tangible benefits to society and economy*'.[69]

The PCP Expert Group recommended priority areas for the deployment of PCP: healthcare, social inclusion, e-government, security and transportation. Within these areas, the PCP Expert Group provided examples of broad topics which were suitable for cross-border collaborative PCPs.[70]

In the health area, the following specific topics are mentioned: electronic patient records supported by smart electronic health cards and e-prescriptions based on health information exchange networks.

Within the area of social inclusion, the Study mentions the following topics: ambient assisted living for elderly, children, etc., design for all workplaces, total conversation communication technologies, multi-platform information society access for groups at risk of exclusion e.g. in remote or deprived areas.

In the area of e-government the following topics are considered to present suitable challenges for cross-border collaborative PCP procedures: digital identities,

[66] PCP Expert Group 11.

[67] PCP Expert Group 6.

[68] Only recently, there has been increased attention for more measurement methodologies of the impact of demand-side policies. These may provide solid proof on the impact of PCP in the EU and may offer suggestions for improvements in its implementation. See Edler et al. 2012, 21.

[69] Commission 2007b, 3.

[70] PCP Expert Group.

workflows for inter-administration business processes (distributed secure software tools) and interactive multi-channel multimedia government to consumer/business architectures.

In the security and transportation areas, PCP could be used to solve challenges within the following topics: border security, risk management systems e.g. for large scale bioterrorism attacks, attacks on utility resources etc., automatic inspection in electronic customs/taxation systems, traffic control systems for freight (for secure cargo tracking and managing freight movements), integration of traffic control systems over different transport modes, communication between car and road infrastructure, advanced driver assistance systems ADAS, automatic emergency call from vehicles.

The European Commission embraced the experts' recommendations in the PCP Communication and in the accompanying PCP Staff Working Document.[71]

In the following years, the Commission continued to formulate policy measures to encourage the use of PCP. In its 2009 ICT Strategy, it set the target to triple the use of pre-commercial procurement in ICT by 2020 and it pointed out that socially desirable technologies, such as environmental technologies, should be given priority.[72]

In order to achieve the above mentioned target, the Commission started in 2009 to fund under different funding programmes (in RFEC, FP7 and CIP programmes)[73] the establishment of networks of public authorities. The Commission made more than € 1.2 million available. These networks were intended to raise awareness on the PCP instrument, to facilitate exchanges of experiences and to eventually facilitate cross-border collaborations for implementation of pre-commercial procurement procedures.

In 2010 it became clear that the goals and targets formulated within the framework of the Lisbon Strategy had not been reached. The data published by the European Commission in the Innovation Union Scoreboards between 2001 and 2010 confirmed that the gap between Europe on the one side, and the United States and Japan on the other side, has consistently been widening along several dimensions of innovation. At the same time, the BRIC economies (Brazil, Russia, India and China) were quickly catching up in terms of key indicators of innovation performance, such as education, patents and investment in R&D.[74] Moreover, despite the fact that Europe featured similar levels of public R&D spending on

---

[71] Commission 2007b.

[72] Commission 2009, 6, 11.

[73] RFEC is the Regions for Economic Change programme is a European Commission initiative for the 2007–2013 period aiming at funding good regional practices with a particular focus on innovation. FP7 (Framework Programme 7) is EU's programme aimed at funding research and covering the period 2007–2013. CIP (Competitiveness and Innovation Framework Programme) is EU's funding framework for innovation activities, with a focus on small and medium-sized enterprises (SMEs). CIP runs from 2007 to 2013 as well.

[74] UNU-MERIT 2011, 20 http://ec.europa.eu/research/innovation-union/pdf/iu-scoreboard-2010_en.pdf Accessed 26 March 2013.

GDP to the US, Japan and China, the difference was substantial in private spending. The effect was less innovation brought to the market.[75]

In response to this negative evaluation, the Commission adopted the new innovation strategy for 2020 (Innovation Union Flagship).[76] The Innovation Union Flagship considers demand-side instruments such as standardisation, public procurement and regulation crucial. The fact that the current low level of investment in R&D in Europe (below 2 % of GDP) compared to the US (2.6 % of the GDP) and Japan (3.4 % of the GDP) is mainly due to lower levels of private investment, led the Commission to conclude that public R&D investment in Europe does not trigger the desired incentive effect. As a solution the Commission proposes to improve the impact and composition of public research spending. It also proposes to improve the broader conditions for private sector R&D in the EU.[77] The new Strategy maintains the focus on the great challenges Europe is facing in the fields of climate change, energy and resource efficiency, health and demographic change.

Within the new Strategy, PCP is considered a suitable means to create procurement markets for innovation of at least €10 billion a year across the EU. To achieve this, the Commission announces its intention to support Member States in setting aside dedicated budgets for PCPs and contracting authorities in deploying joint procurements.[78]

The Strategy makes clear that PCP is suitable to catalyze innovations that improve the efficiency and quality of public services, while addressing the major societal challenges. Suitable areas for implementation are the six Lead market Initiative areas (e-Health, sustainable construction, protective textiles, bio-based products, recycling and renewable energies) or the areas for European Innovation Partnerships (energy security, transport, climate change and resource efficiency, health and ageing, environmentally-friendly production methods and land management).

The concept of European Innovation Partnerships (not to be confused with the 'Innovation Partnership' procedure) was for the first time introduced by the Innovation Union Flagship. These partnerships are a complex combination of supply- and demand-side instruments which should mobilise key actors at both national and EU levels to develop and bring on the market innovations with potential social benefits. From the scant and vague description of the European Innovation Partnership, it could be concluded that its aim is to coordinate and integrate the existing instruments and existing initiatives beyond the existing Joint Technology Instruments (JTIs). The Partnerships would therefore act across the whole research and innovation chain (from R&D efforts to demonstration and pilots, all the way to the market). PCP is one of the available instruments to be used within the Partnerships.[79]

[75] Ibid.

[76] Commission 2010a.

[77] COM 2010b, 14.

[78] COM 2010a, commitment no. 17.

[79] Commission 2010a, 25.

Besides the "Innovation Union Flagship Initiative",[80] other documents ('flagships') that form part of Europe's overall development strategy, announce Commission measures in support of PCP (e.g. co-financing of cross-border collaborative PCPs, guidance to Member States in reserving procurement budgets for PCP competitions etc.).[81]

As already mentioned in the previous section, the European Council of February 2011[82] endorsed the innovation strategy proposed by the Commission and invited the Commission to explore the feasibility of a Small Business Innovation Research Scheme. A subsequent study on the feasibility of a Small Business Innovation Research Scheme was performed in 2012.[83] Based on interviews with contracting authorities and policy-makers across Europe, the study argued that EU suport is key in coordination of cross-border procurement projects, in spreading knowledge and in drafting procurement specifications, while assessing the bids should be left to the procurers. The procurement initiatives could both target broad common-EU policy objectives, as well as procurers' concrete needs.

The study's findings were not implemented in the form of a PCP program under EU coordination. Instead, (3) years later (in 2015), the Commission launched the SME Instrument, a grant scheme designed to support SMEs with high growth potential in commercialising their innovations. The SME Instrument is emulating the procedural steps of the US SBIR and whenever the competitions target public needs, the participating SMEs are encouraged to identify public customers. However, the SME instrument is run directly by the European Commission, without the direct participation of a public procurer.[84]

More direct support to the deployment of PCP competitions has been offered since 2011 under various EU funding instruments. Consortia of contracting authorities from different Member States may receive up to 90 % of the procurement costs.[85] The Commission's support for PCP is further discussed in Chap. 6.

More recently, the Commission has succeeded to introduce a reference to pre-commercial procurement in the 2014 Procurement Directives.[86] This enhances the visibility as well as the legitimacy of this procurement model. Other important legislative amendment intended to encourage innovation–oriented practices after the pre-commercial stage, are: the simplification of the grounds for application of the competitive dialogue procedure and the competitive procedure with negotiation

[80] Commission 2010a.

[81] Commission 2010c, d. Key action 9 states that the Commission will try to leverage more private investment through the strategic use of pre-commercial procurement.

[82] Council 2011.

[83] Rigby et al. 2012.

[84] Bertrand Wert 2015.

[85] See http://cordis.europa.eu/fp7/ict/pcp/calls_en.html.

[86] Recital (47) Directive 2014/24/EU and Recital (57) Directive 2014/25/EU.

and the legal guidance on the applicable rules in case of cross-border procurements. The 2014 Procurement Directives include another notable novelty: the Innovation Partnership procedure. Arguably, this new procurement model was not endorsed by the Commission, due to its potentially distortive effects on fair competition within the Internal market. For a critical analysis of the legislative choices regarding this instrument and its relation to PCP, see Chap. 7.

Concurrently, the Commission intensified efforts to mainstream pre-commercial procurement. In 2014, it endorsed a study quantifying the impacts of PCP in Europe. However, the study went to great pains to identify procurement practice that fits the PCP model and ended up outlining estimations of expected benefits.[87]

In the same year, the Commission launched the *eafip* initiative, its latest attempt to support those national policy-makers and individual procurers, who are contemplating the deployment of innovation procurement (in the form of pre-commercial procurement or procurement of innovative solutions). The *eafip* initiative provides the practical tools to engage in innovation procurement: detailed guidance to national policy-makers on how to set-up innovation procurement policy; comprehensive guidance to procurers on how to implement PCP, starting from needs identification and ending with contract management; a network of experts and local lawyers to advise on concrete implementation aspects.[88]

In conclusion, since 2005 the Commission has undertaken various measures to stimulate public procurers to act as demanding customers of highly innovative solutions. These ranged from drafting the PCP Commission, to funding networks of procurers as well as collaborative cross-border PCPs and ending with comprehensive operational guidance and free assistance in the implementation. Whether these efforts are indeed achieving their aim, is discussed in Chap. 7.

2.4 European Parliament's Support

The European Parliament has also engaged in the debate around PCP. In a resolution of 2007, it identified pre-commercial procurement as an '*untapped opportunity in Europe to use public needs as a driver for innovation*' and encouraged Member States to use PCP to develop innovative solutions for specific problems of public interest.[89]

In a later report of 2009, the Parliament endorsed the PCP Communication and the Commission's efforts to fund exchanges of good PCP practices, but expressed concerns that this procurement model remained little understood by SMEs and largely underutilized by public authorities particularly at the regional and local

[87] Bedin et al. 2015.

[88] See: https://ec.europa.eu/digital-agenda/en/news/training-promotion-and-local-implementation-assistance-pcp-and-ppi Accessed 7 June 2016.

[89] European Parliament 2007.

levels.[90] The Parliament called on the European Commission to undertake additional measures (e.g. financial incentives, improved guidance and the set-up of a European pilot project), with the aim to encourage public procurers to engage in PCPs.[91] The report underscored the need to identify and prioritize medium and long-term public challenges[92] and to detect those technological areas that hold potential solutions and should be targeted by PCP.[93]

In 2010, the European Parliament's Committee on Industry, Research and Energy on Innovation Union[94] reiterated its support for PCP and urged Member States to strategically use public procurement in order to develop innovative, sustainable and eco-efficient solutions to important public challenges. The Commission was invited to review the opportunities for PCP within the current legislative proposals, to financially incentivize regional and local public authorities to engage in PCPs and to draft best-practice guidelines and training programmes to developed the needed skills.[95]

In another more recent resolution, the European Parliament expressed again its support for PCP and listed the important objectives PCP may potentially achieve: creating new markets for innovative and green technologies, improving the quality and effectiveness of public services and creating competitive advantages for small European businesses.[96]

In conclusion, the Parliament has joined the group of EU institutions that support PCP. The Parliament simply reiterates support for the already undertaken initiatives. However, its political support offers the Commission the additional justification to stimulate the use of PCP.

2.5 Summing-Up Policy Support for PCP

The EU is trying to catalyze a technological revolution in order to cope with the numerous and stringent challenges of the not so far-away future. Increased R&D investments are identified as a necessary pre-condition. However, the EU has been less successful than the US in incentivizing private actors to scale up their own R&D investments, despite similar amounts of public R&D investments. The EU policy-makers concluded that US SBIR-type of measures held the

---

90 European Parliament 2008, paras 6, 29.

91 European Parliament 2008, paras 33–36.

92 European Parliament 2008, para 21.

93 The Parliament stressed the importance of the EU Technology Platforms and of continuous knowledge transfer between technologically innovative universities, institutes and contracting authorities for finding suitable technology areas for PCP. European Parliament 2008, p. 7.

94 European Parliament 2010.

95 European Parliament 2010, para 140.

96 European Parliament 2011.

key to incentivizing private R&D investment. As a consequence, they decided to explore whether pre-commercial public procurement could be beneficial to the EU economy. Pre-commercial procurement has not found its way into legislation, but has been anchored in public policy. All main EU institutions (European Council, European Commission and the European Parliament) have expressed their support for PCP. PCP is viewed by the EU policy-makers as a suitable instrument (i) to increase both public and private investments in R&D, (ii) to steer private R&D efforts towards innovative solutions for important and complex public problems and (iii) to indirectly enhance the innovative capabilities of (small) European businesses.

The initial focus on the implementation of PCP procedures in the ICT sector was justified by the beneficial effects the ICT sector has on economic growth and social welfare and by the innovative and dynamic character of this sector in the EU, which makes it responsive to innovation policy measures.

Subsequently, the Commission broadened the scope of PCP into areas wherein the government plays an important role in funding R&D, such as transport and defence, or holds a responsibility to tackle stringent problems: e-Health, sustainable construction, protective textiles, bio-based products, recycling and renewable energies, energy security, transport, climate change and resource efficiency, health and ageing, environmentally-friendly production methods and land management.

The main EU institutions have expressed their expectations that PCP can contribute to the achievement of the EU innovation goals in the above mentioned sectors. The expectations from the performance of PCP are thus high. These policy expectations are based on research papers commissioned by the EU with a handful of experts. It is difficult to conclude whether these studies are objective or rather serve the purpose of confirming the political decisions which they underpin. In the next Chapter, I will investigate whether the policy expectations are realistic by comparing them against relevant economic theories and studies beyond those commissioned by the EU.

References

Aho E, Cornu J, Georghiou L, Subira A (2006) Creating an innovative Europe. http://ec.europa.eu/invest-in-research/action/2006_ahogroup_en.htm. Accessed 26 Mar 2013

Bedin S, Decarolis F, Iossa E (2015) Quantifying the impact of pre-commercial procurement (PCP) in Europe based on evidence from the ICT sector (SMART: 2014/0009)

Business Decisions Limited (2003) The power of customers to drive innovation ftp://ftp.cordis.europa.eu/pub/innovation-policy/studies/studies_the_power_of_customers_to_drive_innovation.pdf. Accessed 26 Mar 2013

Commission (2002) More research for Europe, towards 3 % of GDP. COM 499 final

Commission (2003) Investing in research: an action plan for Europe. COM 226 final/2

Commission (2005a) Implementing the Community Lisbon Programme: more research and innovation—investing for growth and employment: a common approach. COM 488 final

Commission (2005b) Working together for growth and jobs, a new start for the Lisbon Strategy. COM 24 final

Commission (2005c) More research and innovation—investing for growth and employment: a common approach. COM 488 final
Commission (2006) Putting knowledge into practice: a broad-based innovation strategy for the EU. COM 502 final
Commission (2007a) A lead market initiative for Europe. COM 860 final
Commission (2007b) Pre-commercial Procurement: Driving innovation to ensure sustainable high quality public services in Europe. COM 799 final
Commission (2007c) Guide on dealing with innovative solutions in public procurement—10 elements of good practice. SEC 280
Commission (2009) A strategy for ICT R&D and innovation in Europe: raising the game. COM 116 final
Commission (2010a) Europe 2020 Flagship Initiative: Innovation Union. COM 546 final
Commission (2010b) Europe 2020, a strategy for smart, sustainable and inclusive growth. COM 2020 final
Commission (2010c) An integrated industrial policy for the globalisation era. COM 614 final
Commission (2010d) A digital agenda for Europe. COM 245 final
Commission (2013) Measuring innovation output in Europe: towards a new indicator. COM 624 final
Council (2001) Goteborg European Council, 15 and 16 June 2001, http://www.consilium.europa.eu/ueDocs/cms_Data/docs/pressData/en/ec/00200-r1.en1.pdf. Accessed 26 Mar 2013
Council (2002) Barcelona European Council 15–16 March 2002 http://ec.europa.eu/invest-in-research/pdf/download_en/barcelona_european_council.pdf. Accessed 5 June 2016
Council (2003) Brussels European Council of 20 and 21 March 2003 http://www.consilium.europa.eu/uedocs/cms_data/docs/pressdata/en/ec/75136.pdf. Accessed 27 Jul 2011
Council (2004) Brussels European Council 25–26 March 2004 http://www.consilium.europa.eu/uedocs/cms_data/docs/pressdata/en/ec/79696.pdf. Accessed 11 Apr 2013
Council (2005) Brussels European Council, 22 and 23 March 2005. Conclusions http://www.consilium.europa.eu/uedocs/cms_data/docs/pressdata/en/ec/84335.pdf. Accessed 27 June 2011
Council (2006a) Brussels European Council, 23/24 March 2006. Conclusions http://www.consilium.europa.eu/uedocs/cms_data/docs/pressdata/en/ec/89013.pdf. Accessed 28 Jul 2011
Council (2006b) Council conclusions on a broad-based innovation strategy: strategic priorities for innovation action at the EU level http://www.consilium.europa.eu/uedocs/cms_Data/docs/pressdata/en/intm/91989.pdf. Accessed 26 Mar 2013
Council (2007) Brussels European Council, 8/9 March 2007. Conclusions http://register.consilium.europa.eu/pdf/en/07/st07/st07224-re01.en07.pdf. Accessed 28 Jul 2011
Council (2008) Brussels European Council, 13/14 March 2008. Conclusions http://register.consilium.europa.eu/pdf/en/08/st07/st07652-re01.en08.pdf. Accessed 28 Jul 2011
Council (2010) European Council 17 June 2010. Conclusions http://www.consilium.europa.eu/ueDocs/cms_Data/docs/pressData/en/ec/115346.pdf. Accessed 11 Apr 2013
Council (2011) Brussels European Council, 4 February 2011. Conclusions http://www.consilium.europa.eu/uedocs/cms_data/docs/pressdata/en/ec/119175.pdf. Accessed 26 March 2013
Council (2013a) European Council 24/25 October 2013. Conclusions https://www.consilium.europa.eu/uedocs/cms_data/docs/pressdata/en/ec/139197.pdf. Accessed 2 June 2016
Council (2013b) European Council 19/20 December 2013. Conclusions https://www.consilium.europa.eu/uedocs/cms_Data/docs/pressdata/en/ec/140245.pdf. Accessed 2 June 2016
Council (2015a) European Council meeting (19 and 20 March 2015) http://www.consilium.europa.eu/en/meetings/european-council/2015/03/19-20/. Accessed 3 June 2016
Council (2015b) European Council meeting (25 and 26 June 2015) http://www.consilium.europa.eu/en/meetings/european-council/2015/06/25-26/. Accessed 5 June 2016
Directive 2004/18/EC of the European Parliament and of the Council of 31 March 2004 on the coordination of procedures for the award of public works contracts, public supply contracts and public service contracts, OJ L 134/114
Directive 2014/24/EU of the European Parliament and of the Council of 26 February 2014 on public procurement and repealing Directive 2004/18/EC

Directive 2014/25/EU of the European Parliament and of the Council of 26 February 2014 on procurement by entities operating in the water, energy, transport and postal services sectors and repealing Directive 2004/17/EC
Edler J, Georghiou L (2007) Public procurement and innovation—resurrecting the demand side. Res Policy 36
Edler J, Georghiou L, Blind K, Uyarra E (2012) Evaluating the demand side: new challenges for evaluation. Res Eval 21
Ernst & Young and CEP (2011) Next generation innovation policy, The future of EU innovation policy to support market growth http://www.google.nl/url?sa=t&rct=j&q=&esrc=s&frm=1&source=web&cd=3&ved=0CEMQFjAC&url=http%3A%2F%2Fwww.siliconrepublic.com%2Fdownload%2Ffs%2Fdoc%2Freports%2Finnovation-20report-lr.pdf&ei=uj4NUb7ECcHs0gXftIDABw&usg=AFQjCNE20kBwzEgEf_ryTG90zL4vBk6ODA&sig2=j0Xz_TvF_v3KJFyUYCvWyw. Accessed 2 Feb 2013
European Innovation Scoreboard 2007—Comparative analysis of innovation performance (2008)
European Parliament (2007) Resolution on specific problems in the transposition and implementation of public procurement legislation and its relation to the Lisbon Agenda. 2006/2084(INI)
European Parliament (2008) Report on pre-commercial procurement: driving innovation to ensure sustainable high-quality public services in Europe. 2008/2139(INI)
European Parliament (2010) Report on Innovation Union—transforming Europe for a post-crisis world. 2010/2245(INI)
European Parliament (2011) Resolution on an industrial policy for the globalised era. 2010/2095(INI)
Expert Group on 'Knowledge for Growth' (2006) Globalisation of R&D: linking better the European economy to 'foreign' sources of knowledge and making EU a more attractive place for R&D investment http://ec.europa.eu/invest-in-research/pdf/download_en/foray_report.pdf. Accessed 12 Dec 2012
French, German, UK Governments (2004) Towards an innovative Europe. A paper by the French, German and UK Governments. http://www.hm-treasury.gov.uk/media/C0B/BF/towards_innov_europe_200204.pdf. Accessed 26 Mar 2013
Gallup Organization (2009) Innobarometer 2009: Analytical Report http://www.proinno-europe.eu/sites/default/files/Innobarometer_2009.pdf. Accessed 26 Mar 2013
Gheorghiou et al (2003) Raising EU R&D intensity: improving the effectiveness of public support mechanisms for private sector research and development: direct measures (2003) http://ec.europa.eu/invest-in-research/pdf/download_en/report_directmeasures.pdf. Accessed 26 Mar 2013
Gulbrandsen M (1999) Convergence between Europe and America: the transition from industrial to innovation policy. J Technol Transfer 24
ISTAG (2006) Shaping Europe's future through ICT http://www.cordis.lu/ist/istag.htm. Accessed 26 Jan 2012
Joint Research Centre (2008) Mapping R&D investment by the European ICT business sector http://ftp.jrc.es/EURdoc/JRC45723_RR.pdf. Accessed 26 Mar 2013
Kok W et al (2004) Facing the challenge. The Lisbon Strategy for growth and employment http://ec.europa.eu/research/evaluations/pdf/archive/fp6-evidence-base/evaluation_studies_and_reports/evaluation_studies_and_reports_2004/the_lisbon_strategy_for_growth_and_employment__report_from_the_high_level_group.pdf. Accessed 26 Mar 2013
National IST Research Directors Forum on Public Procurement in support of ICT Research and Innovation (PCP Expert Group) (2006) Pre-commercial procurement of innovation: a missing link in the European innovation cycle ftp://ftp.cordis.europa.eu/pub/fp7/ict/docs/pcp/precommercial-procurement-of-innovation_en.pdf. Accessed 12 Nov 2012
OECD (2009) Measuring the relationship between ICT and the environment http://www.oecd.org/sti/43539507.pdf. Accessed 26 Mar 2013
Pro Inno Europe (2007) Paper No. 6 http://ec.europa.eu/enterprise/policies/innovation/files/proinno/eis-2007_en.pdf. Accessed 11 Apr 2013

Rigby J, Boekholt P, Semple A, Deuten J, Apostol R, Corvers S, Edler J (2012) Feasibility study on future EU support to public procurement of innovative solutions: obtaining evidence for a full scheme http://ec.europa.eu/enterprise/policies/innovation/policy/lead-market-initiative/files/meeting-procurement-feb2012/study-eu-support-public-procurement-innovative-solutions_en.pdf. Accessed 2 Feb 2013

Technopolis (2011) Trends and challenges in demand-side innovation policies in Europe http://ec.europa.eu/enterprise/newsroom/cf/_getdocument.cfm?doc_id=7011. Accessed 26 Mar 2013

UNU-MERIT (2011) Innovation Union Scoreboard 2010. The Innovation Union's Performance Scoreboard for Research and Innovation http://ec.europa.eu/research/innovation-union/pdf/iu-scoreboard-2010_en.pdf. Accessed 26 Mar 2013

Wert B (SME Support) (2015) Presentation. http://www.spaceinfoday.eu/system/h2020-space-infoday/files/main-p_03_EASME_Bertrand_Wert.pdf?1443786705. Accessed 7 June 2016

Wilkinson R et al (2005) Public procurement for research and innovation http://ec.europa.eu/invest-in-research/pdf/download_en/edited_report_18112005_on_public_procurement_for_research_and_innovation.pdf. Accessed 26 Mar 2013

Chapter 3
The Economic Rationale for PCP

Contents

3.1 Introduction

In Chap. 2, I presented the policy context that led to the adoption and subsequent support for PCP. I concluded that the following rationale justified the EU policy-makers support for PCP: Europe faces important collective challenges that cannot be solved with available solutions. The right innovations may emerge if sufficient R&D investments are unleashed and early commercialization is incentivized. But despite various R&D policy efforts, Europe had been less successful than the US in attracting large private investments in risky R&D projects and consequently in converting new inventions into new products and jobs. Demand-side policies in general and US SBIR-type of measures, in particular, were identified as the key ingredient to unleash private R&D investments at similar levels to the US and to catalyze the development of desirable innovations, that can safeguard Europe's welfare and advancement.[1]

However, as shown in Chap. 1, the EU PCP differs in important ways from the US SBIR: it is open to participation by both small and large companies, it targets both technological and services areas, it denies commercial purchase of the innovative results and it imposes limitations on the funding share. Moreover, PCP is not set-up in the form of a mandatory and centrally coordinated program.

[1] Commission 2007a, b, 3–5. PCP Expert Group 2006, 5, 24.

R. Apostol, *Trials and Tribulations in the Implementation of Pre-Commercial Procurement in Europe*, DOI 10.1007/978-94-6265-156-2_3

Based on the above, I identify the following most important economic assumptions that underlie the policy choices concerning PCP:

1. Innovation leads to (social) welfare;
2. (Public) R&D investment is a determinant of innovation;
3. European venture capital markets do not sufficiently invest in (risky) R&D;
4. Public needs/demand can influence firms' strategies for creativity and innovation;
5. PCPs is a suitable instrument to develop technological, as well as services innovations.

The Commission did not present a detailed economic rationale for PCP and did not identify conditions for its successful deployment. The policy documents endorsing PCP, leave difficult value-judgments regarding effective implementation to the implementing authorities. However, the EU policy-makers attached high expectations to the deployment of PCP.

Against this background, the purpose of this chapter is twofold: to test whether the policy expectations are realistic and to identify under which economic conditions PCP can be expected to be effective. To this end, I will compare the above mentioned assumptions against authoritative economic theories and studies, beyond those commissioned by the EU policy-makers.

Before doing that, I reflect on the problematic nature of the economic methodologies used to measure the impacts of public intervention on innovation or to predict the influence of certain conditions/factors on innovation (Sect. 3.2).

While keeping in mind that current economic methodologies display significant limitations, I subsequently test the first two assumptions (in Sect. 3.3). To this end, I outline the evolution of the economic thought regarding the role of innovation in the economy and the role of (public) R&D investment among the various determinants of innovation. I also summarize the economic rationale advanced by different economic theories, for public intervention in the innovation area.

In the next Sect. 3.4, I analyse the economic theories regarding the role of venture capital markets in support of innovation (third assumption) and I reflect on the complementary role of government funding of high-risk R&D.

In Sect. 3.5, I compare the fourth assumption that public needs/demand can influence firms' strategies for creativity and innovation against the economic theories on the role of demand in the innovation process. I conclude on the pre-conditions for effectively employing public demand in support of innovation.

In Sect. 3.6, I test the fifth assumption against a limited number of economic theories and studies concerning the dynamics of the innovation process in services. This will shed light on the relevance of PCP for services innovation.

In Sect. 3.7, I draw conclusions on PCP's potential to achieve its objectives and I summarize the most important pre-requisites for a successful implementation.

As this is primarily a legal research, I will not provide a critical analysis of the concerned economic literature, but purely an overview of some of the most important economic theories and empirical studies. The analysis is largely limited to economic literature on innovative technologies and covers only to a limited extent economic theories on innovation in services.

3.2 Innovation Policy as Decision-Making Under Uncertainty

The challenge to provide the policy-makers with a sound analytical framework to predict whether an envisaged policy does more good than harm has not (yet) been met by economics.[2] Economics are limited in predicting or even determining in hindsight with scientific exactness whether a certain public policy has triggered technological evolution,[3] for the reasons presented below.

The ideal measurement method is to identify the likely evolution of a certain industry in the absence of the public innovation policy and to determine whether the industry would have innovated as rapidly and in the same way.[4] For obvious practical reasons, this is an impossible approach to apply.

A method considered manageable by economists, is to compare the evolution and innovative efforts of an industry following the public intervention against the *expectations* of how the respective public policy would impact/(create incentives for) innovation.[5] To this end, economists use a series of indicators to measure/determine the effects (or outputs) of certain policies on innovation, such as changes in the innovation strategies of businesses, number of patents, number of patent citations, sales, firm growth, R&D expenditure etc. There are numerous problems in using such indicators and I will enumerate some of the most important below.[6]

Firstly, it is difficult to find pure indicators, which establish exclusively the effects on innovation of the public policy under study, and do not (partly) capture the effect of other types of public interventions.

Secondly, factors such as R&D spending regard an input to the innovation process, not an output of innovation while the knowledge spill-overs are impossible to measure.[7]

Thirdly, patents are problematic, for being only weakly related to actual innovation performance. Not all innovations are patented and not all patents regard qualitative innovations (or R&D), or the (social) value of an invention may be greater than the value of a patent indicates.[8]

Fourthly, the problem with using the national gross domestic product (GDP) as indicator is that the positive effects of innovative products may show long after their introduction.[9] Moreover, GDP as an indicator does not sufficiently reflect the

---

[2] Manne and Wright 2009, 10–1.

[3] Beinhocker 2006; Taleb 2010.

[4] Baker 2007.

[5] Ibid.

[6] A comprehensive outline of the limitations of economic measurements is offered by Freeman and Soete 2007.

[7] Scotchmer 2004, 282.

[8] Gilbert 2007a, 17; Ottaviano et al. 2003, 18–9.

[9] Basu et al. 2003.

value of investment in R&D, as innovation may in many cases lower the price or may not create value for the private actor at all (particularly when the innovation is made publicly available).[10]

Regarding the capability to predict the best policy choices, Lipsey remarks that *'there does not exist a unique set of formally determined, optimum public policies with respect to technological change'*.[11] By looking at the technological evolution throughout the history of mankind, Lipsey concludes that the economic development of the Western part of the world should in large proportion be attributed to historical accidents and not to intentional public intervention. In the Western world, pluralism and separation of powers (science from religion) were major factors in stimulating the advancement of the society, together with the re-discovery of the Greek science, at a moment when it could escape the censorship of religion. He underlines in this context the important role of independent knowledge institutions which provided an *'effective memory'*, essential for *'cumulative scientific advances'*.

As a consequence, when attempting to trigger technological change through public policy, Lipsey proposes to use a *'mixture of theory, measurement and subjective judgment'*.[12] Due to the limitation of science to predict whether and which type of intervention is the most effective, other economists consider that the use of political decision and participatory decision-making (which involves large parts of the population and those most affected by the consequences of a certain policy) offer as good of an option as any.[13]

Taleb[14] finds that the current economic models used to predict economic outcomes are inherently flawed for being based on limited samples of past information, insufficient to capture rare events (such as the 2008 financial crisis) that can trigger extreme/catastrophic impacts. The economic models tend to qualify such rare events (so-called Black Swans) as improbable, although they can be envisaged. Taleb warns for the danger in relying decision-making on such economic models and draws the attention to the potential extreme impact that large variations in random economic variables may have in the context of the global society characterized by increased interdependencies and nonlinearity.

Taleb develops the *'theory of the fourth quadrant'*, an area characterized by high uncertainty and extreme variations in certain atypical variables (which are rare and have an exponential impact on the end outcome), as well as by potential complex payoffs (whether positive or negative). Instead of trying to predict the probability of occurrence of Black Swans, Taleb advices to rather focus on precautionary measures in the eventuality of such events. He particularly advices to avoid

---

[10] Scotchmer 2004, 269.

[11] Lipsey 2007, 5–28.

[12] Lipsey 2007, 25.

[13] Freeman 1982, 216–20; Coombs et al. 1987, 30.

[14] Taleb 2010.

decision-making driven by short-term profit, and he supports the idea to build-in necessary redundancy (as opposed to optimization/efficiency).

Taleb's argument is not new. Already in 1945, Frederick von Hayek, the Austrian policy philosopher reflected on decision-making under uncertainty.[15] He argued that no policy-maker can possibly possess the necessary knowledge on the political, social, technological and economic variables which can potentially influence the working of their policies in the real world, particularly on a long-term. However, this does not absolve the policy-maker from evaluating the costs of the policy or its long-term value. Von Hayek criticised mathematical economics, which over-simplified things by often not taking into consideration the equally important *'knowledge of people, of local conditions, and of special circumstances'*. In his view, economics often disregard change in some variables and overly rely on *'statistical aggregates, which show a very much greater stability than the movement of the detail'*. Hayek used his observations as an argument against the central planning of an economy and as a praise of the price mechanism as one available conveyor of necessary relevant knowledge, which although not completely understandable or controllable, performs better than any known alternatives.

However, his reflections underline the limited predictive capabilities of economic models and the limited capacity of a human to process enormous amounts of information in decision-making (even if all the necessary information would be available). He concluded that economic theories can only provide *'very general statements or "pattern predictions"'*, but no predictions of individual events.[16] While economists/statisticians can observe certain regularities in investments, price levels etc., such regularities do not always apply, while economics cannot name the preconditions for such regularities. Theorems of macrotheory are certainly valuable in order to generate predictions in the presence of insufficient information. But they are not more than assumptions which may be proven wrong.[17]

Complexity economist Beinhocker eloquently summarizes it:

> The economy is too complex, too nonlinear, too dynamic, and too sensitive to the twists and turns of chance to be amenable to prediction over anything but the very shortest of terms. Even if we were as rational as possible and had all the information we could want, the computational complexity of the economy is such that the future would happen before we would have time to predict it.[18]

Behavioural economists confirm that individuals perform poorly at computing large amounts of information, while they are good at interpreting ambiguous information and at learning.[19] These theories are backed by psychologists who demonstrate that rational models for decision-making (such as logics or statistics) are

---

15 Von Hayek 1945, 519–30.

16 Hayek 2002, 11–2.

17 Hayek 2002, 11–2.

18 Beinhocker 2006, 323.

19 Tversky and Kahneman 1974.

in situations of uncertainty (when not all the determinants of a certain outcome can be known or calculated) less reliable than simple heuristics.[20] They confirm the view that the application of rational models to situations characterised by imperfect information may lead to disaster, as even small deviations from the model conditions may have an impact.[21] Although the theory is not as developed as to identify the generic conditions under which heuristics always work better than rational models, Gigerenzer suggests that beyond a certain point, more information may be harmful to making a correct decision. Beyond this point, experience plays a crucial role in selecting the proper heuristics from the adaptive toolbox of an individual (such as recognition heuristic, fluency heuristic, hiatus heuristics etc.).[22]

Complexity economists suggest another solution to policy-making in the context of insufficient information and uncertainty. They argue that public policy should focus on supporting institutions and societies to adapt quicker to changing complex situations (through infrastructure, network etc.), while leaving the selection of the successful innovations to the market forces.[23] Moreover, public policy should focus on setting ambitious goals and defining a portofolio of alternative trajectories/policies to work towards those goals. This entails though that the government should be prepared to *'experiment, collect feedback and change course, none of which is ever politically easy'*.[24] Scotchmer adds that, because results of R&D projects are inherently uncertain, assessments of the success and efficiency of public investments schemes in R&D should not be focused on the failed projects or comparison to better ideas developed after the investment decision. According to her, it is important to use mechanisms that can lead to good decision-making and to adopt a failure-tolerant approach.[25]

Solutions for decision-making in case of uncertainty are also provided by the precautionary principle, which has made its way into many international agreements, particularly in the field of environmental protection.[26] The precautionary principle advices the adoption of precautionary measures in case of uncertainty or risks with irreversible or catastrophic consequences. Uncertainty in the context of the precautionary principle entails that the outcome can be envisaged with a certain degree of plausibility, but it cannot be attributed any probabilities. In the case

[20] Gigerenzer and Gaissmaier 2011, 451. Heuristics can be defined as 'a strategy that ignores part of the information, with the goal of making decisions more quickly, frugally, and/or accurately than more complex methods'.

[21] Gigerenzer and Gaissmaier 2011, 451–2. Davidson 2009, 35–43.

[22] Gigerenzer and Gaissmaier 2011, 450.

[23] Beinhocker 2006, 426.

[24] Beinhocker 2006, 324, 334.

[25] Scotchmer 2004, 56–7.

[26] See for example, the 1992 Rio Declaration or the United Nations Framework Convention on Climate Change. One common definition sounds as follows: *'Where there are threats of serious or irreversible damage, lack of full scientific certainty shall not be used as a reason for postponing cost-effective measures to prevent environmental degradation'*.

of risks, the outcomes can be identified and probabilities can be assigned.[27] The precautionary principle in its stronger forms, entails a low threshold for the plausibility of an uncertain outcome.[28]

The adopted precautionary action should be sufficient to protect flexibility of decision-making in the future, when more knowledge on the harm becomes available and should reflect the magnitude of the *irreversible* or *catastrophic* harm if precautionary action is not taken. However, action should be based on a cost-benefit analysis of the various options (including inaction).[29]

Economists also agree that it is not possible to take precautions against all uncertain outcomes or risks, as these are present in almost any human activity and precautionary measures may themselves create new uncertainty or new risks.[30] Whenever precautionary measures may create new uncertainty with catastrophic or irreversible outcomes, the precautionary measures should not be taken in the first place (such as a preventive war on terrorism that may increase terrorism).[31]

Actions adopted within the framework of innovation policy can often be regarded as precautionary measures intended to address uncertain outcomes or risks with catastrophic and/or irreversible consequences (such as climate change, loss of resources etc.). However, innovation policy may create itself new uncertainty or risks. For example, public intervention in the form of funding of R&D from the demand side (such as envisaged by PCP) may, on the one side, solve the problem of insufficient funding of innovative firms, but may on the other side, deter rather than encourage competitive investments in R&D (when public funding of R&D strengthens the market position of a certain undertaking and reduces the profit perspectives for other undertakings and implicitly their incentives to invest in R&D). Public R&D funding may also encourage inefficient companies and distort competition (by enhancing the market power of some companies which will discourage their competitors to invest in R&D themselves) and may divert needed funds from real needs (when their impact on stimulating private actors to become more entrepreneurial and invest more in R&D is low or non-existent). These outcomes are uncertain, but their consequences can hardly be qualified as catastrophic or irreversible. Therefore, there is no ground to argue that innovation policy should not be undertaken, particularly because the striven objective justifies action.

In conclusion, innovation policy-making is a form of decision-making under uncertainty. It cannot rely on economic mathematical models for answers, due to the fact that these do not and cannot compute all relevant information. Economists propose to employ experience and learning besides available information and to retain needed redundancy/alternatives as well as avoid distortions to judgments by short-term pay-offs.

---

[27] Sunstein 2005, 37.

[28] Sunstein 2005, 9.

[29] Sunstein 2005, 55.

[30] Sunstein 2005, 12.

[31] Sunstein 2005, 55.

The fact that economic models are not capable to determine with scientific exactness what triggers innovation poses thus difficulties to policy-makers, but does not justify inaction. In the following sections, I will analyse what relevant lessons can be drawn by the policy-maker from the available economic knowledge.

3.3 Relation Between Innovation and (Public) R&D Investments

In this section I will test the first two economic assumption, that innovation leads to (social) welfare and that (public) R&D investments are a key determinants of innovation. To this end, I will describe how the economic thought on the role of innovation in the economy and on the determinants of innovation evolved. I will also describe the different economic theories on the role of the government in inducing innovation through public R&D investments.

Innovation Leads to (Social) Welfare
Already in 1776 economist Adam Smith[32] observed that innovation contributes to wealth creation (or economic growth). He saw innovation as exogenous, an external random phenomenon that is not determined by economic factors and cannot be predicted more accurately than weather.

It was in 1934 that a more in-depth economic theory was developed by Schumpeter regarding the role of innovation in the economic system, based on a historical analysis of large, sweeping changes that fundamentally restructured industries and markets.

Schumpeter concluded that innovation had a dual role: creating new wealth-generating structures and destroying the old ones.[33] He saw economy as an equilibrium system. He considered that introduction of an innovation in a static economy creates a disequilibrium. This starts as a period of prosperity but changes gradually into a recession. As the economy adapts to the changed situation. The innovation weakens and the forces of competition and self-interest trigger increased production. This second wave of changes turns into a period of depression when inefficiencies and false expectations transform into unfavourable expectations. Depression is however accompanied by two favourable effects: the wide spread of the benefits of the innovation and the elimination of inefficient enterprises. Among the negative effects is that wages and prices, production and consumption fall far beyond the equilibrium values. A period of recovery follows under the effects of the forces of equilibrium (these are forces in the market which absorb the destructive effects triggered by innovation and adapt to them), which

[32] Smith 1904, para I.1.9.

[33] Schumpeter 1954, 83.

eventually leads to a new equilibrium.[34] Later, he admitted that other causes besides innovation may trigger the cyclicality of the economy.[35]

Schumpeter saw innovation as endogenous to the economic system and considered the entrepreneur to be its main driver. Moreover, he saw innovation as evolutionary. In Schumpeter's view, the evolutionary character is related to the selection of the viable innovations through competition and the cumulative character of knowledge which leads to innovation (innovations being often the result of cumulative efforts by many inventors and developers). He also believed that large firms have a crucial role in producing innovations. Subsequent empirical studies confirmed that the most innovative companies are large firms, and they deliver much more innovations than small firms in the pharmaceutical and aircraft industries. However, small firms appear to contribute with more innovations in certain industries (e.g. computers and process control instruments).[36]

As classical economist, Schumpeter believed that *'technical progress is a simple time trend'* that cannot be influenced by intentional action such as government intervention.[37] He believed that non-intervention was more advantageous on a long term for the level and speed of performance.[38] Schumpeter also did not believe there was a linear process between invention and innovation. He thought that *'innovation is possible without anything we could identify as invention and invention does not necessarily induce innovation'*.[39]

In a 1957 article, the Nobel Prize winner for economy Robert Solow added the mathematical dimension to Schumpeter's theory on innovation and sparkled renewed interest in the economic study of innovation.[40] He considered that growth was a function of physical capital and human labour and he believed that shifts in the function were caused by technological change.[41] He argued thus that technological progress is the key driver of growth. However, he considered technical progress to be an exogenous variable (as a time trend similar to population growth) to which the economy continuously adjusts and is driven in a state of dynamic equilibrium. His theory became known as the exogenous growth theory.

The idea of innovation contributing to social welfare was expressed by non-economists since 1924. Economic historian Godin identifies the industrialist Carty (1924), followed by the English evolutionary biologist J. Huxley (1935), the Irish mathematician J.D. Bernal (1939) and US policy-maker V. Bush (1945), as being the first supporters of the idea that science should and could be steered towards

34 Schumpeter 1939.

35 Schumpeter 1939; Allen 1991, 71–87.

36 Acs and Audretsch 2010.

37 Freeman and Soete 2000, 325.

38 Reference found in Gortz 2001, 236.

39 Schumpeter 1939, 84.

40 Beinhocker 2006, 40–1. Solow 1956; Solow 1957, 312–20.

41 Output (Y) is a function of the quantity of physical capital (K) and human labour (L): $Y = F(K, L)$.

playing a powerful role in curing social injustice and meeting real social desires. Implicitly they supported public research funding focused on long-term benefits to the consumer and to the individual citizen.[42]

In the 60s–70s, there was increasing attention to the social impact of technology.[43] However, social innovation as reaction/adjustment to the undesired effects of technical innovations, intended to meet social/public needs has gained momentum on the twenty-first century, but captured the interest of policy-makers rather than economists.[44]

(Public) R&D Investment Is a Determinant of Innovation

In the 1980s, neo-classics started to show more interest in the black box of innovation. Paul Romer was the first neo-classical economist to model innovation as an endogenous factor to the economy and he put the basis of the endogenous growth theory.[45] He did not attribute the source of growth to the entrepreneur, but to the nature of the technology. Technology has a cumulative, accelerating feature. The more knowledge is accumulated, the higher are the payoffs. This was coined as the 'increasing return' phenomenon. The endogenous growth theory also found support in the perceived success of massive public spending in R&D in the aircraft, nuclear, space and security sectors during and after the Second World War. Public R&D spending was considered the source of remarkable innovations,[46] as well as the source of broader economic growth.[47]

By now economists have not succeeded to empirically prove that R&D investments are essential to growth.[48] OECD admitted that attempting '*to attribute so much economic growth to technical advance, so much to capital formation, and so much to increased educational attainments of the work force, is like trying to distribute the credit for the flavour of a cake between the butter, the eggs and the sugar. All are essential and complementary ingredients.*'[49] Economists did find though that developed countries and within those, most innovative industries (e.g. computers, pharmaceuticals and instruments), invest most in R&D and in new knowledge.[50] But the correlation between R&D investments and innovative outputs becomes less compelling when calculated at company level. In other words, many innovative companies do not necessarily invest significantly in R&D.

---

[42] Quoted from Godin 2009, 18; Godin and Lane 2013.

[43] Quoted from Godin 2012; Mesthene 1969; OECD 1972.

[44] Godin 2012, 36–7.

[45] Romer 1990.

[46] During the Second World War, government funded R&D successfully led to the development of weapons and of medical treatment for infectious diseases. Nelson 1990, 209.

[47] Davidson 2009, 13–8.

[48] Godin 2009, 91, 94.

[49] Godin 2009, 96; OECD 2001, 4.

[50] Audretsch 1995; OECD 1992a, 1992b, 1996, 2016.

Audretsch argues that this is due to spill-overs from R&D and new knowledge at industry level, which can be exploited by third-parties.[51]

Nevertheless, economists broadly accept that R&D is one of the key determinants of innovation and economic growth.[52]

These economic conclusions underlie the recent Lisbon call for the EU (who relies on innovation to drive growth) to invest 3 percent of its annual GDP in R&D.[53] At the same time, economists warn that a simple increase in R&D investment is not enough, due to the complexity of the innovation process. The R&D expenditure target should therefore be accompanied by incentives to develop science-based solutions for relevant problems.[54]

In conclusion, economists consider that innovation (technological advance) leads to economic growth and that R&D investments constitute an essential, but not sufficient condition to support innovation. In the next section, I outline what role economists think that the government should assume in relation to R&D investment.

Economic Justification for Public R&D Investment

In this section, I will outline the different economic justifications for public intervention in stimulating innovation, particularly in the form of R&D investments. I will compare these economic justifications against the market failures that PCP allegedly seeks to address.

World War II marked a dramatic increase in government support for basic, commercial and military R&D in the US. The upsurge in public funding for R&D yielded major technological advances and built the strong research capacity (particularly in the private sector) that turned the US into the unchallenged industrial global leader.[55] In the postwar period, the US government continued to spend massive R&D budgets, compared to its earlier history and to the other industrial economies. In contrast to the prewar period, most of the federal funded R&D was performed by private industry in the defense sector and was largely devoted to development and only to a small extent to basic and applied research.[56] Mowery and Rosenberg (1993) note that the military procurement has played a major role next to military R&D funding in enhancing the innovative capabilities of US firms in the postwar period and in lowering the barriers to commercialization.[57]

---

[51] Audretsch and Thurik 2003, 41.

[52] Ulku 2004, 4–5; Griffith et al. 2000.

[53] Yusuf 2007, 10-1. Two-thirds (2 % of GDP) should come from the private market.

[54] Wessner 2004.

[55] Mowery and Rosenberg 1993, 39.

[56] In 1985, only 12 % was performed in federal laboratories, while 73 % was performed by private industry. Mowery and Rosenberg 1993, 41–2.

[57] Mowery and Rosenberg 1993, 46.

The federal R&D investment reached a peak of two thirds of the total R&D investment in the US in the mid-1960s.[58] By then, Friedmann's and Arrow's neo-classical theories[59] gained tremendous prestige and the costs and benefits of public R&D investments were increasingly being scrutinized.[60] Neo-classical theories argued that the market mechanism, although often wasteful and inefficient in the choice of the winning innovation, had been a viable mode of bringing remarkable technological advances[61] and that the government should intervene when the outcomes are inconsistent with the expectations of the society.[62] This is the case when the price mechanism does not capture social value, and occurs mainly in the following situations:[63] (1) when innovations presents the characteristics of a public good; (2) when innovations entail positive externalities;[64] (3) when information asymmetries are present; or (4) when monopolies are formed.[65]

(1) An innovation has the characteristics of a public good if, once disseminated, users cannot be denied further use and cannot be mandated to pay for it. Among the innovation activities, basic research is one of the purest forms of public goods. It requires big investments, while it does not produce an economic advantage (as it has no concrete commercial application in sight) on a short term and can often not be appropriated.[66] A free market underinvests in basic research. Public investments are generally accepted by neo-classics, as long as the government does not restrict the choice of scientists regarding which research to pursue.[67]
(2) Innovations may present spillovers (or positive externalities) which cannot fully be translated into benefits for the producers or can only partially be

[58] 80 % of the federal R&D funds were dedicated to defense research in the 1960s. In 1983, only around 14 % of the military R&D budgets were dedicated to basic and applied research, while nearly 86 % went to development of weapon system, construction and testing of prototypes. Mowery and Rosenberg 1993, 43.

[59] Friedmann 1962; Arrow 1962, 619.

[60] Freeman 1982, 15.

[61] Nelson 1990; Aghiou et al. 2005, 701–28; Boone and Van Damme 2004, 71–92.

[62] Such as when innovation contributes to depletion of natural resources instead of enabling their conservation. Cooter et al. 2011, 11–2; Yusuf 2007, 3. Stiglitz argues the need for public intervention, justified by the fact that the relation between fluctuations in the economy and fluctuations in innovation goes both ways, and by the fact that the free market left to itself will not always choose the most positive equilibria resulting from the positive feedback between economy and innovation. See Stiglitz 1994, 121–54.

[63] Gilbert 2007b.

[64] Externalities are about benefits (and costs) of private economic activity that those who make the relevant decisions do not see as benefits (or costs) to them'. See Nelson 2004.

[65] Commission 2006; Inman 1987, 647–777; Baarsma et al. 2010.

[66] Swann 2003, 335–60; Brynjolfsson and Zhang 2006, 3.

[67] Polanyi 1962, 54–72.

exploited (e.g. due to easiness in copying the products, insufficient intellectual property rights, mobility of knowledge workers etc.).[68] Environmental innovations for example, generate environmental benefits (e.g. clean air), for which the society or other economic agents cannot are not paying. In this context, an unaided market will not invest sufficiently in the creation of new knowledge. Economists take the view that knowledge externalities are desirable for the emergence of innovation and public intervention in the form of funding can encourage private actors to invest in R&D and produce sufficient amounts of knowledge, despite these externalities.[69]

(3) In case of information asymmetries, the private investment market fails to engage sufficient funds in highly experimental and uncertain innovations that may potentially yield large economic and social benefits, because it lacks information on the innovative capabilities of the innovator, is not aware of the innovator's existence or does not understand the new ideas.[70]

(4) A market failure may also arise when the monopolist does not have sufficient information on whether the consumers are ready to pay the fixed costs of the production of a certain product. In this case, public intervention in the form of funding of basic research is likely to stimulate the monopolist to invest in innovation.[71]

In summary, neo-classics believe that performing innovative activities and bringing innovative solutions to the market remains principally the role of the private market.[72] Even when the market or systemic failures occur, government's intervention often comes with high costs[73] as policy decisions are not always sufficiently informed and unbiased to achieve better results than the private market.[74] As a consequence, they believe that the government should only fund basic research and should leave the choice of the research topic to the researcher.

Thus, neo-classic theories do not support the idea of government support of applied research, as envisaged by PCP.

In spite of the popularity of the neo-classical theories, the US SBIR found large political support in the '70s. This happened on the background of increased foreign competition and economic slowdown, which caused a decline in private returns to

---

[68] Lipsey 2007, 5–28.

[69] Benjamin and Rai 2008, 12. See also Romer 1994, 20–1.

[70] Wessner 2004 points out that few investors in the 1980s understood Bill Gates vision for Microsoft.

[71] Swann 2003, 335–60.

[72] Baarsma et al. 2010, 39–40.

[73] The public costs of correcting market failures are high because the public intervention will try to bring about private transactions between partners with non-reciprocal interests. See also B. Baarsma et al. 2010, 39–40.

[74] Hans W. Friederiszick, Lars-Hendrik Roller, and Vincent Verouden, 'European State Aid Control: An Economic Framework' 2005, 637 http://ec.europa.eu/dgs/competition/economist/esac.pdf Accessed 8 April 2013; Baarsma et al. 2010.

R&D investments and led to a decrease of private R&D investments. Concerns were also expressed that new product development became increasingly costly, particularly in the biotech and microelectronics sectors, while venture capital excessively focused on short-term projects. This weakened opposition to public funding of commercial applications of scientific knowledge and led to the adoption of the SBIR program in 1982 (see also description in Chap. 4, Sect. 4.2).[75]

While neo-classical theories dominated the US, in Europe, the idea of direct government intervention in the economy was more widely accepted. The desire to deal with unemployment and to make national industry more competitive on the global market were among the most invoked justifications for funding R&D by national companies.[76] Subsequently, the focus of public innovation policies shifted towards improving the quality of innovations and *'contribut[ing] to social welfare, conceived in a wider sense'*.[77]

During the 1970s, the innovation system theories became influential in Europe. These theories argued that 'system failures' explain the suboptimal results in innovation: infrastructural failures (when the infrastructure for certain desirable economic activities such as universities, labs etc. are too costly to be funded by private actors),[78] institutional failures (when the legal system (IP protection system) or the political and social culture and values do not create a climate supportive of innovation),[79] interaction failures (no ties between complementary technologies or actors or existing ties between non-complementary actors),[80] transition, capability and learning failures (when firms are not capable to adapt to changes in their environment, such as new technologies).[81]

In order to address system failures, the system of innovation theorists advocated a more detailed and comprehensive public intervention than accepted by neo-classics. In their view, the government should facilitate interactions and

---

75 Mowery and Rosenberg 1993, 55–8.

76 Magnus Gulbrandsen and Henry Etzkowitz, 'Convergence Between Europe and America: The Transition from Industrial to Innovation Policy' 1999 Journal of Technology Transfer 24.

77 Freeman 1982, 198–201.

78 Edquist C., 'Innovation Policy: a Systemic Approach', in D. Archibugi and B.Å. Lundvall (eds) *'The Globalizing Learning Economy'* OUP 2001; Smith K., 'Innovation as a Systemic Phenomenon: Rethinking the role of Policy' 2000 1 *Enterprise and Innovation Management Studies* 1, 73–102.

79 Carlsson B. and S. Jacobsson, 'In Search of Useful Public Policies: Key Lessons and Issues for Policy Makers' in B. Carlsson (ed) *'Technological Systems and Industrial Dynamics'* Kluwer Academic Publishers 1997.

80 Malerba F., R. Nelson, L. Orsenigo and S. Winter, 'History-friendly models of industry evolution: the computer industry' 1999 8 *Industrial and Corporate Change* 1, 3–40.

81 Chaminade C. and C. Edquist, 'From Theory to Practice: The Use of the Systems of Innovation Approach for Innovation Policy' in J. Hage and M. Meeus (eds), *'Innovation, Science and Institutional Change'* OUP 2006.

identify technological opportunities.[82] This entails a change in the narrow and vertical focus of public institutions involved in stimulating innovation.[83]

In the 21st century, the increased recognition of the complexity of the economy and of the limitations of economics in measuring or predicting the effects of public intervention on the decisions of firms to innovate, has led to new economic approaches to innovation policy.

Complexity economists, for example, reject the neo-classics assumption that the economy is an orderly system made of perfectly rational individuals tending towards equilibrium. They argue that the economy is a complex adaptive system with many dynamically interacting parts and networks, and with imperfect individuals who '*use inductive rules of thumb to make decisions*' and '*are subject to errors and biases*', but also capable to adapt to changing circumstances.[84] The evolution 'algorithm' (differentiate, select, amplify) explains, in their view, the growing order and complexity of the economic system and of the innovation process.[85]

They propose to completely drop the debate on state versus private markets and concentrate on an effective interplay between the two forces to create an effective evolutionary system, that applies the evolution algorithm.[86] In this evolutionary system, the innovation policy-maker is an adaptive agent, subject to evolution through policy experimentation and policy learning. He stimulates the emergence of a variety of innovations, that are subsequently exposed to the selection process in the marketplace.[87] This implies a certain degree of tolerance to '*redundancy, overlap and excess capacity*'.[88]

In the same line of thought, Mazzucato suggests that the state is capable to play a more active role on the innovation scene than correcting market failures and creating the right infrastructure and linkages between innovation actors.[89] By investing in early stage, highly uncertain projects, it can drive the innovation process rather than just incentivize it.[90]

According to Mazzucato, the US government invested in forward-looking innovations through its Small Business Innovation Research ('SBIR') programme, and managed to play a leading role in bringing about innovative breakthroughs. US state investment in different types of risky and uncertain research (whether basic or applied research) was available far earlier than private investment.[91] Mazzucato

82 Freeman 1982.

83 Edler et al. 2002, 5.

84 Beinhocker 2006, 97.

85 Beinhocker 2006, 11–2, 17–8.

86 Beinhocker 2006, 427. Bakhshi et al. 2011.

87 Metcalfe and Georghiou 1997, 7.

88 Beinhocker 2006, 339–40.

89 Mazzucato 2013, 18–9.

90 Mazzucato 2013, 49.

91 Mazzucato 2013, 49.

relies on evidence from two empirical studies, conducted by Ruttan and by Block and Keller. Based on the analysis of state investments in six technology areas (the US 'mass production' system, aviation technologies, space technologies, information technology, internet technologies and nuclear power) Ruttan shows how the US government engaged funds in the most risky and uncertain early research in areas where it spotted a window of technical and commercial opportunity, and continued to oversee the innovation process up to commercialization. He concludes that government investment particularly sparkled the creation of technologies that require large investments at early stages (such as nuclear power).[92] Block and Keller's study shows that between 1971 and 2006, 77 out of 88 of the most important innovations[93] were in their early stages but also beyond, heavily funded by the federal government.[94]

In conclusion, economists disagree on the situations when public intervention in the innovation processes is justified and on the extent to which it should be employed. Both neo-classics and systems of innovation theorists admit that private innovation efforts do not always lead to the desired result. Neo-classics delineate specific circumstances (market failures) under which intervention is justified. According to them the government is only entitled to funding basic/fundamental R&D, while the topic of research should be left to the free choice of the researchers. Systems of innovation theorists adopt a broader view on the conditions and means of intervention. More recent complexity theories advise to drop the debate altogether and focus on the effective interplay between the state and private actor. In other words, the government is entitled to fund technological opportunities (irrespective of the R&D phase), as long as it behaves as an adaptive agent, capable of learning from exploratory policies.

However, regardless of the embraced theoretical argumentation, a withdrawal of public support for innovation in Western countries can hardly be conceived.[95] Innovation policy is not always based on an economic calculation of size of a market failure and of costs and benefits of a planned public measure. Often, decisions are based on political considerations, such as in the case of US SBIR.

---

92 Ruttan 2006.

93 They rate the importance of the considered innovations based on R&D Magazine's annual awards.

94 Block and Keller 2010.

95 Scotchmer 2004 argues: 'In the US, for example, R&D performed by industry now comprises a hefty three-fourths of the total. Nevertheless, the R&D performed by universities and the federal government is also substantial. Most industrial R&D is applied, while most R&D in universities is basic research. Even though universities perform only 14 % of R&D, they perform about half of total basic research. Federal government funds 26 % of total R&D, including grants to universities, firms, and federally funded research and development centers, which are run by firms and universities but are not owned by them. Only ¼ of the federally funded research takes place intramurally in government laboratories. Even though the federal government funds 26 % of R&D, its employees perform only 7 % of the total R&D. This is why industry and universities perform much more R&D than they fund. Industry only receives 10 % of its R&D budget from the government.'

3.4 European Venture Capital Markets—Investments in (Risky) R&D

The PCP Communication and the preceding PCP Expert Group report argued that PCP is necessary due to underinvestment by private venture capitalists in risky R&D projects. In this section, I outline some of the most important economic studies concerning the role of venture capital markets in the innovation process in the US and in the EU. Concurrently, I highlight the economists conclusions concerning the role of public R&D investments to compensate for less well functioning financial markets. This will provide guidance to public procurers on how to effectively deploy PCP.

In general, venture capital is attributed the merit of mitigating the problem of access to finance of young innovative firms and of spurring their growth.[96] Venture capital is largely considered the most efficient financial institution to operate under conditions of uncertainty and information asymmetries which characterize innovative projects in young firms.[97]

In the US, venture capitalists address the uncertainty and information asymmetry problems through intensive scrutiny of business plans and operations and through staged funding.[98] The existence of an efficient financing system with a mature venture capital market is believed to be the reason for the sustained economic growth in the US in the 1990s.[99] Based on a study of twenty industries in the US over a period of three decades, Kortum and Lerner conclude that venture capital funded firms perform better than large firms with R&D divisions, or compared to projects financed through private R&D funds.[100]

However, several economists point out the limitations of venture capital investments.

Kortum and Lerner point out that venture funding does not have an uniform impact. During 'hot' financial periods, the impact decreases, as venture capitalists tend to overestimate the value of projects and over-invest in similar projects, or tend to increase the size of their investment, at the cost of reducing their capability to keep control.[101]

Gans and Stern emphasize that venture capitalists are driven not only by technological opportunity, but also by the capability of the small firm to turn the R&D results into economic returns. This leads to concentration of investments in only a few sectors. In the 1990s in the US, the authors noticed a skewed distribution of

[96] Engel 2002.

[97] Caselli et al. 2006, 6.

[98] Gompers and Lerner 1999, 11.

[99] Caselli et al. 2006.

[100] Kortum and Lerner 2000.

[101] Kortum and Lerner 2000, 686. Gompers and Lerner 1999, 8.

R&D investments in innovation by small technology-based firms, with high rates of R&D investments in few sectors, such as software development, telecommunications and biotechnology. Jacobs also remarks that venture capitalists are prone to herding tendencies and focus on technologies that already have a high probability of success (low risk and close to market).[102]

Kline and Rosenberg confirm that venture capitalists do not invest in potentially breakthrough innovations when the envisaged costs of development are high and the needed efforts are uncertain and unpredictable. The authors also emphasize the trend of increasing development costs of new products in many high tech sectors.[103] Years later, Lerner observes an increase in the size of venture capital investments. But, according to the author, this trend leaves small businesses that generally need small investments without a solution.[104]

That venture capitalists do not invest in radical innovations is attributed by Mazzucato to internal policies regarding management fees and bonuses for high returns. These drive venture capitalists to focus on shorter term investments (of 3 to 5 years, although the venture capital funds are usually set up for period of 10 years).[105]

According to Chemmanur et al., this issue is less apparent in Corporate Venture Capital ('CVC') in the US.[106] CVC (defined as venture capital made available by companies to source innovations from external sources, instead of solely relying on in-house R&D) performs better in nurturing innovation in the funded firms than independent venture capitalists. According to the authors, this is due to less concerns related to short-term financial returns (e.g. CVC managers are paid a fixed salary plus corporate bonuses) as well as due to the unique knowledge they possess on the industry. These features allow the corporate venture capitalist to be more open to experimentation and more tolerant to failure. CVCs appear to generate more innovation productivity (in terms of number of patents and citations) than independent venture capital.[107] However, CVCs are not always a reliable funding source, as internal projects may be preferred to the detriment of the external ones, as required by company strategy or unavailability of surplus capital.[108]

Other studies have also pointed out that tolerance to early failure is important particularly to firms exposed to high failure risks (such as recession periods, early development stages and highly uncertain innovations).[109] Economists argue that technological revolutions are preceded by a period of increased experimentation in the economy, which comes along with inevitable failure of numerous start-ups and

[102] Jacobs 2002.

[103] Kline and Rosenberg 1986, 295.

[104] Lerner 1999.

[105] Mazzucato 2013, 41.

[106] These are internal VC funds established by corporations as subsidiaries.

[107] Chemmanur et al. 2012; Lantz and Sahut 2010, 8.

[108] Lantz and Sahut 2010, 39.

[109] Tian and Wang 2011, 3.

destruction of mature firms and which necessitates highly active financial markets, which are willing to fund new firms even if the failure risk is high.[110] However, economic growth will only be generated if a sufficient number of high-growth start-ups emerge from among the new firms. In this context, the youngest and most experimental firms are impacted by the financial risks even in times of financial equilibrium and are most vulnerable to financial shocks.[111]

Unlike in the US, European venture capital has not been associated with support of innovation, but rather with exploitation of existing technological capabilities of funded firms.[112] Moreover, economists noticed that in times of depression, the level of venture capital investments at seed and start-up stage tends to fall abruptly in Europe.[113] The lack of early-stage venture capital for young companies in Europe was considered as one of the most important reasons why Europe has fewer young firms as leading innovators in high-tech sectors as compared to the US.[114]

Another aspect increasing the difficulties of young innovative firms in funding innovative projects, has been the lack of large public budgets for high-tech R&D such as have been available in the US.[115] According to Auerswald and Branscomb the amount of US government funding just for early stage technology firms, equaled by 2003 the total investments of 'business angels' and was approximately two to eight times larger than private venture capital.[116]

In the US, the government has acted as an entrepreneurial venture capitalist through the Small Business Innovation Research (SBIR) programme and has played a vital role beyond the basic research phase of projects.[117] Mazzucato points out that US SBIR agencies have sometimes invested in highly uncertain, high risk projects in fields such as genomics or ICT, long before venture capital funding was available. According to Mazzucato, the key to the US program's success in stimulating technologies which escaped the attention of the traditional venture investor, was the decentralized institutional set-up, with program managers looking to fulfill very specific technical needs of the Federal agency.[118]

Economists warn that in public venture capital programs such as the SBIR the same pitfalls as in the private venture capital arena may occur. The impact of the public funding proves to be low when short-term reward mechanisms lead public

---

110 Nanda and Rhodes-Kropf 2011, 1–2.

111 Stam 2008, 34, 40–1; Nanda and Rhodes-Kropf 2011, 5, 38. Spiegel and Tookes 2008, 3; Stiglitz and Weiß 1981; Binks and Ennew 1996, 17–25.

112 Caselli et al. 2006, 22.

113 In 2002, the level of venture capital investment has fallen from € 6.7 billion in 2001 to € 4.2 billion. See Independent Expert Group 2003, 6.

114 Veugelers and Cincera 2010.

115 PCP Expert Group 13.

116 Auerswald and Branscomb 2003, 3–4.

117 Mazzucato 2013, 41.

118 Lerner 1999, 17.

managers to choose firms with better prospects of success and already sufficiently funded by venture capitalists[119] (for an outline of the studies that evaluate the impact of the US SBIR, see Chap. 4).

In conclusion, venture capital often leaves the youngest and most experimental firms without funding, particularly in case of large development costs and long-term returns on investment. This confirms the assumption that PCP is needed to compensate for underinvestment by venture capitalists in risky R&D projects. This implies the need for the government to fund these firms both in times of financial equilibrium and in times of recession. Government funding should though present tolerance to failure and investment decisions should be made by managers with in-depth knowledge of the targeted sector and in line with very specific technical needs of their agency.

3.5 The Impact of Public Needs/Demand on Firms' Strategies for Creativity and Innovation

In the 1940s, the belief that basic science (or basic research) was the source of inventions and discoveries dominated in the US. This belief was based on the conclusion that breakthrough innovations had resulted from the massive public investments in basic research during and after the Second World War. It was moreover reinforced by the observation that technology became increasingly complex and dependent on scientific content, and that throughout history innovation efforts tended to concentrate in specialized public or private research and development laboratories.[120]

MIT economist W. Ruper Maclaurin developed in this period, the linear model of innovation.[121] According to his model, innovation starts with basic science, and is followed by the subsequent stages of invention, innovation, finance, acceptance/diffusion.[122] The linear model of innovation was generally accepted at the time.[123] This changed in the 1960s, when several studies commissioned by US Federal Agencies,[124] concluded that concrete agency needs triggered innovation more often, than undirected science (or basic research). The studies recommended to

[119] Mazzuccato 2013.

[120] Scientific content can be defined as the body of learning which is a necessary precondition of future innovations. This is a departure from initial innovative processes which were exclusively associated with the persons involved in the production. Freeman and Soete 2007, 10.

[121] Godin 2010, 6.

[122] Maclaurin 1953.

[123] According to Freeman, the massive public investments in R&D during and after the WWII brought breakthrough innovations.

[124] Based on the analysis of major weapon technologies, one study concluded that only 0.3 % of the innovations derived from basic research. Sherwin and Isenson 1967, quoted from Godin and Lane 2013, 8–9.

'couple scientific discoveries with needs'.[125] This was confirmed by Schmookler's book 'Invention and Economic Growth', in which he argues that market demand (or extent of the market potential) is the most important driver of the inventive activity.[126]

This was the sparkle of modern economic theories on the role of demand in the innovation process.[127] In economic terms, 'demand' encompasses trade-offs between quantity, price and performance and entails the willingness and ability of customers to buy and use an innovation.

In the 1970s, Freeman, the founder of the systems of innovation theory, argued that neither R&D, nor market demand is the main driving factor behind innovation activity. He believed that innovation was a 'coupling process' between supply (technological knowledge) and demand, that takes place in an evolving environment with imperfect information where uncertainty prevails and *'chance plays a much greater role in competitive survival and in growth than it is comfortable to admit'*.[128]

Later, his theory was refined. Innovation was depicted as a non-linear process that is influenced by interdependent interactions between firms and other organizations. The emphasis was laid on the role of institutions (such as firms, public laboratories, universities, financial institutions, government bodies etc.) in a national innovation system. Systems of innovation were defined as *'the network of institutions in the public and private sectors whose activities and interactions initiate, import, modify and diffuse new technologies'*.[129] Innovation is not only influenced by the independent elements of the systems, but also by the relations between these elements.[130]

But the landmark economic contributions on the role of market demand on innovation came from Mowery and Rosenberg (1979), Kline and Rosenberg (1986), Urban and von Hippel (1986) and Porter (1990).

In a 1979 study, Stanford economists Mowery and Rosenberg, distinguished between the role of demand at different moments in the innovation process. They admitted that demand had a dominant role at the diffusion phase, but criticized the overemphasis of the role of demand in determining the emergence of innovative solutions. The decision of firms to innovate is not always caused by the existence of customers' demand or the likelihood of future demand.

They concluded that market demand, defined as willingness of customers to pay for purchasing innovative solutions, is not always and definitely not the only factor motivating firms in investing efforts in the desired innovations. They argued

125 Godin and Lane 2013, 8–9.

126 Schmookler 1966.

127 Mowery and Rosenberg 1979. Demand can be defined as the 'willingness to pay a certain price for the satisfaction of a need or want'. See Edler 2013, 8.

128 Freeman 1979, 213.

129 Freeman 1995, 19.

130 Edquist and Hommen 1999, 66.

that additional and at least equally important supply-side conditions were necessary, such as new technological opportunities/capabilities which lower production costs and make it possible to bring to the market the desired innovation.[131] Moreover, they expressed doubts on whether firms have the capabilities to perceive the demand curve for products[132] and observed that the most radical innovations responded the least to market 'needs'.[133]

They concluded that there is an important role for the government to give a decisive impulse to the innovation process in areas in which the market does not generate the necessary incentives or R&D resources to determine the emergence of innovative solutions for urgent social needs. However, public demand will be effective in those areas where the technological basis is ripe as a consequence of nourishment though supply-side measures.[134]

They also signaled the importance of exchanges of information regarding desired products and product characteristics, between users and producers and between non-commercial basic research institutions and private firms and laboratories.[135]

In 1986, Rosenberg teamed up with Stanford mechanical engineering professor Kline and conceptualized the chain-linked innovation models. They concluded that innovation is triggered by either research or the existence of a potential market,[136] and goes through the following stages: invent and/or produce analytic design, detailed design and test, redesign and produce and distribute and market. Important feedback loops are created between these stages.[137] When science does not provide the necessary knowledge, an innovator starts with a repetitive process of trial and error of several combinations of existing knowledge. This process follows the following steps: the first best estimate of a workable design, build it, test it, incorporate learning, redesign, retest, incorporate learning and so on. They pointed out that this process is costly and justifies continuous investment by the government in basic research.[138]

Even when innovation is triggered by basic research, it still needs to be coupled to market needs in order to be commercially successful. Kline and Rosenberg quote from the journal of Thomas Edison, who, after inventing a vote counting machine only to find out later that the Congress was not interested, allegedly said that he would never again spend time on an invention with no sound market prospect.[139]

---

131 Mowery and Rosenberg 1979, 142.

132 Mowery and Rosenberg 1979, 145.

133 Mowery and Rosenberg 1979, 143–4.

134 Mowery and Rosenberg 1979, 149.

135 Mowery and Rosenberg 1979, 149.

136 Kline and Rosenberg 1986, 286.

137 Kline and Rosenberg 1986, 286.

138 Kline and Rosenberg 1986, 296.

139 Kline and Rosenberg 1986, 278.

The same view of innovation models is shared by complexity economist Brian Arthur. He explains that innovations occur sometimes when the scientific phenomena are not understood (for example, the bicycle was invented when the physical laws of equilibrium were not understood); other innovations emerge as applications of the scientific knowledge (for example the synthetic dyestuffs industry that emerged in Germany at the end of the 19th century as a direct result of knowledge advances in organic industry[140]). But in the context of increasingly complex technologies, science and technologies co-evolve. Arthur uses the concept of 'combinatorial evolution' to capture the idea that technologies are often made of numerous sub-technologies that emerge from existing knowledge, while new knowledge is also created during the development process. Certain major innovations require decades of sequential innovations (little fixes and advancements) before they can compete with incumbent competitors.[141]

In the same year, MIT economist von Hippel outlined his 'lead-users' theory.[142] He argued that manufacturers experience significant benefits when they identify the most experienced and leading-edge users ('lead-users') and involve them in the product development process. He defined 'lead-users' as individuals, firms or organisations which present early needs (months or years before they become general needs in the market place) and tend to benefit significantly from obtaining an early solution to these needs. Based on empirical studies in the chemical and computer industries, he concluded that lead-users may contribute to the innovation process not only with sharing data regarding their needs (and future general needs) but also with *'rich insight to working and tested prototypes of the desired novel product, process, or service'* and even with the development of solutions.[143] Lead users will also tend to be early adopters[144] of the innovations, due to the significant benefits they gain from adoption.[145]

Harvard economist Porter studied in 1990 the role demanding and sophisticated markets (as opposed to individual lead-users) play in creating global competitive advantages for local companies. Based on a four-year study of internationally successful industries in ten important trading countries (Denmark, Germany, Italy, Japan, Korea, Singapore, Sweden, Switzerland, the UK and the US), Porter concluded that the quality, and to a lesser extent the size of demand in the markets where firms are located have a significant influence on the innovation rate of the industry and as a consequence on their competitive advantages on a global level.[146] He explained that local markets which give early and clear signals of

[140] For a detailed account of the emergence of these innovations, see Johann Murmann 2000.

[141] Arthur 2010, 157–9.

[142] Urban and von Hippel 1986.

[143] Urban and von Hippel 1986, 19.

[144] However, lead users are not the same as early adopters. Lead users feel the need before the product is available on the market, before early adopters.

[145] Urban and von Hippel 1986.

[146] Porter 1990.

emerging buyer needs help build a competitive advantage of local firms on foreign markets. The most significant effect is observed when the needs are stringent and the lead market widely embraces the resulting products. In addition, the needs of the local buyers have to *'anticipate or even shape those of other nations'*, which happens when a nation is *'exporting its values and tastes as well as its products'*.[147] He advocated the legitimate role of the government in challenging firms and rewarding the most innovative ones, without falling into the industrial policy pitfalls, such as protecting inefficient companies from foreign competitions.[148]

The theories of von Hippel and Porter inspired Georghiou to develop the concept of 'lead markets'.[149] These are markets with multiple or large single users who are willing to adopt innovations early and pay the premium price for them. In addition, a lead market provides *'the more general conditions favourable to innovation such as an efficient and responsive regulatory structure, security for intellectual property* etc.'.[150] The European Commission has embraced this approach and has launched several lead-market initiatives, focused on the early uptake of innovations.[151] However, the EU concept of lead-market is a diluted version of the demanding and sophisticated market in Porter's study. EU lead-markets entail early adoption of innovations, but do not cover definition of advanced requirements to influence the early investment decisions of the innovating companies.

The above described studies argue thus that companies are incentivized to engage in innovative activities when sophisticated end-users articulate advanced and stringent needs, and adopt the developed innovation at an early stage and on a sufficiently large scale. Although they do not refer to the involvement of the end-user in *funding* the R&D trajectory, these studies show that for demand to have an impact on the innovative activities of private actors, it needs to entail the involvement of the end-users and a clear prospect of early commercialization at a sufficiently broad scale.

Other studies that investigate how *public* demand shapes the innovation process, focus on the role of public agencies in financing the R&D stages and in adopting the resulting innovation at an early stage.[152]

They warn that the decision of a public agency to support one specific innovation at an early R&D phase should be based on a solid knowledge on the technological trajectory and market trends, in order *'to avoid lock-into a technology that is premature or for which accompanying business infrastructure is not ready'*.[153] Otherwise, the public agency should fund parallel development trajectories.[154]

[147] Porter 1990, 82.

[148] Porter 1990, 87.

[149] Georghiou 2006.

[150] Gheorghiou 2006, 13.

[151] http://ec.europa.eu/enterprise/policies/innovation/policy/lead-market-initiative/#h2-3.

[152] Nesta 2010, 14; Edler 2013.

[153] Izsak and Edler 2011, 18.

[154] Cabral et al. 2006.

As early-adopter, a public agency can significantly benefit the innovating company in the following ways:

- by paying a premium for the early use of innovations, the public purchaser ensures early revenues for the innovating firm, which allows the firm to develop the technology up to the point when it is competitive compared to established technologies available on the market.[155]
- by providing important feedback to innovators,[156]
- by providing credibility to small firms.[157]

In conclusion, economists agree that public demand can effectively be employed to incentivize the emergence of innovations and to redirect private innovation efforts towards such desired innovations. Based on the review of relevant economic literature, Dalpé et al.[158] summarize the following cumulative conditions for an efficient use of public procurement at both the R&D stage and at the early-adoption stage:

- It is employed at the early stages in the life cycle of a product and of an industry;
- competition is maintained throughout the whole innovation process;
- the government is itself a technologically advanced end-user of the innovation;
- the government is capable to offer a sufficiently sizeable market for the developed innovation;
- the adaptation of the product to larger markets is not cumbersome.

Using *public* demand to drive innovation in the context of PCP requires thus the existence of a potential public end-user, who has the willingness and ability to purchase and use the innovation, if developed to expected levels of performance and price.

Other Empirical Studies

A number of articles present case-studies of public procurement (both PCP and commercial procurement) being used as innovation policy instrument, while others rank public procurement against other innovation policy instruments depending on its role as determinant of innovation. Several of the most relevant are presented below.

One of the most used examples by economists to demonstrate that public R&D procurement can compensate for customers' distrust of the reliability of a new product which is objectively superior to the more established competing products,

---

155 Malerba et al. 2008, *67*.

156 In the UK, for example, studies show that in many sectors, a large share of spending on innovation is oriented towards marketing and preparing the market, rather than on understanding the needs and preferences of customers. See DTI 2006.

157 Edler and Georghiou 2007, 955.

158 Dalpé et al. 1992, 252.

finds itself in the transistors sector.[159] The initial transistors were not competitive in terms of quality and price against vacuum tubes. The financial support from the US Department of Defense ('DoD') within the US SBIR for the continuous improvement of the technology, which by mid 1970s had eliminated vacuum tubes from the market. A similar example is that of the jet engines. Although it cannot be argued that the technology would not have emerged without the SBIR funding by the DoD, it is widely accepted that DoD speeded the time to the market of jet engines. Jet engines eventually replaced piston engines in the civil aircraft industry. The same happened in the case of Internet, after DoD required the development of a packet/switch network instead of the existent circuit/switched network.[160]

In Europe, the most well-known example of a successful use of public demand (or technology procurement) to steer private R&D efforts towards environmentally friendly solutions in the household appliances sector comes from Sweden.[161] Between 1988 and 1998, the Swedish Energy Authorities applied catalytic procurement to stimulate technological advancement in the energy sector. More concretely, it coordinated end-users, in the residential, the service, and the industrial sector and technology experts in identifying potential technological improvements in terms of energy efficiency and articulating procurement requirements for such improved products. Through a competitive procedure, the best prototype which met the requirements was then selected and awarded.

The program was accompanied by unique combinations of policy instruments for each developed technology, such as subsidies for the installation costs, training of maintenance personnel, information campaigns, labeling. The catalytic procurement program was also characterized by intensive interaction between the actors involved and by an ongoing monitoring and learning process. Thus, failure in the process of technical change was identified at an early stage and action was taken to redesign or terminate the policy intervention.

The economic analysis of the Swedish programme concludes on its success in bringing improvements in technological performance and in some cases cost reduction. The program proved less effective in impacting other outcome indicators such as increasing sales data, market share, changes in manufacturers' assortment, change in knowledge, attitudes and behaviour of important actors. Moreover, not all of the 30 procurements of technologies included in the program scored positively in terms of outcome.

Economists who evaluated the Swedish program admit though the limitation of the available data necessary for the evaluation, such as lack of information on the levels of the outcome indicators before the start of the program. Moreover, by using outcome indicators, the evaluation of the program reflects the impact of all the public instruments used without distinguishing between them.

---

159 Mowery and Rosenberg 1979, 148.

160 Malerba et al. 2008.

161 Neija and Åstrand 2006; Neija 2001.

Other studies assess how the prospect of having a public customer at the end of the R&D trajectory impacts the innovative efforts of the industry. Beise and Rennings[162] conclude on the basis of case-studies of fuel-efficient passenger cars and wind energy that legislation (imposing technological performance requirements) combined with anticipation of international demand created the proper conditions for innovation. International demand appears to have a positive impact on innovation efforts in the vaccine industry as well. A study by Smita Arinivas on the evolution of the vaccine industry in India concludes that technical advance is most stimulated by international procurement when the sector is free from accusations of protectionism and when delivery terms are long and the number of competing suppliers is large. Besides demand, prior learning, enhanced by open dissemination of technical standards and regulations and the participation of developers and manufacturers in networks, is essential.[163]

Other studies, based on surveys of private firms/innovators reach positive conclusions regarding the role of public procurement as determinants of innovation. It is however, not clear whether these studies cover innovation-oriented procurement programs.

For example, based on a survey of Finnish innovators from different sectors, Palmberg[164] concludes that public procurement was the least valuable among different sources of innovation. Miles et al.[165] show that UK firms, out of the seven wider conditions that matter for innovation, rate the intensity of competition and demand for new products and services as the most important after availability of human resources. The study concludes that firms are willing to innovate when innovation delivers them economic and competitive advantages. The extent of these advantages depends on the demand for innovation and the intensity of competition they encounter on the market within which they operate. The stronger and the more clear the demand for innovation in a market, the more willing the firms will be to innovate.[166]

Based on qualitative and quantitative analyses of public demand, Rothwell and Zegveld[167] and Geroski[168] show that on a long-term, public procurement had a more positive impact on innovation than R&D subsidies. Other studies bring evidence that the impact of public procurement on market success of innovations

---

162 Beise and Rennings 2005.

163 Arinivas 2006.

164 Palmberg 2004.

165 In a functional model of innovation systems the seven conditions which influence innovation are: qualitative public research, openness (of individuals to seek and share knowledge and the existence of physical infrastructure which facilitates effective exchange of knowledge), commercial motivation and entrepreneurship, demand for innovation, a competitive market that facilitates entry, rewards successful innovators and selects out poor performers, access to finance and available and qualitative human resources. See Miles et al. 2009, 11–2.

166 Miles et al. 2009, 16–7.

167 Rothwell and Zegveld 1981.

168 Geroski 1990, 182–98; Dalpé 1994, 16.

(indicated by turnover from sales of products which are new to the market) is similar in Germany to the impact of university knowledge spilling over to firms, and scores better than regulation and subsidies.[169] The same study indicates that regular procurement rather than defence procurement has a stronger influence and that its impact is most clear on small firms in economically challenged regional markets, with limited financial resources.

A more recent survey performed on 10 % of the public sector suppliers in the UK, shows that public procurement is the second most important incentive for innovation, following changes in the market demand and preceding internal R&D or private buyers. The survey also concludes that 51.4 % of the suppliers who had performed R&D in the previous three years, had increased their R&D expenses as a result of participation in a public award procedure.[170]

The empirical studies support thus the conclusion that public R&D contracts and the prospect of an early public customer can trigger and/or speed up the emergence of innovations.

3.6 PCP for the Development of Innovative Services

The 2007 PCP Communication and the accompanying PCP Staff Working Document are not clear on whether PCP is a suitable instrument for the development of innovative services, particularly when they are not built around a(n innovative) technology. On the one hand, the policy documents talk about the role of PCP to assure the development of technological solutions to meet challenging societal needs.[171] On the other hand, they indicate that the result of a PCP can be either an innovative product or an innovative service.[172]

In this section I test the fifth assumption that PCP is a suitable instrument to stimulate technological, as well as services[173] innovations, against relevant economic studies.

Some economists consider that a 'one-size-fits-all' innovation cycle applies to all service sectors,[174] while others argue that innovation in services does not have

---

[169] Aschhoff and Sofka 2008.

[170] Georghiou et al. 2013, 7.

[171] Commission 2007a, 4, 9, 10; Commission 2007b, 2–3, 10–1.

[172] Commission 2007a, 2–3, 8; Commission 2007b, 3–4, 8.

[173] Services are difficult to define. According to Bryson et al. service functions/activities 'refer to tasks that are being carried out in connection with productive processes and consumption of both goods and services'. Bryson et al. 2004.

[174] Barras 1986 concluded that service innovations are characterized by a reverse product cycle (RPC) made of three stages: (1) improved efficiency phase, which means an investment in new technology to increase the efficiency of delivery of existing services; (2) improved quality phase, in which technology is used to improve the quality of services; and, ending the cycle, the stage (3) new products phase, which consists, basically, of the generation of new services.

a uniform pattern and that innovation intensity in specific service activities and in specific types of companies may actually be higher than the manufacturing average.[175]

For example, based on empirical data from Spain, Un and Montoro-Sanchez[176] conclude that small- and medium-sized companies (employing fewer than 200 workers) and start-ups have a greater tendency to innovate, both in products (whether in goods or services) and in processes. Moreover, the companies with a greater tendency to implement process innovations are those in the financial sector.[177] In contrast, real estate and transport companies prefer not to innovate in services. This conclusion is confirmed by Hollenstein[178] based on the Swiss case. He identifies the causes of the low innovativeness of these services sectors in the weak demand prospects, strong price competition, low appropriability and innovation opportunities, and relatively poor human capital endowment.

Business services[179] more generally are identified by other economists as highly innovative services.[180] Innovation in this sector appears to be the result of combinations of knowledge from different sources (mainly tacit knowledge).[181] Innovation in this sector is positively influenced by intense level of interaction and the high level of interface with clients. The banking, insurance, and other financial services are also sensitive to the innovation coming from suppliers of new technologies and ICT.[182]

The PRO-INNO study[183] came in 2009 to the conclusion that the innovation patterns of knowledge intensive service firms[184] in Europe—which present an R&D intensity above the average of manufacturing companies—are similar to those of manufacturing firms. However, innovation in other services than knowledge intensive ones, is more incremental rather than radical. Compared to the

[175] Vence and Trigo 2009.

[176] Un and Montoro-Sanchez 2010, 137.

[177] The most important are: online banking, telephone monitoring tools, new or enhanced software or computer networks, application of new methods of risk diversification, optical-electronic document filing, paper-free office management, improved points payment systems, introduction of point-of-sale marketing policy and introduction of new rating or scoring methods.

[178] Hollenstein 2003.

[179] *'Business services cover a broad spectrum of services principally traded in business-to-business transactions. These intermediary services range from software development to temporary-labour agencies, from equipment rental to economic consultancy, and from translation services to accountancy'*. See Commission 2009, 17.

[180] Vence and Trigo 2009.

[181] Hipp and Grupp 2005.

[182] Abreua et al. 2010, 115.

[183] Commission 2009, 9.

[184] Examples of knowledge intensive service activities (KIS) include: research and development (R&D), management consulting, ICT services, human resource management and employment services, legal services (including those related to IPR) accounting, financing, and marketing-related service activities.

manufacturing sector, less service firms develop internal R&D activities and most new ideas in service companies come from employees and customers.

Other economists advocate that innovation in services should be treated as a completely different field from innovation in manufacturing, thus requiring new theories and instruments of analysis,[185] because the traditional indicators of innovation inputs (levels of R&D expenditures) and innovation outputs (the number of patents) do not reflect the *'hidden parts'* of innovation in services. Innovation in services is often not related to R&D activities and tangible results as defined in the context of technological innovation.[186] Innovation in services is instead often determined by users and tacit knowledge rather than by research.[187]

Based on empirical data from the UK, Abreua et al.[188] remark that organisational innovation is a substantial part of the *'hidden'* dimension of innovation in services, especially in three sectors: financial intermediation, computer services and research and development services. These sectors introduce more major changes in organisation and business structure than either manufacturing or other services. Abreua considers that although there are a number of key drivers of innovation in services, there is no one dominant pattern or model of innovation. Therefore, the most efficient form of public intervention in support of innovation is to incentivize trainings for high-level skills. This is recommendable for two reasons. Firstly, labour skills are crucial for the innovative capacity of service firms. Secondly, service firms tend to underinvest in training and staff development due to the intensive movement of labour.

Some economists[189] mention commercial public procurement as a means to reduce uncertainty problems (caused by asymmetry of information) and to increase the number of active service providers in a market.

In conclusion, most economic studies analysed in this section point out that innovative services are not typically the result of activities that qualify as R&D in the traditional sense. Economists identify the following most important drivers of innovation in services: quality of the human capital (including tacit knowledge), intense levels of interaction with clients and use of innovative (ICT) technologies. Economists agree that mainstream policies (such as incentives for training of high-level skills etc.) positively impact innovation in services, often more than those policies aimed directly at innovation in services. Among policy measures aimed directly at innovation in services, economists mention: increased access to external finance and commercial public procurement.

Due to the fact that PCP may only be employed when the majority of the activities deployed qualify as R&D services, I can conclude that PCP/public R&D procurement is not a relevant tool for generating innovative services.

---

185 Un and Montoro-Sanchez 2010; Barras 1986.

186 Griliches 1992; Abreua et al. 2010; Vence and Trigo 2009.

187 Commission 2009, 34–5.

188 Abreua et al. 2010, 99–118.

189 Rubalcaba and Den Hertog 2010.

3.7 Conclusion

This chapter has tested 5 of the most important economic assumptions that lie at the foundation of PCP, against authoritative economic theories and studies encompassing but going beyond those embraced by the EU innovation policy-makers.

I concluded that there is broad support in economic theory for the first assumption that innovation leads to (social) welfare. Economists also broadly support the second assumption, that R&D investment is a necessary pre-condition of innovation, although it may not be the only or the most important one.

Economists differ mostly on the role the government can play as investor in R&D. According to neo-classics, public R&D investments is only justified in the case of basic research and researchers are in the best position to make such decision. They do not support public intervention in support of applied research (which forms the focus of PCP). More recent complexity theories propose to completely drop the debate on state versus private markets and concentrate on an effective interplay between the two forces, in order to create an effective evolutionary system, open to experimentation, learning and adaptation. Based on this theory, public R&D funding should:

- stimulate the emergence of a variety of innovations to be subsequently exposed to the selection process in the marketplace;
- choose the most successful innovative trajectory when uncertainties are much lower;
- tolerate redundancy, overlap and excess capacity;
- learn from policy experiments and adapt the policy.

This chapter also tested the assumption that PCP is needed in the EU, due to insufficient investments by venture capitalists in risky R&D projects. Based on a comparative analysis of theories and studies dealing with the role of venture capital in the US and the EU, I concluded that this third assumption is correct. The reviewed literature indicates that private venture capitalists are reluctant to invest in projects which involve high failure risks, large research and development costs, or long-term return on investment. The shortage of venture capital for risky R&D projects becomes more acute in times of economic downturn.

As a consequence, there is a clear justification for the government to fill the gaps left by EU venture capitalists. However, government funding should embed tolerance to failure and investment decisions should be made by managers with in-depth knowledge of the targeted sector and in line with very specific technical needs of their agency.

This chapter also showed that there is wide support among economists for the fourth assumption, that demand is a key determinant of innovation. Based on several landmark economic studies, I concluded on the following prerequisites for effective use of demand:

- needs should be clearly signaled to private actors at an early stage;
- the customer should ensure early and sufficiently wide adoption of the resulting innovation;
- the government should reward the most innovative firms, breaking away from the industrial policy pitfalls, such as protecting inefficient companies from foreign competitions.

This chapter has also tested the fifth assumption that PCP is a suitable instrument to stimulate technological, as well as services innovations. Based on relevant studies, I concluded that innovative activities related to services do not normally qualify as R&D, which leads to the conclusion that PCP remains mainly relevant for technologically demanding solutions and only to a very limited extent for innovation in services.

Based on the above, I summarize the following economic preconditions for an effective PCP:

1. The PCP portfolio includes a large number of high-risk R&D projects, which entail large costs at early development stages and long-term returns on investment;
2. PCP programs focus particularly on young companies that experience difficulties in obtaining (sufficient amounts of) private capital;
3. PCP budgets are increased in times of economic downturn;
4. The selection of PCP projects is based on a careful consideration of technological trajectories and market trends such as to avoid lock-in. This entails that competition is maintained until uncertainty decreases and it becomes clear which innovation is the most valuable.
5. Managers in charge of PCP deployment possess or gain in-depth knowledge of the relevant technological area.
6. Failure is tolerated to a certain extent, in order to encourage PCP managers to choose risky R&D projects, instead of commercially promising (close-to-market) projects. For example, PCP programs should allow multiple sequential awards to the same company and for the same project, to allow the further development of a technology following the first PCP contract.
7. The public end-user is closely involved: provides data regarding their needs, provides input on tested prototypes, even helps with the development of the solutions.
8. The public end-user is willing to pay the premium price for the early use of the developed innovation and is capable to offer a sufficiently sizeable market for the developed innovation;
9. PCP should challenge and reward the most innovative companies, instead of shielding inefficient companies from foreign competition.
10. Innovative technologies rather than innovative services are targeted;
11. Scrutiny/measurement of the impact of PCP is regularly performed and lessons are codified.

This chapter sets the scene for the following outline of the differences between the US SBIR, and the PCP procedure and for the discussion on the significance of these differences for the successful deployment of PCP in Chap. 4.

References

Abreua M, Grinevich V, Kitson M, Savona M (2010) Policies to enhance the 'hidden innovation' in services: evidence and lessons from the UK. The Service Ind J 30:99–118

Acs ZJ, Audretsch DB (2010) Entrepreneurship, innovation and technological change. Rev Soc Econ

Aghiou P, Bloom N, Griffith R, Howitt P (2005) Competition and innovativeness: an inverted-U relationship. Q J Econ 701–728

Allen RL (1991) Opening doors: the life and work of Joseph Schumpeter, vol 1. Transaction Publishers, Piscataway

Arinivas S (2006) Industrial development and innovation: some lessons from vaccine procurement. World Dev 34:1742–1764

Arrow K (1962) Economic welfare and the allocation of resources for inventions. In: Nelson RR (ed) The rate and direction of inventive activity. Princeton University Press, NJ

Arthur B (2010) The nature of technology—what it is and how it evolves. Free Press, New York

Aschhoff B, Sofka W (2008) Innovation on demand—can public procurement drive market success? ZEW Discussion Paper No 08-052. ftp.zew.de/pub/zew-docs/dp/dp08052.pdf. Accessed 8 Apr 2013

Audretsch DB (1995) Innovation and industry evolution. MIT Press, Cambridge

Audretsch DB, Thurik AR (2003) Entrepreneurship, industry evolution and economic growth. In: Koppl R, Birner J, Kurrild-Klitgaard P (eds) Volume 6: Austrian economics and entrepreneurial studies

Auerswald PE, Branscomb LM (2003) Valleys of death and Darwinian seas: financing the invention of innovation transition in the United States. J Technol Transf 28:227–239

Baarsma B, Koopmans C, Theeuwes J (2010) Beleidseconomie: een rationele onderbouwing van overheidsingrijpen. Amsterdam: Pallas Publications

Baker JB (2007) Beyond Schumpeter vs. Arrow: how antitrust fosters innovation (Washington College of Law). http://ssrn.com/abstract=962261. Accessed 12 Dec 2012

Bakhshi H, Freeman A, Potts J (2011) State of uncertainty—innovation policy through experimentation. NESTA Provocation 14. http://www.nesta.org.uk/library/documents/Provocation_14_State_of_Uncertainty_v7.pdf. Accessed 27 Mar 2013

Barras R (1986) Towards a theory of innovation in services. Res Policy 15:161–173

Basu S, Fernald JG, Oulton N, Srinivasan S (2003) The case of the missing productivity growth: or, does information technology explain why productivity accelerated in the US but not the UK? NBER Working Paper No 10010. http://www.nber.org/chapters/c11441.pdf. Accessed 26 Mar 2013

Beinhocker ED (2006) The origin of wealth, evolution, complexity and the radical remaking of economics. Harvard Business School Press, Brighton

Beise M, Rennings K (2005) Lead markets and regulation: a framework for analyzing the international diffusion of environmental innovations. Ecol Econ 52:5–17

Benjamin SM, Rai AK (2008) Fixing innovation policy: a structural perspective. George Wash Law Rev 77:12

Binks M, Ennew CT (1996) Growing firms and the credit constraint. Small Bus Econ 8:17–25

Block F, Keller M (2010) Where do innovations come from? In: Block F, Keller M (eds) State of innovation: the US government's role in technology development. Paradigm, Columbia

Boone J, Van Damme E (2004) Marktstructuur en innovatie. In: Jacobs B, Theeuwes JJM (red), Innovatie in Nederland – De markt draalt en de overheid faalt (Koninklijke Vereniging voor de Staathuishoudkunde Preadviezen)

Brynjolfsson E, Zhang XM (2006) Innovation incentives for information goods. MIT Sloan School Working Paper 4780-10. http://seeit.mit.edu/Publications/brynjolfsson-zhang6-14-06.pdf. Accessed 27 Mar 2013

Bryson J, Daniels P, Warf B (2004) Service worlds. People, organisations, technologies. Routledge, Abingdon

Cabral LMB, Cozzi G, Denicolò V, Spagnolo G, Zanza M (2006) Procuring innovation. CEPR Discussion Paper Series No 5774. www.cepr.org/pubs/dps/DP5774.asp.asp. Accessed 8 Apr 2013

Caselli S, Gatti S, Perrini F (2006) Are venture capitalists a catalyst for innovation, or do they simply exploit it? http://papers.ssrn.com/sol3/papers.cfm?abstract_id=890669. Accessed 8 Apr 2013

Chemmanur TJ, Loutskina E, Tian X (2012) Corporate venture capital, value creation, and innovation. Rev Financ Stud http://papers.ssrn.com/sol3/papers.cfm?abstract_id=1364213. Accessed 8 Apr 2013

Commission (2006) Community framework for state aid for research and development and innovation. 2006/C 323/01

Commission (2007a) Pre-commercial procurement: driving innovation to ensure sustainable high quality public services in Europe. COM 799 final

Commission (2007b) Staff working document accompanying COM(2007) 799 final

Commission (2009) Challenges for EU support to innovation services—fostering new markets and jobs through innovation. SEC 1195 final

Coombs R, Saviotti P, Walsh V (1987) Economics and technological change. Rowman & Littlefield, Lanham

Cooter R, Edlin A, Litan RE, Priest GL (2011) The importance of law in promoting innovation and growth. In: The Kauffman task force on law, innovation and growth, 'rules for growth—promoting innovation and growth through legal reform'. Ewing Marion Kauffman Foundation, Kansas City

Dalpé R (1994) Effects of government procurement on industrial innovation. Technol Soc 16:65–83

Dalpé R, DeBresson C, Xiaoping H (1992) The public sector as first user of innovations. Res Policy 21: 252

Davidson P (2009) The Keynes solution. Palgrave Macmillan, Basingstoke

DTI (2006) Innovation in the UK: indicators and insights. DTI occasional paper No 6. http://www.dti.gov.uk/files/file31569.pdf. Accessed 8 Apr 2013

Edler J (2013) Review of policy measures to stimulate private demand for innovation. Concepts and effects. London: Nesta

Edler J, Georghiou L (2007) Public procurement and innovation—resurrecting the demand side. Res Policy 36

Edler J, Kuhlmann S, Smits R (2002) New governance for innovation, the need for horizontal and systemic policy co-ordination. Report on a Workshop held at the occasion of the 30th anniversary of the Fraunhofer Institute for Systems and Innovation Research

Edquist C, Hommen L (1999) Systems of innovation: theory and policy for the demand side. Technol Soc 21:63–79

Engel D (2002) The impact of venture capital on firm growth: an empirical investigation. ZEW Discussion Paper No 02-02. ftp.zew.de/pub/zew-docs/dp/dp0202.pdf. Accessed 8 Apr 2013

Freeman C (1979) The determinants of innovation. Futures 213

Freeman C (1982) The economics of industrial innovation. Frances Pinter Publishers Limited

Freeman C (1995) The "national system of innovation" in historical perspective. Camb J Econ 19:5–24

Freeman C, Soete L (2000) The economics of industrial innovation, 3rd edn. MIT Press, Cambridge

Freeman C, Soete L (2007) Developing science, technology and innovation indicators: what we can learn from the past. UNU-MERIT Working Paper Series 2007-001. http://arno.unimaas.nl/show.cgi?fid=6680. Accessed 26 Mar 2013

Friedmann M (1962) Capitalism and freedom. The University of Chicago Press, Chicago

Georghiou L (2006) Effective innovation policies for Europe—the missing demand-side. In Economic Council Secretariat (eds) Globalisation challenges for Europe, 18 edn. Prime Ministers Office Publications, Finland

Georghiou L, Edler J, Uyarra E, Yeow J (2013) Choice, design and assessment. Technol Forecast Soc Change 7

Geroski PA (1990) Procurement policy as a tool of industrial policy. Int Rev Appl Econ 4

Gigerenzer G, Gaissmaier W (2011) Heuristic decision making. Annu Rev Psychol 62:451

Gilbert RJ (2007a) Competition and Innovation. http://escholarship.org/uc/item/9xh5p5p9. Accessed 26 Mar 2013

Gilbert R (2007b) Holding innovation to an antitrust standard. Compet Policy Int 3:2

Godin B (2009) The making of science, technology and innovation policy: conceptual frameworks as narratives, 1945–2005, Montreal

Godin B (2010) "Innovation studies": the invention of a specialty (Part II). Project on the Intellectual History of Innovation Working Paper No 8

Godin B (2012) Social innovation: utopias of innovation from c. 1830 to the present. Project on the Intellectual History of Innovation Working Paper No 11

Godin B, Lane JP (2013) "Pushes and pulls": the hi(story) of the demand pull model of innovation. Project on the Intellectual History of Innovation, Working Paper No 13

Gompers P, Lerner J (1999) Capital market imperfections in venture markets: a report to the advanced technology program, Department of Commerce

Gortz E (2001) Public and private expenditure and the Faroese business cycle. In: Eliasson G, Karlson N (eds) The limits of government, policy competence and economic growth. Transaction Publishers, Piscataway

Griffith R, Redding S, van Reenen J (2000) Mapping the two faces of R&D: productivity growth in a panel of OECD industries. The Institute for Fiscal Studies Working Paper 02/00. http://eprints.ucl.ac.uk/4074/1/4074.pdf. Accessed 26 Mar 2013

Griliches Z (1992) The search for r&d spillovers. Scand J Econ 94

Hayek FA (2002) Competition as a discovery procedure (translation). Q J Austrian Econ 5:9–23

Hipp C, Grupp H (2005) Innovation in the service sector: the demand for service-specific innovation measurement concepts and typologies. Res Policy 34:517–535

Hollenstein H (2003) Innovation modes in the Swiss service sector: a cluster analysis based on firm-level data. Res Policy 32:845–863

Independent Expert Group (2003) Raising EU R&D intensity—improving the effectiveness of public support mechanisms for private sector research and development. EUR 20717

Inman R (1987) Markets, governments and the "new" politial economy. In: Auerbach AJ, Feldstein M (eds) Handbook of public economics, vol II. Elsevier 1987, Amsterdam

Izsak K, Edler J (2011) Trends and challenges in demand-side innovation policies in Europe thematic report 2011 under specific contract for the integration of INNO policy trend chart with ERAWATCH (2011–2012). http://ec.europa.eu/enterprise/newsroom/cf/_getdocument.cfm?doc_id=7011. Accessed 2 Feb 2013

Jacobs T (2002) Biotech follows dot.com boom and bust. Nature 20:973

Kline SJ, Rosenberg N (1986) An overview of innovation. In: Landau R, Rosemberg N (eds) The positive sum strategy—harnessing technology for economic growth. National Academy Press, Washington, DC

Kortum S, Lerner J (2000) Assessing the contribution of venture capital to innovation. Rand J Econ 31:674–692

Lantz JS, Sahut JM (2010) Corporate venture capital and financing innovation. Probl Perspect Manag

Lerner J (1999) Public venture capital. In: Wessner C (ed) National Research Council 'The small business innovation program: challenges and opportunities'. National Academy Press, Washington, DC

Lipsey RG. (2007) Technological transformation, intellectual property rights and second best theory. Rev Econ Res Copyr Issues 4:5–28

Maclaurin WR (1953) The sequence from invention to innovation and its relation to economic growth. Q J Econ 67(1)

Malerba F, Orsenigo L, Nelson R, Winter S (2008) Public policy and changing boundaries of firms in a history-friendly model of the coevolution of the computer and semiconductor industries. J Econ Behav Organ 67:355–380

Manne GA, Wright JD (2009) Regulating innovation: competition policy and patent law under uncertainty. Cambridge University Press, Cambridge

Mazzucato M (2013) The entrepreneurial state. Demos

Mesthene EG (1969) Foreword. In: Rosenbloom RS, Marris R (eds) Social innovation in the city: new enterprises for community development. Harvard University Press, Cambridge

Metcalfe JS, Georghiou L (1997) Equilibrium and evolutionary foundations of technology policy. CRIC Discussion Paper No 3. Available at http://www.cric.ac.uk/cric/Pdfs/dp3.pdf. Accessed 28 Dec 2013

Miles N, Wilkinson C, Edler J, Bleda M, Simmonds P, Clark J (2009) The wider conditions for innovation in the UK—how the UK compares to leading innovation nations. NESTA Report. https://www.nesta.org.uk/sites/default/files/wider-conditions-for-innovation-report.pdf. Accessed 27 July 2016

Mowery DC, Rosenberg N (1979) The influence of market demand upon innovation: a critical review of some recent empirical studies. Res Policy 8:105

Mowery DC, Rosenberg N (1993) The U.S. national innovation system. In: Nelson RR (ed) National innovation systems—a comparative analysis. Oxford University Press, Oxford

Murmann P (2000) Knowledge and competitive advantage in the synthetic dye industry: 1850–1914: the coevolution of firms, technology and national institutions in Great Britain, Germany, and the United States. Enterp Soc 1(4):699–704

Nanda R, Rhodes-Kropf M (2011) Financing risk and innovation. Working Paper 11-013. http://papers.ssrn.com/sol3/papers.cfm?abstract_id=1657937. Accessed 8 Apr 2013

National IST Research Directors Forum on Public Procurement in support of ICT Research and Innovation (PCP Expert Group) (2006) Pre-commercial procurement of innovation: a missing link in the European innovation cycle. ftp.cordis.europa.eu/pub/fp7/ict/docs/pcp/precommercial-procurement-of-innovation_en.pdf. Accessed 12 Nov 2012

Neija L (2001) Methods to evaluate market transformation programs—experience of the Swedish market transformation program. 29 Energy Policy

Neija L, Åstrand K (2006) Outcome indicators for the evaluation of energy policy instruments and technical change. Energy Policy 34:2662–2676

Nelson RR (1990) Capitalism as an engine of progress. Res Policy 19:195

Nelson RR (2004) The market economy, and the scientific commons. Res Policy 33:462

Nesta (2010) Demand and innovation. How customer preferences shape the innovation process. The Work Foundations Working Paper. http://www.nesta.org.uk/library/documents/Working-Paper-Demand-and-Innovation-v7.pdf. Accessed 8 Apr 2013

OECD (1972) Science, growth and society. OECD Publications Service, Paris

OECD (1992a) Technology and the economy: the key relationships, Paris

OECD (1992b) Science and technology policy outlook, Paris

OECD (1996) Technology and industrial performance, Paris

OECD (2001) The new economy: beyond the hype

OECD (2016) Research and Development Statistics (RDS). http://www.oecd.org/innovation/inno/researchanddevelopmentstatisticsrds.htm. Accessed 26 July 2016

Ottaviano GIP, Pinelli D, Maignan CJ (2003) Economic growth, innovation, cultural diversity what are we all talking about? A critical survey of the state-of-the-art. FEEM Working Paper No 12.2003, 18–9. http://papers.ssrn.com/sol3/papers.cfm?abstract_id=389042. Accessed 26 Mar 2013

Palmberg C (2004) The sources of innovation—looking beyond technological opportunities. Econ Innov New Techn 13:183–197

Polanyi M (1962) The republic of science. Minerva 1
Porter ME (1990) Competitive advantage of nations. Harv Bus Rev 81
Romer PM (1990) Endogenous technological change. J Polit Econ 98
Romer P (1994) The origins of endogenous growth. J Econ Persp 8:3
Rothwell R, Zegveld W (1981) Government regulations and innovation—industrial innovation and public policy. In: Rothwell R, Zegveld W (eds) Industrial innovation and public policy. Pinter
Rubalcaba JG, Den Hertog P (2010) The case of market and system failures in services innovation. 30 Serv Ind J
Ruttan V (2006) Is war necessary for economic growth?: Military procurement and technology development. Oxford University Press, Oxford
Schmookler J (1966) Invention and economic growth. Harvard University Press, Cambridge
Schumpeter J (1939) Business cycles: a theoretical, historical and statistical analysis of the capitalist process. McGraw-Hill, New York
Schumpeter J (1954) Capitalism, socialism and democracy, 4th edn. Unwin University Books, London
Scotchmer S (2004) Innovation and incentives. Massachusetts Institute of Technology, Cambridge
Sherwin CW, Isenson RS (1967) Project Hindsight. Science 156:1571–1577
Smith A (1904) An inquiry into the nature and causes of the wealth of nations, 5th edn. Methuen & Co., Ltd, London. http://www.econlib.org/library/Smith/smWN.html. Accessed 27 Aug 2012
Solow R (1956) A contribution to the theory of economic growth. Q J Econ 70:65
Solow R (1957) Technical change and the aggregate production function. Rev Econ Stat 39
Spiegel M, Tookes H (2008) Dynamic competition, innovation and strategic financing. http://www4.gsb.columbia.edu/filemgr?file_id=72705. Accessed 8 Apr 2013
Stam E (2008) Entrepreneurship and innovation policy. Jena Economic Research Papers 006. http://papers.ssrn.com/sol3/papers.cfm?abstract_id=1115262. Accessed 8 Apr 2013
Stiglitz JE (1994) Endogenous growth and cycles. In: Shionoya Y, Perlman M (eds) Innovation in technology, industries and institutions-studies in Schumpeterian perspective. The University of Michigan Press, Ann Arbor
Stiglitz JE, Weiß A (1981) Credit rationing in markets with imperfect information. Am Econ Rev 71:393–410
Sunstein CR (2005) Irreversible and catastrophic. John M. Olin Law & Economics Working Paper No 242. http://www.law.uchicago.edu/files/files/242.crs_.catastrophic.pdf. Accessed 26 Mar 2013
Swann GMP (2003) Funding basic research—when is public finance preferable to attainable 'club goods' solutions? In: Geuna A, Salter AJ, Steinmueller WE (eds) Science and innovation– rethinking the rationale for funding and governance. Edward Elgar Pub, Cheltenham
Taleb NN (2010) The Black Swan. The impact of the highly improbable, 2nd edn. Random House Trade, New York
Tian X, Wang TY (2011) Tolerance for failure and corporate innovation. Rev Financ Stud. http://papers.ssrn.com/sol3/papers.cfm?abstract_id=1399707. Accessed 8 Apr 2013
Tversky A, Kahneman D (1974) Judgement under uncertainty: heuristics and biases. Science 185:4157
Ulku H (2004) R&D, innovation, and economic growth: an empirical analysis. IMF Working Paper, No 185. http://papers.ssrn.com/sol3/papers.cfm?abstract_id=879010##. Accessed 26 Mar 2013
Un CA, Montoro-Sanchez A (2010) Public funding for product, process and organizational innovation in service industries. Serv Ind J 30:137
Urban GL, von Hippel E (1986) Lead user analyses for the development of new industrial products. http://web.mit.edu/evhippel/www/papers/Lead%20Users%20Eric%20von%20Hippel%20and%20Glen%20Urban%20-%201988.pdf. Accessed 8 Apr 2013

Vence X, Trigo A (2009) Diversity of innovation patterns in services. Serv Ind J 29:1635–1657
Veugelers R, Cincera M (2010) Europe's missing yollies. Bruegel Policy Brief 2010/06
von Hayek F (1945) The use of knowledge in society. Am Econ Rev 35(4):519–530
Wessner CW (2004) Entrepreneurship and the innovation ecosystem policy. Lessons from the United States. Discussion Paper on Entrepreneurship, Growth and Public Policy 4604
Yusuf S (2007) From creativity to innovation. World Bank Policy Research Working Paper 4262. http://www-wds.worldbank.org/servlet/WDSContentServer/WDSP/IB/2007/06/21/000016406_20070621101544/Rendered/PDF/wps4262.pdf. Accessed 26 Mar 2013

Chapter 4
The US Model of R&D Procurement—Lessons for PCP

Contents

4.1 Introduction

As already mentioned in Chap. 1, the European Commission designed the PCP model with the aim to emulate the perceived success of the US Small Business Innovation Research ('SBIR') program, in pulling valuable R&D projects into the commercialization phase and enhancing the competitive position of its suppliers on the global market. The US SBIR had allegedly achieved this by creating a demanding environment for innovations and stimulating private investors to increase their share of R&D funding.[1]

In this Chapter, I will investigate whether the European Commission's perception of US SBIR's success is correct, by analyzing the most reputable assessment studies. I will conclude there is compelling evidence of the program's positive impacts and I will identify the features that are associated with its success. I will point out where these are in line with the prerequisite identified in Chap. 3 and whether they are reflected in the EU PCP.

[1] Commission 2007.

R. Apostol, *Trials and Tribulations in the Implementation of Pre-Commercial Procurement in Europe*, DOI 10.1007/978-94-6265-156-2_4

First, I will describe the features of the US SBIR program and the rationale for its adoption (Sect. 4.2). Subsequently, I will outline the outcomes of the different evaluations of the SBIR program (Sect. 4.3). I will point out throughout the text the relevant differences between the EU PCP and the US SBIR. In Sect. 4.4, I will sum-up the differences between the two programs and I will highlight whether these are related to the prerequisites for effective PCP implementation (as identified in Chap. 3).

4.2 The Features of the US SBIR Program

4.2.1 Legislated Set-Asides

The US SBIR program was set-up in 1982 through the Small Business Innovation Development Act (Act).[2] The Act mandated Federal agencies with yearly extramural R&D budgets in excess of $100.000.000 to reserve certain percentages of these budgets for contracts and grants to small businesses.[3] The Act represented a codification of prior practice at the National Science Foundation (NSF).[4]

This type of federal institutions with large and stable R&D budgets cannot be found within the EU. Although some organisations were set-up in order to facilitate the collaboration of EU Member States in R&D projects (such as the European Defence Agency), they have an obvious intergovernmental character. Decisions to proceed with an R&D project depend on the approval of national defence ministries of the EU Member States.[5] The different set-up of the EU as compared to the US is described in Chap. 7, Sect. 7.2. A detailed institutional analysis remains however outside the scope of this research.

Since 1982, the SBIR program has been repeatedly reauthorized, and amended.[6] The mandatory set-aside percentage grew from 0.2 to 1.25 % between 1982 and 1988 and was established at 2.5 % in 1992.[7]

In December 2011, the latest Reauthorization Act extended the SBIR program for a period of six (6) years up to September 30, 2017 and brought significant

---

[2] Small Business Innovation Development Act of 1982.

[3] Small Business Act of 1958, section 9(f)(1).

[4] Obermayer 2009; Patterson 2009; NRC 2008, 16–7.

[5] European Defence Agency 2013.

[6] Small Business Research and Development Enhancement Act of 1992, reauthorizing the SBIR program until September 30, 2000. The Small Business Reauthorization Act of 2000 reauthorized the program until September 30, 2008. Subsequently, Congress passed numerous extensions, before the latest SBIR/STTR Reauthorization Act of 2011.

[7] NRC 2008, 16–7. In 1992, a related program, the Small Business Technology Transfer program (STTR), was set-up for projects undertaken in collaboration with universities. This program benefited from additional set-asides from external R&D budgets. Discussion on this related program falls outside the scope of this chapter.

changes which implement most of the recommendations made in an extensive evaluation report by the National Research Council (NRC).[8] Among others, the Reauthorization Act of 2011 provided for a gradual increase in the minimum set-asides for the period 2012–2017: 2.6 % in 2012 and an increase by 0.1 % point each fiscal year until it reaches 3.2 % for fiscal year 2017.[9]

SBIR is the largest source of R&D funding for small and medium-sized businesses in the US.[10] Over 4000 SBIR awards are made each year, for a total of around $2 billion annually.[11] By 2009, over 112.500 awards had been made since the inception of the programme, for a total amount of more than $26.9 billion.[12] 11 federal departments and agencies are currently mandated to conduct SBIR programs: Department of Agriculture, Department of Commerce, Department of Defense, Department of Education, Department of Energy, Department of Health and Human Services, Department of Homeland Security, Department of Transportation, Environmental Protection Agency, National Aeronautics and Space Administration (NASA), and National Science Foundation.

The largest SBIR funding agency is the Department of Defense (DoD), with approximately 57 % of the total budget and 57 % of the number of awards. NIH is the second largest programme with 30 % of the programme's expenditure and 19 % of the number of awards. Other 3 agencies NASA, DOE and NSF amount for another 10 % of the total expenditure. The other 6 agencies only spend 3 % of the total dollar amount of the programme.[13]

Other Federal agencies than those mentioned above may voluntarily participate in the SBIR Program, upon written approval by SBA.[14]

Differences with the PCP

Unlike the US SBIR, PCP is a voluntary instrument. The EU does not have the competence to regulate such budgetary aspects of Member States. Moreover, the Lisbon Treaty does not offer a ground for legislative action in the field of research and development,[15] nor in the field of strengthening the competitiveness of EU industry. It rather allows the EU to adopt policy and coordinating action.[16] Mandatory set-asides are left to the discretion of each Member State.[17]

---

[8] SBIR/STTR Reauthorization Act of 2011, section 493.

[9] SBIR/STTR Reauthorization Act of 2011, section 5102 (a)(1).

[10] Gans and Stern 2000, 18–9.

[11] OECD 2010, 2.

[12] See SBA website http://www.sbir.gov/about/about-sbir. Accessed 18 December 2013.

[13] Based on data acquired by NRC in 2005. See Allen, Layson and Link 2012, 107.

[14] SBA 2012, 34.

[15] Articles 4(3), 179(2), 181(2) TFEU.

[16] Article 173(1) TFEU provides for example, that the EU shall ensure the proper conditions for the competitiveness of the Union's industry by 'fostering better exploitation of the industrial potential of policies of innovation, research and technological development'.

[17] Some states (such as the UK) have already adopted such minimum set-asides for their PCP-like programs. For details, see discussion in this chapter.

4.2.2 The Rationale Behind the SBIR

Background to Adoption

The idea for the set-up of the US SBIR program emerged at the end of the 1970s, when the US was confronted with a significant loss of international competitiveness. Increased globalization (enhanced by the telecommunication revolution) had taken away the comparative advantage of traditional manufacturing industries in the US, against countries with low wage levels. This led US-based firms to shift production to low-cost manufacturing countries, which resulted in a significant loss of jobs in the US.

The US understood that the best alternative to high unemployment rates or lowering wages, was to shift the economic activity away from high-cost manufacturing industries and into knowledge-based economic industries, which were compatible with high wage levels.[18] Economic activity based on new knowledge would also respond to demand for improved solutions for national defense.

But, concerns were growing that the US was lagging behind against its main competitor, Japan, in the development and exploitation of emerging technologies. The reason was found in the inability to commercialize innovative technologies in global markets.[19]

On this background, the proposal to support small business in accessing federal budgets for risky R&D projects found considerable support in the political arena. Several studies had by then documented the role of small businesses as 'a very important source of job growth'.[20] Moreover, small businesses were identified as particularly strong players in knowledge-intensive sectors, "*capable of cost-effective performance of research and development and capable of transforming research and development results into new products*".[21] Despite their important role in the innovation process, small businesses appeared unable to access sufficient funding for risky R&D project, particularly from federal budgets.[22] The difficulties to access finance appeared to be especially acute for small starting businesses, who lacked a record in innovative activities, who performed small

---

[18] Audretsch 2003, 130. An illustrative example is the increase in employment by 15 % in Silicon Valley between 1992–1996, despite average income being 50 % higher than the rest of the US.

[19] Mogee 1991, 27.

[20] Birch 1981. Based on the analysis of approximately 600 innovations introduced in the US between 1970–1979, Gellman (1982) finds that small firms contribute 2.45 times more innovations per employee than do large firms.

[21] Small Business Innovation Development Act of 1982, section 2(a). This conclusion was based on previous research by Birch 1981, who showed that scientists and engineers in small businesses produce 14 times more patents than their counterparts in large businesses. These patents were also more likely to be cited, which was an indication of their superior quality.

[22] The SBIR agencies are currently required to find 'a portofolio balance between exploratory projects of high technological risk and those with greater likelihood of success'. See SBA 2012, 28. See also Technopolis 2010, 114.

projects of limited interest to private investors, and who lacked information or means to come in contact with potentially interested investors.[23]

Economic Justification

The program's justification was therefore found in the failure of the private market to fund promising but risky projects by small businesses. The strong focus on technological and scientific performance for selecting the awardees suggested that the program would primarily support basic research.[24] This argumentation didn't raise controversies in the US, as it was in line with influential neo-classical economic theories about the role of the government in addressing market failures (as shown in Chap. 3). Whether the program stayed true to its initial objectives is discussed in Sect. 4.3 below.

The US SBIR was thus based on the following arguments:

- innovation is the driver of competitiveness, new jobs and higher living standards;
- small businesses are more effective in innovation activities than large businesses;
- public investments in R&D positively influence the innovation process.[25]

NRC singles out the economic theory of innovation ecosystems as justification for the government intervention through SBIR. The theory of innovation ecosystems is similar to the 'systems of innovation' theory which became influential in the EU in the 1970s. The theory of innovation ecosystems is based on the idea that '*complex synergies among a variety of collective efforts [are needed to] bringing innovation to market*'.[26] These are internal as well as collaborative efforts of numerous actors: large and small businesses, universities, and research institutes and laboratories, as well as venture capital firms and financial markets and government policy.[27] Moreover, multiple institutional variables influence the efficiency of an innovation process: e.g. rules that protect property (including intellectual property) and the regulations and incentives that structure capital, labor, and financial and consumer markets. Also the *'shared social norms and value systems — especially those concerning attitudes towards business failure, social mobility, and entrepreneurship'* impact the innovation ecosystem.[28]

---

23 NRC 2008, 31–3.

24 Gulbrandsen and Etzkowitz 1999, 6.

25 Link and Scott 2012, 656.

26 NRC 2008; The idea of an innovation ecosystem builds on the concept of a National Innovation System (NIS), was popularized by Richard Nelson of Columbia University. According to Nelson, a NIS is 'a set of institutions whose interactions determine the innovative performance ... of national firms'. See Nelson and Rosenberg 1993.

27 Mogee 1991, 28.

28 Interesting to note here is that Europeans seem to have, for example, a greater fear of entrepreneurial failure than Americans. See the NRC 2008, 29; Commission 2004.

In line with the 'systems of innovation' theory, public innovation policies were designed to strengthen links within the system. In this context, SBIR was set-up as an intermediate institution whose purpose was to bring together venture capitalists, entrepreneurs and other participants in the innovation eco-system in achieving desired national objectives.[29] The US SBIR is thus not viewed in terms of demand-side or supply-side approach, but as a measure to create the links between the relevant actors in the innovation eco-system. In Sect. 4.2.3.7 below, I point out that the US SBIR covers both demand-side and supply-side measures.

Objectives

The SBIR program was established with the following objectives: (1) to stimulate technological innovation; (2) to use small businesses to meet federal research and development needs; (3) to foster and encourage participation by minority and disadvantaged persons in technological innovation; and (4) to increase private sector commercialisation of innovations derived from federal research and development.[30]

The 1992 Act that reauthorized the SBIR program moved the commercialization goal up the above mentioned list. This led analysts to raise concerns that the programme was drifting away from its initial focus on risky projects that did not receive sufficient private capital (this is further discussed in Sect. 4.3 below).

SBIR agencies were expected to support projects that responded to agency missions. However, since 1990, they were required to give priority to specific areas identified as critical to national security and economic prosperity.[31] On the basis of this obligation, various lists of National Critical Technologies were produced by the National Critical Technologies panel or by the Secretary of Defense.[32] Such technologies were identified as crucial in enhancing the competitive advantage of

---

[29] *The Valley of the Death is* the period of transition when a developing technology is deemed promising, but too new to validate its commercial potential and thereby attract the capital necessary for its continued development.

[30] Small Business Innovation Development Act of 1982, section 2 (b).

[31] According to the United States Code 1991, Title 42 The Public Health and Welfare such reports should be issued biannually by the National Critical Technologies Panel and should include not more than 30 of the most economically important emerging civilian technologies for the next 10 years, including an estimation of the current and future size of the domestic and international markets for products derived from such technologies (section 6683(a)–(b)). National critical technologies are those technologies which have the potential 'to further long-term national security or economic prosperity of the United States' (section 6683(b)). The Secretary of Defense is mandated by the same legislation to identify technologies for the defense area. (10 U.S.C. 2522) Section on Armament retooling and manufacturing. See also Executive Order 13329 of February 24, 2004. Section 2 mandates the heads of SBIR agencies to give priority to manufacture-related R&D and to report to SBA and to the Office of Science and Technology Policy on the undertaken efforts to implement this executive order.

[32] The obligation to formulate SBIR solicitations is reiterated in SBIR/STTR Reauthorization Act of 2011, section 638 (g)(3).

the US in the global competition, on the basis of such criteria as the importance/criticality of a technology for the national economy or the size of the commercialization market.[33] Many technologies (such as ICT, semiconductors, optoelectronics, artificial intelligence, manufacturing technologies, sensor technologies and high-density data storage) are repeatedly uptaken in different reports and there is considerable overlap between the critical defense technologies and critical commercial technologies.[34]

Nevertheless, whenever contracts are awarded, the concrete and direct needs of the SBIR agency take lead in determining the subject-matter and area of an SBIR call.

Differences Between the US SBIR and the PCP

The goals of the US SBIR are to a certain extent similar to those invoked by the EU in relation to PCP.[35] The public R&D support is meant to stimulate enhanced R&D efforts in areas of public importance that would otherwise not be addressed by private innovators. In addition, the public R&D support is meant to increase the global competitive advantage of national companies and trigger benefits for the national economy. Additionally the EU PCP aims to catalize the development of solutions to societal challenges.

However, the two counterprograms differ in an important aspect. The US SBIR expressly targets the riskiest R&D projects, that do not attract private investors,[36] while the PCP guidance makes no similar pledge, although this is an important prerequisite for effective deployment (see Chap. 3).

Another difference between the 2 programs is the size of the companies allowed to participate. Unlike in the US, the EU does not restrict participation in PCP competition to small companies. However, this difference is less significant in practice, due to the different coverage of the concept of small companies in the US and the EU[37] and due to the possibility to limit the amounts awarded at each PCP Phase, in order to attract in majority smaller companies.

4.2.3 Organisational Features

4.2.3.1 Decentralised Implementation

According to section 9(j) of the Small Business Act, the Small Business Administration (SBA) is endowed with the coordination, monitoring, support and evaluation of the SBIR program.

---

33 Mogee 1991, 20–3.

34 Mogee 1991, 26.

35 Discussed in Sect. 1.2 above.

36 Patterson 2005.

37 Small companies in the US are those with up to 500 employees. IN the EU, small companies have up to 50 employees, while medium companies up to 250 employees. See Commission 2009.

Coordination

SBA fulfills its coordinating role by formulating mandatory guidelines for the Federal agencies which operate SBIR programs.[38] SBA's Policy Directives are meant to bring consistency in the implementation of the SBIR program within the different agencies, while leaving sufficient flexibility to the agencies to adapt the program to their specific needs.

The Policy Directives establish, for example, the 3 phased structure of an SBIR procedure, but leave it to the agencies to formulate evaluation criteria. They also mandate the agencies to exclude applicants with more than 20 Phase I awards or 15 Phase II awards over the prior 5, 10 or 15 fiscal years, who do not achieve sufficient commercialization rates. Yet they allow the agencies to establish the applicable commercialization benchmarks.[39]

SBA also coordinates the release schedules, in order to spread the SBIR competitions throughout the whole year. This allows small businesses sufficient time to submit proposals for more than one topic.[40] However, the SBIR agencies drive the SBIR process. It is the responsibility of each agency to formulate the SBIR calls in line with its needs and its mission. It is also the responsibility of each SBIR agency to carefully consider the priority sectors, when formulating the SBIR calls.[41] The SBIR agencies are responsible for receiving and evaluating SBIR proposals, for signing funding agreements, for publishing award announcements, and for managing the contracts.[42]

Support

In its supporting role, SBA acts as an information hub for the SBIR competitions of all participating agencies. It manages a searchable database of up-coming SBIR competitions from all the involved agencies (topics and closing dates).[43] It also maintains several databases related to: information on ownership and affiliation of SBIR applicants (information submitted and updated by businesses which intend to apply for SBIR awards), including VC, hedge funds or private equity owned small businesses; information on the number of Phase I and II awardees and a database with calculation of Phase I–II transition rates for Phase I awardees and commercialization rates for all Phase II awardees).[44]

---

[38] The latest guidelines (see SBA 2012) came into effect upon their publication on the 6th of August 2012.

[39] SBA 2012, 9–11.

[40] SBA 2012, 15.

[41] Such as the National Critical Technologies as discussed in the previous section.

[42] Small Business Act of 1958, section 9(g). SBA 2012, 28–9, 50.

[43] Ecorys 2011, 47. Small Business Act of 1958, section 9(b) and (j) SBA 2012, 41.

[44] SBA 2012, 4, 12, 39–45.

SBA is also responsible for enhancing the participation in the SBIR of smalls businesses located in states with low record of participation. To this end, SBA is providing assistance in programs and activities employed within these states.[45]

Monitoring

SBA fulfills its monitoring tasks by reviewing the compliance of policies, rules, regulations, interpretations and procedures generated by the SBIR agencies with its own Policy Directives,[46] and by supervising the correct use of discretion, granted to the SBIR agencies and individual program managers.

SBA monitors, for example, the correct calculation of the extramural R&D budgets,[47] the implementation of the recommendations of the Interagency Policy Committee to improve the effectiveness and efficiency of the program,[48] the existence of conflicts of interest when making multiple awards to the same company or awarding an agreement for which only one proposal had been received,[49] the consideration of the critical technologies when defining the SBIR topics,[50] compliance with the maximum thresholds for awards to venture capital (VC), hedge funds or private equity owned small business[51] etc.

Besides assessments and recommendations, SBA has various corrective mechanisms, such as appealing the decision of a project officer with the head of the SBIR agency, or receiving back the funds unrightfully awarded to companies that do not meet the SBIR eligibility criteria from agency's non-SBIR funds.[52] Against the companies that make false declarations during the SBIR competitive procedure, SBA (or the SBIR agency) may pursue criminal, civil or administrative remedies.[53]

Evaluation

Periodic internal and external assessments of program's performance are strongly embedded in the organizational structure.

The agencies regularly formulate concrete targets for improved performance (e.g. by how much to reduce timelines for awards), while SBA provides support in

---

45 Small Business Act of 1958, section 9(s).

46 SBA 2012, 52.

47 SBA 2012, 4, 49.

48 SBA 2012,, 50.

49 Small Business Act of 1958, section 9(l).

50 According to section 9(g)(3) of the Small Business Act of 1958, each Federal agency is required when formulating SBIR solicitations to give special consideration to research topics which further one or more critical technologies, as defined by the National Critical Technologies Panel or the Secretary of Defense.

51 SBA 2012, 18.

52 SBA 2012, 18.

53 SBA 2012, 60. The False Claims Act is attributed an important role in this context. According to the False Claims Act, a penalty of up to three times the value of the SBIR funding may be applied for false certification. See Metzger (2013).

identifying suitable performance metrics.[54] The SBIR agencies are also mandated to report yearly, as well as throughout the year on different aspects of their SBIR program.[55] SBA will bundle these yearly reports and other information provided by the agencies throughout the year and will report back to the Congress on the overall performance of the SBIR program.[56]

But evaluation of certain aspects of the SBIR program (such as commercialization assistance best practices, flexibility in Phase I and II award sizes, etc.) may also be performed externally by the Interagency SBIR Policy Committee, an institution made of representatives from SBIR agencies and SBA. Based on the evaluation, the Committee issues recommendations for the improvement of the program's effectiveness and efficiency.[57] Moreover, every four (4) years, studies of the functioning of the SBIR should be performed by the National Academy of Sciences (NAS) in accordance with the parameters set by the Interagency SBIR Policy Committee.[58]

The US SBIR program is thus a program set up by Federal legislation, with organizational responsibilities shared between SBA and the participating Federal agencies. Moreover, in the US a continuous assessment of the impact of the SBIR program is performed by different institutions and recommendations are implemented in practice. This was identified in Chap. 3 as an important prerequisite for the effective deployment of public R&D funding.

Differences Between the US SBIR and PCP

Unlike in the US, PCP has not been set-up as a mandatory program to be executed by certain EU-wide agencies. PCP has a recommendation status and relies on the will of national contracting authorities to find common needs and engage in the perils of cross-border collaborations. Moreover, in the EU there is no agency endowed with the task to coordinate, monitor or assess the application of PCP. The European Commission has partially assumed such a role. Besides having initiated the drafting of the PCP Communication, the European Commission has commissioned regular evaluations of the status of application of PCP in the EU and has financed dissemination of knowledge and best practice on PCP through the set-up of networks of contracting authorities from different Member States. Recently, the European Commission adopted a more hands-on approach, meant to encourage the creation of best practices in the application of PCP. It funds collaborative cross-border PCPs and it monitors the execution of these funded projects.[59]

[54] SBA 2012, sections 10(i) and 11(d)(5).

[55] SBA 2012, 33, 38, 46–8, 50.

[56] SBA 2012, section 10(g).

[57] SBA 2012, 37.

[58] SBA 2012, 37–8.

[59] For an overview of the current PCP projects funded by the EU, see http://cordis.europa.eu/fp7/ict/pcp/projects_en.html.

However, the subsidiarity principle and the strong national interests in the EU have impeded so far the adoption of a mandatory PCP program coordinated at EU level (these aspects are further discussed in Chap. 7).

4.2.3.2 Eligibility Criteria

The US SBIR sets eligibility requirements regarding the ownership of the company, type and location of the work performed and past performance of SBIR applicants.

Firstly, only 'for-profit' US companies may participate, that are at least 51 % owned by US citizens (or legally admitted permanent resident aliens), or at least 51 % owned by another "for profit" business, that is itself at least 51 % owned and controlled by one or more US citizens. Moreover, the company or its parent company may not have more than 500 employees.[60]

These eligibility criteria need to be complied with at the time of the award, not the proposal, which allows individuals to set-up a company in-between.[61] The 2011 Reauthorization Act has introduced a major change, by allowing the award of maximum 25 % of the SBIR funds of the NIH and National Science Institute, and 15 % of the SBIR budget of the other agencies to firms that are owned in majority by (multiple) venture capitals (VC), hedge funds or private equity companies. In order to make use of this possibility, each agency needs to obtain prior authorization from the SBA. To this end, each SBIR agency needs to show that awards to such companies would not undermine the objectives of SBIR, and would complement rather than substitute the financial means of the VC, hedge fund or equity capital owned company.[62]

Secondly, all the R&D activities funded by SBIR program must take place in the United States, while up to 1/3 of Phase I and 1/2 of Phase II may be performed outside the company concerned.

Thirdly, the project leader of an SBIR project must be for at least 51 % of his/her time employed by the company.[63] This allows researchers from universities or from research institutions to progress towards a commercial business.[64]

---

[60] 13 CFR Ch. I (1-1-01 Edition), section 121.702.

[61] SBA 2012, 17; 13 CFR Ch. I (1-1-01), section 121.704.

[62] Section 5107(a)(dd) of SBA's Policy Directives provides that the head of the Federal agency will explain in written why the award to firms funded in majority by venture capital/hedge fund/private equity firms, will: "(A) induce additional venture capital, hedge fund, or private equity firm funding of small business innovations; (B) substantially contribute to the mission of the Federal agency; (C) demonstrate a need for public research; and (D) otherwise fulfill the capital needs of small business concerns for additional financing for SBIR projects." See also section 5107(c), SBA 2012.

[63] SBA 2012, 18–9.

[64] SBA 2012, 18–9. Connell 2013, 8.

Fourthly, only novel work may be funded within the SBIR program. The same application (or 'essentially equivalent work') may not be funded twice within different SBIR competitions[65] and only work meant to create and/or apply new knowledge may be funded, such as: *'(A) a systematic, intensive study directed toward greater knowledge or understanding of the subject studied; (B) a systematic study directed specifically toward applying new knowledge to meet a recognized need; or (C) a systematic application of knowledge toward the production of useful materials, devices, and systems or methods, including design, development, and improvement of prototypes and new processes to meet specific requirements'*.[66]

Fifthly, the SBIR applicants who have received more than a certain number of Phase I or Phase II awards during the previous 5, 10 and 15 years, from any of the SBIR agencies, must meet certain benchmarks for progress towards commercialization, as well as actual commercialization rates of products resulting from previous SBIR funded projects.[67] Moreover, SBIR applicants who have received in previous 5, 10 or 15 years a certain number of Phase I awards, must meet certain benchmarks regarding the rate of winning Phase II agreements.[68] An applicant who does not meet the commercialization threshold when submitting the application could be excluded from SBIR competitions for one year starting from the date the application was submitted.[69]

These newly introduced eligibility criteria seek to reward applicants that have a good record in proceeding to Phase II and to commercialization.[70] For example, an SBIR agency may decide that an SBIR applicant who received in the last 10 years more than 4 Phase II awards should prove commercialization of at least one of the products developed under one of these SBIR Phase II contracts. In case the SBIR participant is not capable to bring this proof, he may be excluded for one year from participation in SBIR competitions advertised by the agency.

Differences Between the US SBIR and the PCP

Unlike in the US, the European Commission chose to adopt a more open approach to the eligibility criteria for PCP. The Commission recommends in its 2007 Communication that participation in PCP is not be restricted to participation by EU-based or EU-owned companies, but should be left open to participation of businesses from all parties to the Government Procurement Agreement (GPA), provided they locate the majority of their research activities within the EU. The approach of the EU PCP is based on the premise that stimulating technological solutions for societal challenges in international competition (but on the EU territory) will bring the desired growth and welfare and will indirectly contribute to

[65] SBA 2012, 22.

[66] Small Business Act of 1958, section 9(5).

[67] SBA 2012, 10.

[68] SBA 2012, 11.

[69] SBA 2012, 10.

[70] SBA 2012, 9.

enhancing the innovative capabilities of European businesses.[71] However, EU procurers may decide on a case-by-case basis whether competition within a PCP should be limited to EU service providers.[72]

Although the EU PCP does not define any further requirements regarding ownership of the companies allowed to participate in a PCP, EU procurers may seek inspiration into the US SBIR eligibility criteria. Careful consideration is though recommended when deciding to allow participation of companies owned by private equity funds, venture capitals or hedge funds, in order to avoid supporting projects that already attract sufficient private investment. Allowing participation of companies owned by private venture capitals is in line with the conclusion in Chap. 3 that venture capital does not fund the riskiest, but rather the most promising R&D projects.

4.2.3.3 Phases

The SBIR program is a phased program, which awards funds in competition and based on merit.[73] No limitation is imposed on the number of SBIR agreements individual firms may acquire, unless it does not justify the efficient use of the funds through minimum commercialization rates.[74]

The first two of the following three phases outlined below are funded under SBIR[75]:

- Phase I, the feasibility study, can be funded with maximum USD 150 000. Small firms can test during six (6) months the scientific and technical value and the feasibility of their R&D effort.
- Phase II, the R/R&D effort, takes place during two years and involves a funding of maximum USD 1.000.000 for a full R&D effort. However, it is not necessary to exhaust the whole R&D effort needed for commercialization. This means that sequential Phase II contracts may be awarded.
- Phase III, when the firm pursues commercialisation of results from Phases I and II.

Phase III does not receive funds from the SBIR program. This phase may though be funded from other budgetary sources. Studies indicate that about 10 % of projects are supported by other federal research funding.[76] SBIR Phase III awards

71 Commission 2007, 6.

72 When procurers are concerned with aspects related to national security, they may limit competition to European businesses. See Commission 2007, 6.

73 NRC 2008, 65; SBA 2012, 9.

74 NRC 2008, 65.

75 Small Business Reauthorization Act of 2011, section 5103(a)–(c); SBA 2012, 24.

76 NRC 2008.

may be made without competition and there is no limit on the number, duration or amount of Phase III awards and the limitation on the size of the business ceases to apply.[77]

Before the latest Reauthorization Act of 2011, all Phase II recipients must have received first a Phase I award. This requirement was meant to ensure that more advanced research is not favoured to the detriment of more basic research (which forms the subject-matter of Phase I projects).[78] The Reauthorization Act of 2011 introduced the possibility to deviate from this requirement under certain circumstances: when awarding a SBIR Phase II to an STTR Phase I awardee,[79] provided the awardee meets the other eligibility criteria; upon written motivation by the heads of the National Institutes of Health (NIH), DoD and the Department of Education.[80] Moreover, multiple Phase II funding may be provided to continue the initial R&D effort.[81]

Companies that completed a Phase II successfully, can obtain a Phase III status. This entails that they benefit of a preference in case of future purchases of products such as those developed within SBIR projects. A government agency will be able to sole source (purchase without competition) the product from this company. This preference extends to the case when a sub-contractor is involved in the supply or when the business is taken over by a larger company.[82]

However, in practice, it appears difficult to get procurers to buy SBIR products. They often consider the obligation to buy SBIR products as a burden on their budgets and tend to avoid the risks associated with new products. Besides being encouraged by top management to purchase SBIR products, the procurement officers are regularly informed about the available products.[83] The latest Reauthorization Act of 2011 underlines the need to prioritize the purchase of products developed through SBIR.[84]

Moreover, SBA has been mandated by the same Reauthorization Act to monitor and report to Congress all the instances in which an agency pursues the same R&D or production of a technology with another business than the SBIR awardee.[85] In order to implement this obligation, SBA requires SBIR agencies to notify

---

77 SBA 2012, 14.

78 NRC 2008, 82.

79 The Small Business Technology Transfer (STTR) programme is another federal programme that funds R&D performed by small businesses and nonprofit institutions in collaboration with a public research institute.

80 SBA 2012, 12.

81 SBA 2012, 13.

82 NRC 2008, 12.

83 Technopolis 2010, 85.

84 SBIR/STTR Reauthorization Act of 2011, section 5109. Section 9(r) has been amended to include the following: "(4) Phase III Awards—To the greatest extent practicable, Federal agencies and Federal prime contractors shall issue Phase III awards relating to technology, including sole source awards, to the SBIR and STTR award recipients that developed the technology.".

85 SBA 2012, 15.

and motivate their decisions to engage with other businesses than SBIR awardees for the same type of R&D or production. SBA may appeal these decisions, but does not seem endowed to coerce a different course of action.[86]

Differences Between US SBIR and PCP

The structure of the US SBIR and PCP is similar. PCP proposes to divide the contract into three phases: feasibility, development and testing, while the US SBIR limits to feasibility and the full R&D effort (which may involve a testing phase as well).

There are however, two major differences between the US SBIR and PCP.

1. Unlike the US SBIR, PCP does not provide for a 'Phase III' status and an EU contracting authority is not allowed to purchase directly a product resulting from the PCP procedure.[87] Neither does the PCP guidance recommend public authorities to commit to subsequently conduct a commercial procurement procedure. The early uptake of the developed innovation has been identified in Chap. 3 as an important prerequisite for the successful implementation of a demand-side R&D policy. As a consequence, when uptake of the developed innovations is not encouraged, the EU PCP lacks an important efficiency prerequisite.
2. The US SBIR allows and encourages multiple sequential awards of Phase II contracts, in order to stimulate SBIR managers to engage in the most experimental and risky R&D projects. This was identified in Chap. 3 as a prerequisite for effectiveness. The PCP guidance does not mention such a recommendation. However, implementing authorities in EU Member States may avail themselves of this possibility.

4.2.3.4 Percentage of Funded R&D Costs

In the US, there is no requirement of cost-sharing between the Federal agency and the small business, although such a course may be stimulated by certain agencies (however, not allowed as an evaluation factor of the proposal).[88] Most SBIR agreements (whether contracts or grants) fund the full costs of the R&D project, according to cost principles and procedures approved by each agency, plus a 'reasonable fee or profit'.[89] Moreover, agencies have the freedom to make SBIR awards as fixed price contracts or cost type contracts.[90]

However, since 1992, DoD introduced the "fast track" programme, which ensured expedited review of Phase II proposals of those applicants who could

[86] Ibid.

[87] PCP Communication 10.

[88] SBA 2012, 22.

[89] SBA 2012, 23.

[90] Ibid.

commit internal funding or could demonstrate financial or in-kind commitments from third parties. The "fast track" programme essentially ensured continuity of funding between Phase I and Phase II.[91]

Differences Between US SBIR and PCP

The PCP guidance on the other side, initially required contracting authorities to pay a market price for the contracted R&D services. This requirement was subsequently dropped. The 2014 Framework for State aid for R&D&I introduced a presumption that PCP takes place according to market conditions (and does not entail unwarranted aid) whenever the procurer complies with pre-defined criteria of openness and equal treatment. The suitability of this approach is further discussed in Chap. 7.

4.2.3.5 Confidentiality and IPR

The 2011 SBIR Re-Authorization Act and SBA's 2012 Policy Directives provide for confidential treatment of any proprietary information submitted in an SBIR proposal or generated during the performance of an SBIR agreement. The Small Business Act provides for *'retention by a [small business] of the rights to data generated by the concern in the performance of an SBIR award'* (copyrighted material). The SBIR agency is mandated to protect such data from disclosure and non-governmental use for a period of at least 4 years from delivery of last deliverable in any (subsequent) SBIR funding agreement, unless express permission for disclosure is granted by the owner.[92] Data in the sense of these clauses covers 'recorded information', meaning something that can be read (e.g. SBIR Phases I and II final reports, computer code, computer programs, computer documentation, drawings, equations etc.)[93] The Government obtains a royalty-free license *'to use and to authorize others to use on its behalf, these data for Government purposes (…)'*.[94]

In case of patentable innovations developed during the project, the ownership of the innovation goes by default to the company, while no royalty or repayment in case of successful commercialisation is due to the government.[95] The government will not disclose the invention for a period of 4 years, in order to allow the SBIR awardee sufficient time to obtain patent protection. The US government retains a royalty-free license for Federal use of patented inventions and may require—under

91 NRC 2000, 21.

92 SBA 2012, 25–6.

93 Metzger and Riemenschneider (2013)

94 SBA 2012, 75.

95 37 CFR Part 401, Article 14.

certain circumstances—the patent holder to license its IPR and/or to manufacture the invention in the US.[96]

These provisions are mandatory for all SBIR agencies and may not be subject to negotiations with applicants in SBIR competitions.[97] The Bayh-Dole Act,[98] which governs the division of rights to inventions made by small businesses under government funded grants, contracts or cooperative agreements, and is the framework legislation applicable to SBIR contracts, provides detailed control and enforcement mechanisms to be used in SBIR contracts (e.g. time-limits for disclosure of the invention, consequences related to non-disclosure, reporting on the application of the invention after the SBIR contract etc.[99]

The public agency may deviate from the standard legislative IPR arrangements for reasons of national security. The decision to deviate from this standard needs to be motivated and can be appealed by the contractor.[100]

Differences Between US SBIR and PCP

The intellectual property conditions of the SBIR and PCP are similar. However, unlike in the EU, the division of intellectual property rights ('IPR') between the contracting authority and the supplier is in the US mandated by legislation and is also legislated in detail.

4.2.3.6 Flexibility

As already mentioned, the SBA's Policy Directives provide mandatory guidelines to federal agencies on the operation of their SBIR programs and SBA supervises the proper implementation of these guidelines and the exercise of the discretion allowed by the Policy Directives. Within this context, the SBIR agencies retain substantial flexibility in conducting their own SBIR programs.[101]

For example, SBA's Policy Directives indicate which evaluation criteria an SBIR agency must minimally use[102]: (i) technical approach and expected benefits; (ii) adequacy of the proposed effort to achieve the desired solution and the intensity of the relationship to the fulfillment of the solution; (iii) soundness and technical merit of the proposal; (iv) qualifications of the main researchers and other participants; (v) commercialisation potential (based on the following sub-criteria:

---

96 Ibid.

97 SBA 2012, 26.

98 Bayh-Dole Act 1980.

99 For a more detailed discussion on the Bayh-Dole Act see section 5.3.1.2.

100 37 CFR Part 401, art 14.

101 SBA 2012, 3.

102 SBA 2012, 72–3.

commercialization record in previous SBIR projects or other research, existence of third parties funding commitments, existence of Phase III commitments, other indicators of the commercial potential). Each SBIR agency is allowed to further specify these criteria and/or add others.

The SBA Policy Directives also allow deviation from certain rules, upon written motivation and approval from SBA or the head of the SBIR agency. Rules from which deviation is possible regard, for example: the obligation to perform the 1/3 of Phase I activities and ½ of the Phase II activities within the organization of the awardee; obligation for the principal investigator (researcher) to be employed for more than half of his working time by the awardee; the obligation to perform the R&D work within the US territory for both Phase I and II;[103] the obligation to extend the contract period,[104] or the value of the awards.[105] The new Reauthorization Act increases flexibility in funding Phase II agreements from another agency than the Phase I awardee or following an STTR Phase I award.[106] Moreover, a pilot between 2012–2017 allows the National Institutes of Health, the Department of Defense and the Department of Education to provide Phase II awards to a small business which has not previously received a Phase I award regarding the same project.[107]

The allowed flexibility leads to differences between the precise approach to SBIR among the different federal agencies and among the different departments of the same agency (such as among the different departments of DoD), in terms of procedure, amount of funding, degree of innovativeness required, number of calls, broadness or specificity of the topics etc. But the most important differences are between agencies that are purchasing the outputs of their SBIR programmes for their own use (DoD, NASA and part of DoE) and those that do not purchase their SBIR program's outputs (NIH, NSF and parts of DoE), but focus on innovations for use in the private sector.

Hereunder, I provide a summary of the SBIR procedures within the DoD and National Institutes of Health (NIH), the most important agencies in terms of SBIR program size and also with the most diverging approaches.

DoD annually awards around 2000 Phase I and 1000 Phase II contracts,[108] defines its topics in detail, steers the research during the execution of the R&D contract and uses various mechanisms (e.g. purchase of the project result) to stimulate the subsequent commercialization of the resulting innovation.[109] DoD's

---

103 SBA 2012, 18–9.

104 SBA 2012, 24.

105 SBIR/STTR Reauthorization Act of 2011, section 5103(d)(aa).An agency may increase the award guidelines for Phase I and II up to 50 % upon SBA approval. See also SBA 2012, 24.

106 SBIR/STTR Reauthorization Act of 2011, section 5104.

107 SBIR/STTR Reauthorization Act of 2011, section 5106.

108 Deputy under Secretary of Defense (2008). See also http://www.acq.osd.mil/osbp/sbir/about/sbirAnnualReport.shtml#fy11. Accessed 18 December 2012.

109 SBA 2011, slide 12.

SBIR department is organized in a flexible manner, with few overheads and program managers appointed for short periods of four to six years.[110] A DoD program manager is mandated to prepare in advance a Technology Development Strategy that assesses the needs which can be addressed through new SBIR procedures, and outlines support measures for the commercialization of technologies developed during previous SBIR contracts.[111] For each topic a Technical Point of Contact (TPOC) is appointed, which can be contacted for questions and clarifications on the technical aspects of the call for proposals up to the deadline for submission of the proposals.[112]

DoD focuses thus within the framework of the SBIR, on developing technologies meant to fulfill its operational needs. The developed technologies are eventually developed or purchased by DoD as integrated part of weapons systems. SBIR managers at DoD closely interact with the SBIR participant and steer the R&D contract during the execution of the project. Moreover, SBIR liason officers ensure communication between the SBIR contractor and the end-customers within the agency.[113] These are important features for effective R&D demand-side public policies, as identified in Chap. 3.

Within the DoD, the Defence Advanced Research Projects Agency (DARPA) is endowed with the mission to promote the most radical, high risk projects with long-term return expectations.[114] In line with its focus on highly innovative solutions, DARPA has more flexibility than other Department of Defense agencies in conducting the SBIR program.[115] This flexibility allows DARPA to experiment with new strategies, such as increasing the exchange of knowledge across competing research groups, bringing in contact university researchers and entrepreneurs interested to start a new company, small businesses and venture capitalists, SBIR awardees and large companies able to commercialize the developed technology etc.[116] DARPA's approach to fund the most radical, high risk projects, to allow experimentation and to tolerate early R&D failure are characteristics that pay-off on the long-term. Some of the most successful technologies in the market place have been funded by DARPA at very early stages in the R&D trajectory.[117] These features are confirmed by the economic studies analysed in Chap. 3, as being crucial for an effective employment of public R&D funding from the demand-side.

---

[110] Mazzucato 2013, 76.

[111] The needs assessment and needs definition phase involves an integrated and collaborative process between different internal stakeholders, who advice and assist in identifying the needed capabilities and in formulating 'broad, time-phased, operational goals'. The needs assessment is the basis for identifying concrete needed material solutions. See DoD Instructions (2008).

[112] DoD 2004.

[113] NRC 2008, 71–2.

[114] NRC 2008, 21.

[115] Ibid.

[116] Mazzucato 2013, 79.

[117] Ruttan 2006.

Within the DoD, there are three main criteria for evaluating proposals:

- Soundness, technical merit and the level of innovation of the proposed approach, and its incremental progress towards the topic or subtopic solution;
- Qualifications of the firm and team to perform the R&D and commercialize results;
- Potential for commercialisation. This includes evaluation on the basis of past performance of the company with the commercialisation of the results of previous SBIR projects (as indicated by the Commercialisation Achievement Index (CAI), a centralized database at federal level).[118]

Following the evaluation, price negotiations are performed with the best ranked applicants. The Federal Acquisition Regulation provides in article 15.404-1(b)(2) a list of techniques to perform price analysis.

Although for most of the SBIR projects 100 % funding is provided, DoD operates a so-called "Fast Track" policy for some SBIR and STTR projects. This entails that better chances of proceeding to Phase II are given if some matching cash is found by the participating company from outside investors, customers or sponsors. The proportion of projects receiving this treatment is though small (for example, only about 2 % of Army Phase II awards).[119] DoD provides multiple Phase II awards to promising SBIR projects which necessitate additional development, test and evaluation (Phase II Enhancement program).[120]

Since 2006, support is also provided for commercialisation at Phase III. DoD signs, for example, Technology Transition Agreements with SBIR awardees during Phase II, with the objective of increasing the commercialization chances of an SBIR technology. The Technology Transition Agreements identify the stakeholders (acquisition officers within DoD (including the end-customer), SBIR manager and SBIR awardee) and identify, among others, funding sources beyond Phase II, and strategies regarding the integration of the SBIR project result into commercial products.[121]

DoD departments are moreover allowed to set up a Commercialisation Readiness Program (CRP) and provide subsidies for the commercialization phase and encourage subsequent commercial procurements of the developed products. Within this program, the Secretary of each DoD department is authorized to identify research programs funded under SBIR which meet high-priority needs and are close to commercialisation and use incentives to encourage the SBIR program

[118] Each company must submit with any DoD Phase II SBIR proposal a Commercialisation Report which describes the commercialization of the products developed in a previous Phase II project. The content of these reports is automatically computed into the CAI, when four or more projects have completed Phase II. Firms with a CAI in the bottom 10 % may not receive more than half of the evaluation point for the commercialisation criteria. See NRC 2008, 16.

[119] NRC 2008, 15.

[120] Office of the Under Secretary of Defense 2010, 3.

[121] See http://www.acq.osd.mil/osbp/sbir/gov/transition-guidance.shtml. Accessed 18 December 2012.

managers to fund follow-on awards.[122] The Navy, for example, sets aside around 20 % of its SBIR funds for the CPP and by 2009, had supported 129 projects.[123]

Within the context of the CRP, the Navy has for example, set up a Transition Assistance Programme (TAP), which consists concretely in a series of workshops, trainings and briefing meetings which are organized over a 10 month period, to help companies develop their commercialisation plans and present their technology to both DoD and private undertakings. At the end of the TAP, the annual Navy Opportunities Forum gives companies that have successfully completed the TAP programme the opportunity to present their products to a broad audience of around 400-500 representatives of DoD and of the private sector.[124]

In addition, DoD must give preference, including sole-source awards to the SBIR awardees. Whenever R&D contracts or production contracts are pursued with another company than the business which developed the SBIR-technology, report and justification is due to the SBA.[125] However, there are significant differences among the services within DoD. The Navy, for example, shows more consistent links between the SBIR and the acquisition departments.[126]

Unlike DoD, NIH focuses on innovative drugs and medical devices for the private end-user and awards in 95 % of the cases grants instead of contracts. As opposed to the DoD approach, it defines less specified SBIR topics and allows unsolicited proposals as well.[127] During the performance of the project, no substantial involvement with the recipient of the grant occurs.[128] Overall size of grants is the same as within DoD ($100 k Phase I and $750 k Phase II), but in practice individual grants vary widely in amount.

The key evaluation criteria are[129]:

(i) Significance (does the project address an important problem/critical barrier in the field and does the envisaged solution have a high probability of commercialization?);
(ii) The proposed approach (are the proposed strategy, methodology and analyses suitable to lead to the achievement of the envisaged solution?);
(iii) Level of innovation (are novel theoretical concepts, approaches or methodologies, instrumentation, or interventions proposed?);

---

122 SBA 2012, 54–5.

123 Office of the Under Secretary of Defense 2010, 3–4.

124 NRC 2008, 20.

125 Deputy under Secretary of Defense 2008.

126 The Navy accounts for 70 % of all DoD Phase III contracts. See NRC 2009, 29.

127 SBA 2011, slide 12.

128 See http://grants.nih.gov/grants/policy/nihgps_2012/nihgps_ch1.htm#definitions_of_terms. Accessed 2 February 2013.

129 See http://grants.nih.gov/grants/funding/sbirsttr_ReviewCriteria.htm. Accessed 2 February 2013.

(iv) Experience and expertise of the "principal investigator" (main researcher) and research team;
(v) Adequacy of the facilities and resources of the project.

In addition, during the evaluation of Phase II proposals the progress towards meeting the objectives set in the Phase I proposal is taken into consideration.

NIH also operates a so-called "Fast Track" policy for SBIR projects, which entails that better scores are given if commercialization plans are submitted and letters of support from potential commercialisation partners and/or Phase III funders are provided.[130] Moreover, starting in 2014, a database regarding the transition rate to Phase II and commercialization rates of recipients of a certain amount of SBIR awards is expected to be operative and the transition rate and commercialization rate will be taken into consideration in the evaluation of the SBIR applications.

NIH also supports commercialisation of the products developed within SBIR programs and the Phase III financial support is more substantial than within DoD in terms of amount of funding and available coaching on commercialization strategies. This difference is justified by the fact that developing promising drug compounds and medical devices takes much more money and time than is available under the SBIR phases. Thus, within the framework of NIH's Commercialization Assistance Program (CAP), Renewal Applications may be submitted by Phase II awardees. Within the CAP, funds may be provided for subsequent development work, for preclinical studies of drugs or devices, for regulatory approval, etc. These awards generally amount to $1 m per year for up to three years.[131]

Supplementary consulting programs are made available, to assist SBIR awardees with commercialization. At Phase I, NIH provides consulting support related to the potential of the innovation to be commercialised and related to the aspects that need to be taken into consideration, such as competitors, applicable regulation, potential clients and price. At Phase II, one-on-one consulting (from an advisor/industry expert) may be provided for a period of 18 months. This relates to concrete steps towards commercialization, such as finding investors, partnerships, applying for IPR etc.[132]

Differences Between US SBIR and PCP

In conclusion, unlike the EU PCP, the US SBIR program is a large, established program, with experienced personnel that is allowed sufficient flexibility to tailor the support to each project and to adopt a large array of support measures up to the commercialization phase. This is in line with the prerequisite identified in Chap. 3, concerning the benefits of a high degree of experimentation and tolerance to failure.

---

[130] http://grants.nih.gov/grants/funding/sbir_faqs.htm. Accessed 2 February 2013.

[131] http://grants.nih.gov/grants/policy/nihgps_2012/nihgps_ch18.htm#_Toc271265315. Accessed 2 February 2013.

[132] http://grants.nih.gov/grants/funding/cap/. Accessed 2 February 2013.

4.2.3.7 Contracts and Grants

The EU has identified SBIR as a demand-side policy instrument (or a public procurement instrument) used by the US in pulling R&D projects into the commercialization phase. However, the SBIR program covers both demand- and supply-side instruments. According to the Small Business Development Act of 1982, the SBIR program covers '*contracts, grants or cooperative agreements entered into between any Federal agency and any small business for the performance of experimental, developmental, or research work funded in whole or in part by the Federal Government*'.[133]

Agencies such as DoD and NASA mainly focus on topics related to their specific needs and award contracts, while the NIH accepts (unsolicited) applications, that are not directly linked to its operational needs and awards grants.[134]

The grants correspond to what the EU labels as 'subsidies', while contracts correspond to public contracts subject to the EU public procurement rules. The distinction in the US between grants and contracts lies in the purpose of the R&D contract. According to the Federal Acquisition Regulation ('FAR'), contracts are used '*only when the principal purpose is the acquisition of supplies or services for the direct benefit or use of the Federal Government*' and grants are used '*when the principal purpose of the transaction is to stimulate or support research and development for another public purpose*'.[135] SBIR contract awards are more specific than grants and are defined in detail. The SBIR agency awarding contracts gets involved closely in the execution of the SBIR project and is capable of sole-sourcing (purchasing without competition) at a later stage the developed solution.

An SBIR contract is thus awarded when the Federal agency needs a product which is not available commercially on the private market, for fulfilling its own operational tasks. Such an example constitutes the SBIR call launched by NASA, to fulfill its need for a much lighter, energy efficient laser system than available on the market, to be used for a new NASA science mission that would take continuous measurements of CO_2 (carbon dioxide) and O_2 (oxygen) data from space. The data collected by the satellite would form the basis of better-informed policy decisions related to climate change.

Such collection of data would be for the first time achieved by using a satellite rotating around the globe. The laser transmitter module was the crucial component in sensing which areas of the globe are emitting O_2 and/or CO_2. The small company EM4 received an SBIR award to develop this module. They came up with a module 7 times lighter, 3 times more energy efficient and with improved functionalities, which was subsequently used by NASA for its mission.[136]

---

[133] Small Business Innovation Development Act of 1982, section 121.701(c).

[134] NRC 2008, 82.

[135] Federal Acquisition Regulation art 35.003 (a).

[136] http://decadal.gsfc.nasa.gov/documents/10_ASCENDS.pdf. Accessed 2 February 2013.

Differences Between US SBIR and PCP

In conclusion, the US SBIR clearly distinguishes between grants (or subsidies) for the development of solutions whose end-customer finds itself on the private market and R&D contracts for the direct benefit and use by the SBIR agency. Such a delineation is missing in the case of PCP. In the absence of express competences to closely scrutinize the set-up and deployment of PCP(-'like') initiatives by EU Member States, the European Commission uses the state aid rules to prevent distortive deployments of PCP. The result is a muddled concept that does not provide the needed flexibility to stimulate those groundbreaking innovations that Europe so urgently needs. This is further discussed in Chap. 7.

4.3 Quantifying the Impact of the US SBIR Program—The Debate

4.3.1 Impact of US SBIR

Since its inception, the US SBIR has been regularly scrutinized and assessed on its capacity to fulfill its legislative objectives (stimulate technological innovation, encourage commercialization of outputs, encourage participation by women- and minority-owned small businesses, fulfilling agency missions) as well as on other criteria such as its capacity to incentivize additional private R&D investments, to stimulate growth, or to incentivize the creation of new firms.

Qualitative assessments (based on surveys, case studies, interviews), as well as quantitative assessments (based on patents, sales or growth generated after exiting the program) have been performed. Both approaches present difficulties in depicting the real economic impact of the program. The first approach has been criticized, particularly for: (1) being biased by the propensity of successful firms to respond to surveys and to report overly positive results or estimations; (2) not comparing against matching firm that hadn't received SBIR support. The second approach presents three main difficulties: (1) finding comparable firms that did not benefit of SBIR funds; (2) quantifying certain outcomes (e.g. increase in technological innovation; profits from the commercialisation of products developed with SBIR support); (3) reflecting social value which is not captured by quantifiable indicators, such as patents or profit.[137]

Methodological difficulties common to both types of assessments, entail: possibility that results related to commercialization or job creation may show many

137 OECD (2010), 5: '*The Department of Defense for instance is using the company commercialisation report (which requires firms that submit bids for phases I or II to report commercialisation for all previous awards). However, this dataset does not include further growth by award-winners that are ineligible for (or do not apply to) further awards*'.

years after the awards; difficulty to isolate the impact of the SBIR awards from other factors that contribute to the success of the firm.[138]

Hereafter, I will give an overview of the most reputable assessments of the program. I will focus on studies of those SBIR agencies that adopt a procurement-oriented approach and focus on technologies that solve specific agency needs. These are in particular DoD and NASA.

I will focus on the assessment of the following SBIR impacts:

- to commercialize research outputs (sales, revenues);
- to support R&D projects that would otherwise not be funded by the firm or other private investors (in this way complementing rather than replacing private investments);
- to incentivize increased private R&D investments (e.g. by encouraging increased firm investments or by attracting venture capital following the SBIR award);
- to generate valuable research outputs (e.g. outputs that respond to the agency's operational needs);
- to support growth (e.g. employment growth of the SBIR awardees).

An early qualitative assessment of the impact of the SBIR program was performed by Berger et al. in 1992, based on a survey among Phase II SBIR awardees. They found that the SBIR awards had stimulated small businesses to conduct R&D and to commercialise their results. A significant percentage of the responders reported that they wouldn't have conducted the research without the SBIR award and that their project success was due to the SBIR program.[139]

In the same year (1992), Alic et al.[140] published a critical account of the overall US policy in support of technology development. Based on case studies, the authors argued that relying on spin-off from military R&D to ensure US' industrial leadership was an expensive and ineffective approach. They don't deny the scientific value of many projects supported by DoD, but warn that these yield insufficient and diminishing civilian benefits (e.g. innovative civilian technologies or GDP growth), due to its cumbersome procurement systems that favored a pool of established companies and delayed the diffusion of defense-related technologies. In the face of shrinking defense budgets, following the end of the Cold War, as

[138] Roessner 1989.

[139] More specifically, 12 % of the respondents reported that they had successfully commercialized the result of the Phase II SBIR award 4 years after the award. "over 60 % of the respondents attributed nearly all of their projects' success to the SBIR program" and "eighty-four percent stated that the technology development effort would not have been pursued without SBIR". See Berger et al. 1992.

[140] Alic et al. 1992 argued that, due to technological specialization and increased reliance on incremental improvements (rather than radical developments) and substantial costs involved in transferring technology to different uses, the spin-off model weakened.

well as increased foreign competition in the defense sector, the authors argued for more direct support to the development of civil technologies and the wide diffusion of non-proprietary knowledge.

A year later (1993) Mowery & Rosenberg[141] observed that defense-related R&D funding has created bodies of scientific or engineering knowledge which constituted the basis of new technologies with both civilian and defense-related applications (the spin-off effect).[142] However, due to increasingly specific and diverging requirements for technologies in the civil and military sectors, the capability of defense R&D and procurement to spawn commercial applications had diminished.[143]

These concerned were partially damped by the quantitative assessments that were performed in the following years. The first quantitative assessments of the SBIR, and one of the most reputable so far, was conducted by Lerner in 1999.[144] He compared the employment growth and sales of around 900 companies that had received SBIR contracts in the first 3 years of the program with around 500 matching companies that hadn't received any SBIR contract. He came to the conclusion that firms who had received SBIR funds created within 10 years (between 1985–1995) significantly more jobs (an average of 26 employees vs. 6) and sales (an average of $4.0 million vs. $1.1 million) than firms which hadn't received an SBIR award. He found that the relation between SBIR Phase II awardee and employment was stronger as compared to SBIR Phase I awardees and that the relation between the SBIR awards and growth was much stronger in high-technology industries.

The SBIR awardees had also an average higher probability (3.1 %) to attract venture capital following the award, compared to non-awardees, who had only a 0.8 % probability. This was interpreted as a confirmation that the program acted as a certification for the awardees and reduced the information asymmetries between innovators and investors.

In conclusion, Lerner's study found that the SBIR stimulates company growth (in terms of employment and sales) and incentivizes additional private investments. A caveat of the study is that it did not isolate the impact exclusively attributable to the SBIR awards, as oppose to other contributing factors.

Another reputable study was performed by Wallsten in 2000.[145] The author tested whether the SBIR program finances those projects that are socially valuable, but do not attract sufficient private investments, due to their low profitability.

---

141 Mowery and Rosenberg 1993.

142 They consider that defence-related procurement had especially a positive impact on the information technology sector in the US and that technologies such as the jet engine, swept-wing airframe or light-water nuclear reactors are 'spinoffs' from defence-related R&D spending. The author admits that defense-related procurement had a detrimental impact on some products and industries, such as the numerically controlled machine tools.

143 Mowery 2009, 47.

144 Lerner 1999.

145 Wallsten 2000.

The author criticized the use of employment growth and commercial success as indicator of program's effectiveness. Rise in employment is not an accurate indicator as many small awardees often sell or license the right to commercialise their inventions. On the same note, a high ratio of commercial success may signal that insufficient risk is taken and that the program replaces instead of increasing the R&D investments. The author warned that underscoring commercialization as success indicator may deter program managers from engaging in risky R&D projects.[146] In the absence of legislative incentives and of suitable methods to calculate social return on R&D investments, program managers could turn to funding those projects that would have a high probability of commercial success and that would be funded by private investors anyway.[147]

Based on the analysis of 3 samples of firms: 367 that had received SBIR awards between 1990–1992, 90 that applied but did not win an award and 22 that were eligible but did not apply, Wallsten found that firms with more employees and patents win more SBIR grants, but the grants do not appear to enhance employment in firms. Moreover, firms' R&D spending in 1992 decreased compared to the 1990 levels, by approximately the same amount of the SBIR award.[148] The author advanced several interpretations for these findings. Either the SBIR program has no beneficial impact, as it crowds out firm R&D investments. According to Wallsten, alternative explanations may be that SBIR enables firms to use the saved money to continue research that would otherwise be stopped, or to fund the research for a longer period of time. The author doesn't rule out that the SBIR encouraged private investments from other sources than the firm, as the study did not investigate this aspect.[149] Another important caveat of this part of the study is that information on R&D investments were only analyzed for a small dataset of 81 firms that are publicly-traded.

Gans and Stern analysed in 2000 the 'crowding-out' effect of the SBIR program at industry level.[150] Based on a sample of 100 projects funded by the SBIR between 1990–2000, selected from a list of 200 largest recipients of SBIR funding, the authors concluded that the firms that had reported the most technological

[146] Wallten 2000, 86.

[147] Thorough evaluations would combine sophisticated engineering and scientific data with complex economic welfare analysis under conditions of uncertainty. Even if these evaluations could be conducted at a reasonable cost, political overseers might have difficulty determining whether the evaluations were competent and unbiased.

[148] This conclusion holds for those publicly-traded firms, for which information on R&D expenditure is available.

[149] Wallsten 2000, 99.

[150] Crowding out may happen when competitors of the SBIR awardees reduce their R&D funding, as they perceive the government awards to reduce their commercial returns from that product development. Reduction may happen at the level of the specific firm that receives the award, or at industry level. Thus, private firms may not allocate R&D budgets in expectation of public awards in that area. Or private firms displace R&D investments from other ongoing/planned projects and concentrate their investments on the project supported by the SBIR award.

success (in terms of revenues from commercialization and issued patents and employment growth), found themselves in market segments characterized by high rates of private venture capital investments.[151] The authors did not bring evidence that SBIR is funding the same projects that attract (sufficient) venture capital. The authors simply warned that this could be the case.

They admitted though that the SBIR might be supporting the marginal projects in those economic segments, that experience the most serious hurdles in terms of appropriability or access to capital. The fact that firms generally prefer private venture capital to public awards, whenever they have this choice, provided support for the second interpretation.[152]

Later studies continued to focus on commercial success as an indicator of the program's effectiveness.

A qualitative assessment of the DoD SBIR, performed by Audretsch et al. in 2001 on a sample of 112 DoD SBIR awardees who had received Phase II support since 1992,[153] concluded that the program encourages commercialization. They also found that these projects would not have been undertaken in the absence of SBIR support. The authors concluded that DoD SBIR supports projects that are socially worthwhile, but present appropriability hurdles and would not happen without the public support.[154] DoD SBIR appeared particularly encouraging for scientists and engineers who had no previous entrepreneurial experience with knowledge-based small firms.[155]

Based on a survey performed in 1995 on firms (208 survey responses) that had received awards from NASA Langley SBIR programme since its inception in 1982, Archibald and Finifter reached in 2003 similar positive conclusions. Nearly 70 % of their respondents indicated that an innovation with commercial potential resulted from their SBIR contract. However, only 17 % had an innovation that was already available on the market or had already produced sales.[156]

A major cross-agency evaluation of the effectiveness of the SBIR program, was commissioned by the US Congress as part of the 2000 Re-authorization Act.

The SBIR programs of the 5 agencies which account for more than 90 % of the total value of the program (the Department of Defence, the National Institutes of

---

[151] This was measured as the undiscounted amount of venture investment in that market segment between 1985–1992, thus previous to the SBIR award. See Gans and Stern 2000.

[152] As most of the respondents in the survey reported. The SBIR funding can usually be accessed with months of delay, while private venture capital is usually directly available. Additionally, VCs provide services and access to networks and expertise, beyond capital. This makes private venture capital preferable to firms. See Gans and Stern 2000, 16–7.

[153] Additional interviews were conducted with 34 projects of the sample, that had reported sales from the technology developed during the Phase II project.

[154] The authors estimate a 84 % social rate of return for the SBIR funding of the analysed projects. Audretsch et al. 2001, 16–7.

[155] Ibid. 10–1.

[156] Archibald and Finifter 2003.

Health, the National Aeronautics and Space Administration, the Department of Energy, and the National Science Foundation) formed the subject of evaluation. The study was conducted by the National Research Council (NRC) on a sample of 11.214 projects completed from Phase II awards made between 1992–2001, out of which around 1900 completed the surveys with all relevant information.[157] The survey was complemented by case studies, data and document analyses, as well as interviews of program staff and agency officials. The study resulted in a series of reports between 2004–2009.

The general conclusion of NRC was that the SBIR program was '*sound in concept and effective in practice*'.[158] The SBIR program achieved important goals: (1) it led to the creation of new scientific and technical knowledge; (2) it facilitated private investment by signaling quality and thus reducing the information asymmetries between innovators and private investors; (3) it supported the growth of a diverse array of small businesses; and (4) it encouraged the commercialisation of the products developed with public R&D funds; (5) it stimulated the development of technologies which can meet the specific needs of public agencies in health, transport, the environment, and defense.[159]

At NASA and DoD, NRC found that around 46 % of Phase II projects commercialised the outputs. At NASA 17.7 % even generated revenues greater than $1 million and nearly half of the revenues generated through commercialization were achieved from other customers than the federal government, which showed the broader value of the research outputs.[160] Both NASA and DoD SBIR proved to be valuable support for new firm creation,[161] and for expansion of the R&D funding base.[162] Around 70 % of the respondent Phase II awardees indicated they definitely or probably would not have undertaken the research without the SBIR support. At DoD 48 % of the respondent firms attributed more than half of their firm's growth to the SBIR support.[163]

Based on a survey of NASA and DoD Contracting Officer's Technical Representative, NRC also found that a large share of the Phase II projects yielded new scientific and technological knowledge of significant research value.[164]

[157] Link and Scott 2010, 592.

[158] NRC 2008, 54–5.

[159] NRC 2008, 57.

[160] NRC 2009, 6.

[161] 20 % of NASA respondents stated they found their business at least in part due to SBIR. AT DoD the percentage was slightly higher (25 %).

[162] Ibid. 6–7.

[163] NRC 2009, 31.

[164] 63 % of respondent s at Nasa. nearly a quarter of the projects have reported at least one patent filing. And 53 % at DoD. 32 % of DoD survery respondents reported at least 1 peer-reviewed article and nearly 35 %generated at least 1 patent application and just over 25 % had already received a patent related to the project. But NRC warns for the limited relevance of patents as a measure of technological success, as patents have a limited economic value when the firm's primary market is the federal government, who already gained the right for royalty free use of the innovation generated by an SBIR contract. See NRC 2009, 38.

Moreover, the developed technologies significantly contributed to fulfilling agencies' missions (needs).[165]

Several economists have used the same dataset gathered by NRC, to assess the impacts of the SBIR program. Allen et al. (2012) measured the benefits of the SBIR program in terms of producer and consumer surplus, calculated as licensing and sales (measured as the sum of all the Phase I and II awards, including those to firms that did not present any producer or consumer surplus). They concluded that the average net economic value of the SBIR program in the five largest participating agencies was positive.[166]

Qian & Haynes[167] confirmed in 2014 NRC's finding, that the SBIR stimulates the formation of new 'high quality high growth companies' in the high technology sector.[168]

In 2016, NRC released a new series of reports assessing the progress of the SBIR program since the previous assessment. The reports are based on improved surveys,[169] on case studies, agency data and interviews with agency managers and other stakeholders. The report on NASA's SBIR largely confirms the conclusions of the previous 2009 report. The program particularly encourages the creation of technical knowledge (illustrated by patents and peer reviewed publications), and the commercialization of technologies developed through the SBIR contract (46 % of the respondents reported sales). NASA's SBIR also encourages the formation of new companies (40 % of respondents indicated the SBIR award was the only or one of the reasons for founding a company). The Study confirms the previous evidence of the additionality of the SBIR R&D funding: 68 % state that the project would definitely or probably not been initiated without the SBIR support; and 43 % of respondents stated that the project would have been narrower in scope, or behind schedule.[170]

The assessment of the DoD SBIR is also fully in line with the previous 2009 assessment. More than 45 % of the respondent Phase II projects report sales[171] and a further 26 % estimate sales in the future. According to DoD's commercialization database 70 % of Phase II projects commercialise the result of the project. NRC also found an increase in the uptake of the SBIR results by DoD, which suggests that the SBIR fulfils the agency's needs.[172] The report shows that Phase II

---

165 DoD's central mission is for example, "to use the inventiveness of small companies to solve DoD's technical problems, and to develop new technologies that can be applied to the weapons and logistics systems that are eventually used by the Armed Forces". NRC 2009, 25.

166 Stuart Allen et al. 2012.

167 Qian and Haynes 2014.

168 Qian and Haynes 2014, 524–5.

169 The survey was performed on 490 awards out of which 179 responses were received. NRC 2016a, 3.

170 NRC 2016a, 30.

171 30 % of these, reported sales of over $1 million or more. NRC, SBIR at DoD 2014, 61.

172 20 % of Phase II respondents state that their output of their SBIR project was currently in use by the DoD. NRC 2014, 61.

awardees experience some, but not high levels, of employment growth between the time of award and time of survey.[173] Moreover, 13.5 % of the Phase II projects stated that they attracted non-SBIR and non-federal funding (personal funding or venture capital) following the award.[174]

The above analysed evaluation studies reach an overall positive conclusion regarding SBIR's benefits.

In conclusion, there is compelling evidence that the SBIR yields positive results, in terms of commercialization, employment, technological knowledge, incentives for additional private investments. Several studies warn that important pitfalls may weaken the strength of the program: excessive reliance on a limited number of R&D contractors in the defense area, while the development of civil innovation, with potential military applications, is ignored; and the risk of funding precisely those projects that are already attractive to private investors.

4.3.2 Strengths and Points of Improvement

The studies described above point out which features of the SBIR program drive the positive impacts of the program. These are described below.

Selection on Technological Merit

An important aspect underscored by several studies is that the SBIR selection should focus on *technological merit*, rather than commercial potential. This would enhance the program's support for those marginal projects, that have social value but would not happen in the absence of public support, due to their low profitability.

Lerner concludes that an important feature of the programme for the period under scrutiny was the scoring system used to select awardees. It largely focused on the technological merit of the solution proposed, rather than on the commercial potential.[175]

The same point is underscored by Archibal and Finifter, who warned in 1993 that the increased focus on 'likelihood of commercial success' for the selection of SBIR awardees, brought by the 1992 Reauthorization Act could weaken the quality of the program.[176] The authors found that projects performed after the 1992 legislative change showed a significant increase in the rate of commercial success, and a decrease of 10 % in basic research output. They conclude that after 1992, the

173 On average from 17 to 24 employees. NRC 2014, 63.

174 More than 30 % compared to 20 % in 2009. NRC 2014, 64.

175 Lerner 1999, 296.

176 Archibald and Finifter 2003.

projects that presented only technical superiority, without cost/price reduction potential had less opportunities to win an SBIR award. The authors expressed concerns that this may signal a decrease in the quality of the program output, as the focus falls on less expensive rather than technically superior solutions.[177]

Multiple Sequential Awards

A controversial issue remains the award of *multiple sequential SBIR awards* to the same firm. Lerner concluded in 1999 that multiple sequential SBIR contract did not increase the impact of the program, but showed *"rather detrimental effects on the firm"*.[178] NRC, on the other side, singled out the possibility for multiple awards to individual firms as a key feature to the effectiveness of the SBIR program. It argued that multiple DoD SBIR awards and multiple funding sources were needed to bring a technology to the market and that most companies with multiple awards were high performers in meeting the agency's needs and in reaching large amounts of commercial sales.[179]

Flexibility

The NRC studies of 2009 and 2016, singled out another precondition for a successful program: *flexibility* to adapt the structure of the SBIR award procedure. Program managers need to be given room to adapt the program to the needs of specific technologies and unique mission needs (such as waivers on funding size[180] or on amount of support for commercialization, possibility to change the specifications of the call during the R&D project).[181] This is considered the only way to encourage program managers to make a balance between high-risk technologies with important long-term benefits against less radical technologies with promising commercialisation perspectives and immediate benefits.[182] In order to prevent abuse, the 2011 Reauthorization Act has strengthened the possibilities for reporting fraud and for regular assessments of the program performance.[183]

The NRC studies underline several other conditions for improving the program's performance:

- *reduce evaluation times* of SBIR proposals, particularly before Phase II, in order to prevent the funding gap for small high-tech companies with limited

[177] Archibald and Finifter 2003, 614.

[178] Lerner 1999, 312.

[179] More specifically, 10–25 Phase II awards are found to maximize returns. NRC 2009, 9 and 2014. See also NRC 2016a, 34.

[180] The Reauthorization Act of 2011 responded to NRC's recommendations by raising the financial thresholds (Phase I awards to $150.000 and Phase II awards to $1.000.000) and allowing SBIR managers to increase them by a maximum of 50 %, upon motivation submitted to SBA.

[181] NRC 2008, 66.

[182] NRC 2008, 84–5.

[183] Reauthorization Act of 2011, section 313. Reducing vulnerability of SBIR and STTR programs to fraud, waste, and abuse.

own resources;[184] The NRC Studies also praise the Fast Track program of DoD for bringing this funding gap and recommend its adoption by other agencies.[185]
- *simplify rules and procedures* to be followed by bidding firms;[186]
- *provide Phase III support*, particularly when the agency does not acquire the products of the firms receiving the SBIR award.
- test new policy instruments (e.g. new pilot initiatives), followed by regular evaluation of outcomes

The NRC studies also highlight the importance of strengthening the assessment methodology (e.g. develop metrics for measuring the effectiveness and the social benefits of the SBIR)[187] and data availability (e.g. strengthen reporting at agency level, in order to make measurement of the success of the program possible).[188]

4.4 Lessons for the EU

The US SBIR inspired the design of the PCP model. The European Commission attempted in this way to emulate the perceived success of the US in bringing R&D projects into the commercialization phase and increasing the competitive advantages of their firms in the global market. In this chapter, I investigated whether this perception is confirmed by the most reputable assessments of the US SBIR.

I concluded that the performed qualitative and quantitative assessments reached overall positive conclusions concerning the capacity of the US SBIR to:

- stimulate company growth in terms of employment;
- incentivize commercialisation (measured by sales);
- incentivize firms to perform R&D that would not take place in the absence of the SBIR award;
- incentivize additional R&D investments by the participating firm itself or by external investors;
- support the creation of new firms.

---

[184] The Reauthorization Act of 2011 took heed of the recommendation to shorten the evaluation times. SBIR agencies other than the National Institutes of Health or National Science Foundation (to which the term of 1 year is applicable) are required to adopt measures to reduce the evaluation time to 90 days from the application deadline. See SBIR/STTR Reauthorization Act of 2011, section 5126.

[185] This program requires matching funds for Phase II. Wessner (2001) found that the Fast Track Program increases the efficiency of the Department of Defense SBIR program by encouraging the commercialization of new technologies and the entry of new firms to the program.

[186] NRC 2008, 38.

[187] NRC, SBIR at NASA 2016, 38.

[188] Such as excluding a firm from participation in SBIR calls for a period of 1 year from the time of the decision, if winning subsequent Phase II awards or commercialization of SBIR products has not been satisfactory, according to the rules developed by each agency. See section 5165.

The analysed studies point out some of the strengths of the US SBIR program:

- selection of the project based mainly on technological merit, and to less extent on commercial potential or cost of development;
- flexibility to adapt the structure of the SBIR competition (waivers on funding size or on amount of support for commercialization, possibility to change the specifications of the call during the R&D project), while enabling fraud reporting and periodic impact assessment.
- purchase of the resulting innovation or provide financial support for commercialisation outside the SBIR agency.
- periodic assessments of the impact of the program and of new pilot initiatives.

These strengths overlap the prerequisites (1, 6, 8, 9, 10, 11) that were identified in Chap. 3 (see Sect. 3.4) as key to an effective deployment of PCP.

Several studies pointed out potential pitfalls of the program, such as over reliance on military R&D and the risk of funding R&D projects that already attract private investments. However, these studies did not provide undisputable evidence of such negative effects, but rather introduce a note of caution in the debate.

Based, on the overall positive assessments of the US SBIR, I can conclude that the European Commission's initiative to seek to duplicate the same results in the EU is justified.

However, none of the above SBIR strengths are embodied in the PCP structure. PCP does not expressly encourage support to high-risk innovations and is not even limited to technological targets (innovative services may also form the target of PCP competitions). PCP has not been set-up as a fully-fledged program with EU-wide coordination and supervision. Therefore, PCP does not mention the need to allow flexibility to PCP managers such as to encourage them to select high-risk projects and to experiment with new policy strategies. Neither does PCP facilitate the uptake of the developed innovation. Unlike in the US, where innovations developed during an SBIR Phase 2 may be sold to the SBIR agency without competition and SBIR procurers are even required to justify purchases from other firms, in the EU the procurer is obliged to organize a separate procurement procedure in accordance with the EU Procurement Directives. In the same line, PCP does not mention other instruments used by the SBIR agencies to speed up the commercialisation of those projects that meet high-priority needs (e.g. multiple sequential awards within the framework of the SBIR, or additional funding for commercialisation activities outside the scope of the SBIR program).

A final important difference is the conceptualization of the policy instrument. The US SBIR, on the one side, is clearly divided between a procurement-based and a grant/subsidy-based share. The procurement-based share embodies features that were identified in Chap. 3 as key prerequisites for an effective support of innovation from the demand side:

- the SBIR topics are aligned with the procurement needs of the agency;
- close interaction between the SBIR awardees and the SBIR manager;

- SBIR liaison officers ensure communication between the SBIR contractor and the end-customers within the agency;
- early purchase of the developed innovation.

PCP, on the other side, was labelled in its entirety as 'procurement', although it allows the development of innovations for broader public goals (which corresponds to the grant/subsidy-based share of the US SBIR). This muddled concept, leads not only to confusion but also to a less effective implementation (this is further discussed in Chap. 6).

In conclusion, SBIR is an established program, with a strong and flexible structure, that supports strategic technologies up to the commercialisation stage. In the absence of express competences to coordinate, supervise and sanction abuses in the implementation of PCP, the European Commission sought to prevent potential distortive applications by adopting a rigid approach, which is not conducive of effectiveness.

Having identified the main weaknesses of the PCP, I will turn in the next Chapter to the analysis of practical implementations of PCP in the EU and of PCP- or SBIR-like initiatives in three front-runner EU Member States. This analysis will highlight in how far these initiatives incorporate the key prerequisites for effective deployment, as identified in Chap. 3. Finally, this analysis will reveal which PCP features are considered by contracting authorities within the EU as barriers to its wide deployment.

References

Alic JA, Branscomb L, Brooks H, Carter AB, Epstein GL (1992) Beyond spinoff: military and commercial technologies in a changing world. Harvard Business School Press

Allen D, Layson SK, Link AN (2012) Public gains from entrepreneurial research: inferences about the economic value of public support of the Small Business Innovation Research Program. Res Eval 21:110

Archibald RB, Finifter DH (2003) Evaluating the NASA Small Business Innovation Research Program: preliminary evidence of a trade-off between commercialization and basic research. Res Policy 32:609

Audretsch DB, Link AN, Scott JJ (2001) Public/private technology partnerships: evaluating SBIR-supported research. Available at http://www.dartmouth.edu/~jtscott/Papers/01-01.pdf. Accessed 15 May 2016

Audretsch DB (2003) Standing on the shoulders of midgets: the U.S. Small Business Innovation Research Program (SBIR). Small Bus Econ 20:130

Bayh-Dole Act (1980) (P.L. 96–517)

Berger RE, Little CE, Saavedra PJ (1992) Commercialization activities in the SBIR program (part 1). J Technol Transf 17

Birch DL (1981) Who creates jobs. Public Interest 65

Commission (2004) Entrepreneurship—Flash Eurobarometer Survey. http://europa.eu.int/comm/enterprise/enterprise_policy/survey/eurobarometer83.htm. Accessed 18 Dec 2012

Commission (2007) Pre-commercial procurement: driving innovation to ensure sustainable high quality public services in Europe. COM 799 final

Commission (2009) Staff Working Document on the implementation of Commission Recommendation of 6 May 2003 concerning the definition of micro, small and medium-sized enterprises. SEC 1350 final

Connell D (2013) Secrets of the world's largest seed capital fund: how the United States government uses its Small Business Innovation Research (SBIR) programme and procurement budgets to support small technology firms. http://www.cbr.cam.ac.uk/pdf/SBIR%20Full%20Report.pdf. Accessed 5 February 2013
Consolidated version of the Treaty on the Functioning of the European Union (TFEU) [2008] OJ 115/47
Deputy under Secretary of Defense (2008) Memorandum for Secretaries of the Military Departments Directors of Defense Agencies. http://www.acq.osd.mil/osbp/docs/memorandum_sbir_phase_III_guidance.pdf. Accessed 2 Feb 2013
DoD Instructions (2008) 5000.02 User needs and technology opportunities. https://acc.dau.mil/CommunityBrowser.aspx?id=332529. Accessed 2 Feb 2013
DoD 2004.3 SBIR solicitation http://www.acq.osd.mil/osbp/sbir/solicitations/sbir20043/index.shtml. Accessed 18 Dec 2012
Ecory (2011) Study on pre-commercial procurement in the field of security. http://ec.europa.eu/enterprise/policies/security/files/doc/pcp_sec_finalreport_en.pdf. Accessed 29 Jan 2013
European Defence Agency (2013) 2012 Financial Report. http://www.eda.europa.eu/docs/default-source/finance-documents/eda-2012-financial-report-audited.pdf. Accessed 6 Nov 2013
Gulbrandsen M, Etzkowitz H (1999) Convergence between Europe and America: the transition from industrial to innovation policy. J Technol Transfer 24
Gans J, Stern S (2000) When does funding by smaller firms bear fruit? Evidence from the SBIR program. Economics of Innovation and New Technology 12:4
Lerner J (1999) The government as venture capitalist: the long-run impact of the SBIR program. J Bus 72
Link AN, Scott JT (2010) Evaluating the commercialization success of SBIR projects. Research Policy 39
Link AN, Scott JT (2012) Employment growth from public support of innovation in small firms. Economics of Innovation and New Technology 21
Mazzucato M (2013) The entrepreneurial state (Demos)
Metzger DP (2013) SBA's Final SBIR/STTR eligibility rule: a safer harbor for SBIR financing. http://www.arnoldporter.com/resources/documents/SBAs%20Final%20SBIR-STTR%20Eligibility%20Rule_%20CIT.pdf. Accessed 12 July 2014
Metzger DP, Riemenschneider KO (2013) SBIR data: What they are, what they are not, and how to mark them. Transition 10
Mogee ME (1991) Technology policy and critical technologies, a summary of recent reports. National Academy Press, Washington
Mowery DC, Rosenberg N (1993) The U.S. National Innovation System. In: Nelson RR (ed) National innovation systems—a comparative analysis. Oxford University Press, Oxford
Mowery DC (2009) National security and national innovation systems. J Technol Transf 34
Nelson RR, Rosenberg N (1993) Technical innovation and national systems. In: Nelson RR (eds) National innovation systems: a comparative analysis. Oxford University Press
NRC (2000) The Small Business Innovation Research program: an assessment of the Department of Defense Fast Track Initiative. National Academies Press
NRC (2008) An assessment of the SBIR program. The National Academies Press, Washington, D.C.
NRC (2009) SBIR at DoD. The National Academies Press, Washington, D.C.
NRC (2014) SBIR at the Department of Defense. National Academies Press, Washington D.C.
NRC (2016a) SBIR at NASA. The National Academies Press, Washington, D.C.
OECD (2010) Public procurement programmes for small firms—SBIR-type programmes. http://www.oecd.org/innovation/policyplatform/48136807.pdf. Accessed 2 Feb 2013
Obermayer AS (2009) Senator Ted Kennedy's role in the birth of the Small Business Innovation Research program. http://www.zyn.com/sbir/Kennedy_&_SBIR.pdf. Accessed 17 July 2014
Office of the Under Secretary of Defense (2010) Report on Department of Defense Small Business Innovation Research Program Commercialization Pilot Program—Report for Fiscal

Year 2009. http://www.acq.osd.mil/osbp/sbir/docs/FY09-SBIR-Commercialization-Pilot-Program-Report-to-Congress.pdf. Accessed 2 Feb 2013

Patterson F (2005) The SBIR game: how to play it to win. http://www.sbircoach.com/files/The%20SBIR%20Game%20-%20How%20To%20Play%20It%20To%20Win.pdf. Accessed 15 July 2014

Patterson F (2009) Reflections on the birth of the SBIR program. http://sbircoach.blogspot.com/2009/09/reflections-on-birth-of-sbir-program.html. Accessed 17 July 2014

Qian H, Haynes KE (2014) Beyond innovation: the Small business Innovation Research program as entrepreneurship policy. J Technol TRansf 39

Roessner JD (1989) Evaluating government innovation programs: lessons from the U.S. experience. Research Policy 18

Ruttan V (2006) Is war necessary for economic growth? Military procurement and technology development. Oxford University Press

SBA (2011) The Small Business Innovation Research (SBIR) and Small Business Technology Transfer (STTR) program—program overview. http://www.sbir.gov/about/about-sbir. Accessed 18 Dec 2012

SBA (2012) Small Business Innovation Research Program Policy Directive. https://www.federalregister.gov/articles/2012/08/06/2012-18119/small-business-innovation-research-program-policy-directive. Accessed 18 Dec 2012

SBIR Annual Reports. http://www.acq.osd.mil/osbp/sbir/about/sbirAnnualReport.shtml#fy11. Accessed 18 Dec 2012

Small Business Innovation Development Act of 1982 (P.L. 97-219) 15 U.S.C. 638

Small Business Act of 1958 (P.L. 85-536) section 9(f)(1)

Small Business Research and Development Enhancement Act of 1992 (P.L. 102-564), reauthorizing the SBIR program until September 30, 2000

Small Business Reauthorization Act of 2000 (P.L. 106-554)

SBIR/STTR Reauthorization Act of 2011 (P.L. 112–81)

Technopolis (2010) Eerste evaluatie Small Business Innovation Research (SBIR) programma's in Nederland. http://www.google.nl/url?sa=t&rct=j&q=&esrc=s&frm=1&source=web&cd=1&ved=0CDsQFjAA&url=http%3A%2F%2Fwww.rijksoverheid.nl%2Fbestanden%2Fdocumenten-en-publicaties%2Frapporten%2F2010%2F03%2F04%2Feerste-evaluatie-small-business-innovation-research-sbir-programma-s-in--nederland%2F10143501-bijlage.pdf&ei=0fcMUbLUE8bR0QWH3ICYAw&usg=AFQjCNFcmSZhejL8GI8_8vit4TWHliZwvw&sig2=QG8FzAaOfPUZRhG10B2adA. Accessed 2 Feb 2013

United States Code (1991) (42 U.S.C. 6683)

Wallsten S (2000) The effects of government-industry R&D programmes on private R&D: the case of the Small Business Innovation Research Program. Rand J Econ 31

Wessner C (2001) The Small Business Innovation Research Program (SBIR): an assessment of the Department of Defense Fast Track Initiative. National Academy Press

Chapter 5
Placing PCP Within the Legislative Framework

Contents

R. Apostol, *Trials and Tribulations in the Implementation of Pre-Commercial Procurement in Europe*, DOI 10.1007/978-94-6265-156-2_5

5.1 Introduction

As already explained in the introductory chapter, PCP is a procurement model for R&D services where risks and benefits are shared between the contracting authority and the supplier. The procurement of such R&D services contracts is exempted from the scope of application of the EU Procurement Directives.[1] In principle, this allows enhanced procedural flexibility, as compared to the rules laid down by the Procurement Directives. Despite the fact that these contracts had been exempted since the adoption of the first public procurement directives in 1989, by 2005 the R&D procurement had barely started to show on the national and EU agendas,[2] while 2 early initiatives in the UK and the Netherlands raised concerns of market distortion.[3]

In order to encourage wider implementation, for the benefit of the whole EU economy, the European Commission decided to clarify under which legal conditions PCP was allowed. The Commission focused on the applicable legal framework made of: the Treaty on the Functioning of the European Union ('TFEU'), the EU State aid rules and the World Trade Organisation (WTO) Government Procurement Agreement (GPA).

This chapter describes PCP's objectives and features, as defined by the Commission (Sect. 5.2). It points out which features were derived from the applicable legal framework (Sect. 5.3) and concludes on the degree of remaining procedural flexibility as compared to a procedure conducted in accordance with the Procurement Directives. To this end, it analyses relevant case-law of the Court of Justice of the EU concerning contracts (partially) exempted from the Procurement Directives (Sect. 5.4).

This chapter also points out remaining ambiguities and gaps in the EU guidance concerning the implementation of PCP. Section 5.5 seeks additional guidance for the meaning of R&D services, a key concept to a legally compliant use of PCP. To this end, it analyses the Frascati Manual as well as State aid and (defence) procurement laws. Section 5.6 seeks to clarify conceptual delineation between PCP and other (procurement) policy instruments that have been employed to stimulate innovation (performance and/or functional specifications, competitive dialogue, subsidies and forward commitment procedure). Section 5.7 draws conclusions.

5.2 The Features of PCP

5.2.1 Objectives

Since 2000 EU policy-makers had become increasingly aware that major threats to EU's current levels of welfare (e.g. ageing, security threats, shortage of resources, climate change etc.), required substantially improved solutions compared to those

---

[1] See Article 14 Directive 2014/24/EU; Article 32 Directive 2014/25/EU.

[2] Wilkinson et al. 2005, 10.

[3] This is further explained in Chap. 6.

available on the market. Insufficient R&D investment in the economy was identified as one of the major reasons for EU's incapacity to advance its global economic lead. As already explained in Chap. 2, the EU policy-makers realized that supply-side measures, which had been the focus of the EU innovation policy until 2000, were not sufficient to trigger the commercialization of needed innovations. As a consequence, demand-side measures, such as PCP received increased political support.

A group of experts hired by the European Commission in 2006, concluded that pre-commercial procurement was a suitable instrument to increase public demand of innovative solutions and to leverage private R&D investments in the ICT sector as well as elsewhere.[4] This motivated the Commission to '*explor[e] the extent to which pre-commercial procurement could indeed contribute to more R&D and innovation in the EU and, hence, bring tangible benefits to society and economy*'.[5]

More concretely, the PCP Communication defined the following 3 objectives[6]:

- reinforce the innovation capabilities of EU businesses, which will eventually lead to an improved competitive position in the global economy;
- develop innovative solutions to the above mentioned Grand Challenges;
- improve the quality and efficiency of public services.

5.2.2 Non-Mandatory Implementation

PCP is not a mandatory procedure, but a recommendation introduced through a soft-law instrument, the so-called Communication. Contracting authorities who decide to procure R&D and to share the entailing risks and benefits are still free to follow a different procedure, as long as they comply with the applicable EU public procurement and State aid rules.

PCP is also not mandatory in terms of allocated budgets. The European Commission has not recommended (or proposed legislation regarding) the allocation of minimum budgets to the implementation of PCP. This is due to missing competences in the innovation policy area.[7]

The Commission expected that enhancing legal certainty through the PCP Communication would suffice to boost the wide deployment of PCP. Later, it became obvious that a '*recommendation*' status did not adequately enhance contracting authorities' trust in the legality or necessity of the PCP procedure and consequently did not lead to its wide implementation.[8]

---

[4] Commission 2007a, 4–5.

[5] Commission 2007a, 3.

[6] Commission 2007b, 1, 4.

[7] Article 173 TFEU.

[8] For an overview of the state of implementation of PCP, see Chap. 6, Sect. 6.6.

5.2.3 Direct and Catalytic PCP

The European Commission tailored PCP to the situation wherein a group of European procurers share a need and based on an open dialogue with suppliers, conclude that solutions are not yet available commercially. Subsequently, they define a common set of requirements.[9]

The PCP Expert Group emphasized that contracting authorities themselves, and not intermediate institutions, should identify and formulate the needs.[10] However, they did not recommend that PCP should be limited to developing innovations for the direct benefit or use of the involved public authority. Neither does the PCP Communication introduce such a limitation. Instead, it refers to topics of public interest, irrespective of whether the contracting authority is (one of the) potential end-user(s) of the PCP outcome or not.[11]

PCP may thus be used in three distinct situations. The innovative solution may be desired to fulfill a need the government has as exclusive end-user (direct procurement), or it can be intended to develop a solution that contributes to the achievement of a public goal the contracting authority strives for (catalytic procurement). In the second case, the public authority/entity helps an innovative technology/service to reach the market, by organizing the private procurement, but the solution is exclusively intended for private end-users. In between, there is cooperative procurement, which is intended to provide an innovative solution of interest to both the procuring authority/entity and the private consumers as end-users.[12]

In Chap. 4, I concluded that this approach creates confusion on the distinction between PCP as demand-side instrument and subsidies as supply-side instruments. Moreover, it allows innovation agencies in EU Member States to provide financial support to national companies in breach of the EU State aid rules. This raises questions of efficacy in achieving EU's innovation policy goals. A potential solution will be outlined in Sect. 7.4.

5.2.4 Phases

PCP as formulated in the 2007 PCP Communication and accompanying PCP Staff Working Document, provides in one tender the conditions for competitive R&D

---

[9] Commission 2007b, 3, 5.

[10] PCP Expert Group 2006, 27.

[11] Commission 2007b, 5: 'A key characteristic of the approach presented is to solicit multiple companies in competition to come up with alternative solution proposals to address a *particular problem of public interest*' (emphasis added by the author).

[12] The theoretical foundation of these concepts was for the first time laid down in Edquist and Hommen 2000, 22–3.

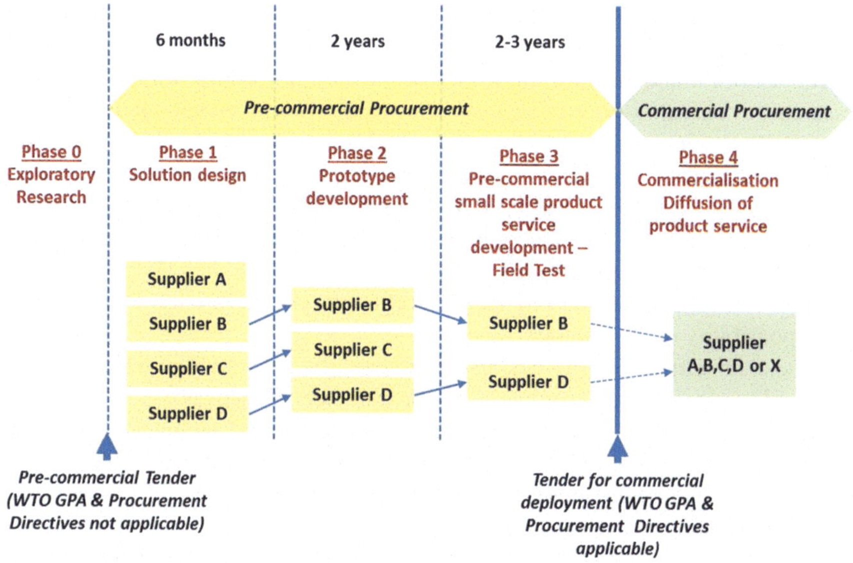

Fig. 5.1 COM/2007/799 & SEC/2007/1668

during three phases, with evaluation moments after phase 1 and phase 2 (see Fig. 5.1).[13]

Phase 1 involves solution exploration. The scope of the solution exploration phase—which takes about 6 month—is to '*verify the technical, economic and organisational feasibility of the proposal against the pros and cons of potential alternative solutions, as well as its ability to solve the problem of public interest*'. The output of this phase should be a technology evaluation, a plan of how R&D will subsequently be conducted and an evaluation of the economic value of the technology.

From amongst the suppliers that satisfactorily finalize phase 1, at least 3 will be selected to continue with the following prototyping phase (phase 2). Phase 2 lasts around 2 years, and covers R&D activities performed up to a prototype. The outputs should be product specifications, a tested prototype, a production plan and a business plan.

Finally, phase 3 covers test series conducted by the best two suppliers, selected at the end of phase 2. Phase 3 lasts 2–3 years and covers the production of a first batch of pre-products/services, their testing in relevant environments and the incorporation of the results of the field testing in a limited series of products, meant to demonstrate the suitability for full-scale quantity production. The outputs are refined production and business plans.[14]

[13] Commission 2007a, 8.

[14] PCP Expert Group 2006, 23.

The final solution should thus be ready for commercialisation within 4.5–5.5 years from the start of the PCP.[15]

The PCP Communication clarifies that PCP is not meant for fundamental research (or '*curiosity driven research*'), but for R&D with certain applications in sight. PCP does not include commercial development activities either. These are defined as '*quantity production, or supply to establish commercial viability or to recover R&D costs, integration, customisation, incremental adaptations and improvements to existing products or processes*'.[16] The field test phase where a first batch of products/services is produced and tested is the last PCP phase. The subsequent commercialization of the innovation developed through PCP remains the responsibility of the supplier.

If the contracting authority desires to purchase the innovation, it needs to open the award to competition according to the Procurement Directives.[17]

The PCP Communication does not recommend specific amounts of funding for the different phases. Member States wishing to implement national PCP programmes, or contracting authorities desiring to conduct specific PCP procedures are free to decide the amounts of funding.

The first phase of the PCP commences with multiple different solutions, which are successively eliminated to yield at least 2 suppliers after the final PCP phase. Maintaining competition up to the final phase is meant to avoid the creation of monopolists. According to the PCP Communication, the precise number of R&D projects to be funded in parallel should be decided based on a comparison between the economic value of the desired solution for the contracting authority and the R&D risks involved.[18]

5.2.5 Eligibility and Award Criteria

PCP was formulated as a transparent and competitive procedure, which allows participation of all interested EU businesses as well as businesses from signatory countries of the GPA or of other international agreements entered into by the EU. The R&D and operational activities required by the PCP call need though to be performed on the territory of the EU or of a partnering country in order to be eligible for PCP participation.[19] However, the PCP Communication recognizes that restricting participation to EU businesses may be decided on a case-by-case basis (e.g. based on national security arguments).[20]

[15] PCP Expert Group 2006, 21.

[16] Commission 2007a, 2.

[17] Commission 2007a, 4.

[18] Commission 2007b, 5.

[19] Commission 2007b, 10.

[20] Commission 2007a, 6.

The PCP Expert Group had proposed 2 additional eligibility criteria, inspired by the US SBIR, but were not uptaken in the PCP Communication[21]:

- only for-profit organizations can participate,
- main researcher is employed by the proposing firm for at least 50 % of his time.

Three diverging criteria from the US SBIR were proposed and were (explicitly or implicitly) included in the PCP Communication:

- companies which locate their R&D and operational activities related to the PCP call within the EU or within the countries that have a Stabilization or Association agreement with the EU in the context of the EU neighbourhood policy, without being European or European-owned, are admissible[22];
- no double funding of the same R&D activities is allowed[23];
- open to both large, medium and small companies.[24]

The Commission recommends the following award criteria[25]:

- ability to address the problem posed in the tender;
- technological quality and innovativeness of the proposal;
- added value for society/economy of the proposal.

5.2.6 Summarizing Remarks

I have analysed in this section the approach proposed by the European Commission to the procurement of R&D services. I showed that due to limited competences in the area of R&D and innovation, the European Commission defined PCP as a voluntary recommendation. This entails that contracting authorities are not mandated to set-aside budgets for conducting PCPs and neither are they bound by the procedural steps recommended by the Commission.

More concretely, the Commission recommends:

- to conduct PCPs in collaboration by contracting authorities (from different Member States);
- to set the PCP up as a three-staged competition, gradually selecting the suppliers who deliver the best R&D results after each R&D stage;
- to focus on innovations that find themselves within 4.5–5.5 years from commercialisation;

---

21 PCP Expert Group 2006, 22.

22 Companies do not need to have their head offices located in Europe or to have European shareholders.

23 In the US a firm may receive funding via SBIR, as well as other funding programs.

24 Nevertheless, subcontracting to SMEs should be required and encouraged.

25 Commission 2007b, 10.

- to allow suppliers from GPA countries or from other countries that signed international agreements with the EU, to participate as long as they perform their R&D within the EU or within the countries that have a Stabilization or Association agreement with the EU in the context of the EU neighbourhood policy;
- to apply award criteria that focus on quality and degree of innovativeness.

A contracting authority may deviate from all these recommendations. The Commission did not recommend any amount of funding per R&D phase, leaving this to the discretion of implementing contracting authorities.

5.3 Legal Boundaries to PCP Implementation

In this section, I highlight the PCP features that according to the PCP Communication and the related Staff Working Document, are a consequence of the applicable legal rules: the Procurement Directives, the EU State aid rules and the GPA. I clarify whether the legal rules allow different choices than recommended by the Commission and I identify gaps in the provided guidance on some of PCP's features and legal conditions.

5.3.1 Compliance with the Procurement Directives

5.3.1.1 Minimum Applicability Conditions

The European Commission designed the PCP procedure to fall under the exemption provided by the Procurement Directives for R&D services whose risks and/or benefits are shared between the contracting authority and the service provider.[26] A PCP procedure may thus be applied when the following two minimum requirements are fulfilled.

Firstly, the procured contract covers in majority R&D services. Which activities qualify as R&D services is not defined in the Procurement Directives. The PCP Communication and the accompanying PCP Staff Working Document provide an overview of the type of activities that qualify for each phase of the PCP. The guidance is not comprehensive, despite the fact that this is a crucial pre-condition for

[26] Articles 14 Directive 2014/24/EU and 32 Directive 2014/25/EU: 'This Directive shall only apply to public service contracts for research and development services which are covered by CPV codes 73000000-2 to 73120000-9, 73300000-5, 73420000-2 and 73430000-5 provided that both of the following conditions are fulfilled: (a) the benefits accrue exclusively to the contracting authority for its use in the conduct of its own affairs, and (b) the service provided is wholly remunerated by the contracting authority.'

reliance on the PCP exemption. Whether the development of a solution covers in majority R&D services or not, can be a complex and often uncertain undertaking. In Sect. 5.5, I provides an analysis of the concept of R&D services, by reference to the PCP Communication, the Frascati Manual[27] and other relevant EU legislation.

Secondly, the procurer should share the benefits of the R&D services with the participating business. If the procurer retains all the benefits (such as intellectual property rights (IPR)) and pays the exclusive costs of development, the procurement of R&D services will fall within the scope of the Procurement Directives.[28]

5.3.1.2 Sharing Risks and Benefits

The sharing of risks and benefits is a crucial element of PCP. Apportioning risks and benefits between the procurer and the service provider provides incentives to both the procurer to engage in PCPs and to the service provider to partly invest itself in R&D and commercialise the resulting solutions.

In addition, sharing risks between collaborating procurers (e.g. costs), provides incentives for each individual procurer to assume the inherent risks of R&D. And finally, sharing benefits with the wider public through publication of the results and participation of the PCP participant in standardization activities ensures spill-over of knowledge.[29]

From a legal point of view, the procurer has the discretion to deviate from the specific PCP guidance, as long as some degree of sharing is ensured. However, the Commission's recommendations are commendable. They are based on general good practice, meant to provide suitable incentives to the procurer and the service provider (see description below).

The procurer may not deviate from the requirement to publish the concrete sharing of risks and benefits prior to the PCP competition and to refrain from any subsequent negotiation of these terms. These obligations flow from the public procurement principles of transparency and equal treatment.[30]

Sharing Risks

The Commission enumerates in the PCP Communication and accompanying PCP Staff Working Document, by way of example, several risks which could be assumed by the service provider: the risk that additional funding beyond the PCP budget will be needed for the development, the litigation/filing costs for IPR

[27] OECD 2002.

[28] Recital (35) Directive 2014/24/EU; recital (42) Directive 2014/25/EU clarify that '*sharing of the results of the R&D or purely symbolic participation in the remuneration of the service provider should not prevent the application of this Directive*'.

[29] Commission 2007a, 6–7; Commission 2007b, 6–7.

[30] Commission 2007b, 9.

emerging during the PCP procedure and the exploitation risks.[31] The main risk assumed by the procurer is project failure and loss of investment.[32]

A later study funded by the Commission concludes that procurers' risk aversion is a serious barrier to engaging in PCPs. The Study provides outlines the types of risks which may arise in the procurement of innovation (technological risks, organisational and societal risks, market risks, financial risks and turbulence risks) and provides guidance on the risk management actions which may be deployed depending on several variables (e.g. the type of risk, the likelihood to occur, the extent of the consequences if it occurs, the potential benefits if it does not occur, the different stakeholders it might affect and their degree of tolerance to risk etc.).[33]

Sharing Benefits

The guidance offered by the Commission in its PCP Communication and accompanying Staff Working Document on sharing benefits only refers to patentable inventions developed during the PCP procedure. The Commission recommends to assign the supplier the ownership of the IP generated during the PCP procedure, with due protection of each procurer's rights as end-user, in the form of royalty-free licenses and the right to require suppliers to license IPRs to third parties under fair and reasonable (FRAND)[34] conditions. The procurer is also advised to retain a call-back option, which allows it to gain the ownership of the generated IPR, in case the supplier is not commercializing the developed solution within a certain period of time after the end of the PCP procedure.[35]

This IPR sharing strategy is based on the assumption that the procurer is not well-suited to pursue commercialization of the solutions developed within an R&D contract. By granting the IPR to the participating business in the PCP and retaining a call-back option, the contracting authority will ensure that the developed innovation is widely used on the market and that it will form the basis of follow-on innovation activities.[36] The main benefit retained by the supplier under these conditions, regards the possibility to commercialise the results of PCP and to obtain the resulting profits, as well as the possibility to re-apply the IP in later projects. According to the Commission guidance, this IPR strategy will motivate the supplier to bare a share of the funding.[37]

[31] Commission 2007b, 7.

[32] Commission 2007b.

[33] Risk is defined therein, as 'measureable uncertainty (likelihood) for something to occur that lets projects fail, decreases their utility or increases their costs and duration'. Expert Group Report 2010, 24.

[34] FRAND means 'Fair, Reasonable and Non Discriminatory' licensing terms. The concept has been developed in the context of IPR in the standard-setting context. See Commission (2011) recital 289.

[35] Commission 2007a, 7.

[36] Commission 2007b, 8.

[37] Ibid., Wilkinson et al. 2005, 39.

By retaining (royalty-free) usage-rights, the procurer will be able to obtain direct benefits in terms of a lower cost offer from the respective supplier in a subsequent procurement, whenever a commercial procurement follows the PCP. This approach can, according to the Commission, also enable the procurer to obtain access to existing technologies which are protected by IPR but were developed prior to the PCP procedure (also called 'background' IPR).[38]

Finally, by requesting the PCP participant to license IPRs to third parties under FRAND conditions, the procurer can ensure knowledge-diffusion.

Although the PCP Communication recommends the above mentioned distribution of IP rights, a contracting authority is free to choose for a different IP strategy,[39] to the extent to which there is no national legislation regarding the division of IPR in government-funded projects. If no mandatory regulations restrict its discretion, the contracting authority may choose to contractually gain the ownership of the IP or leave it to the supplier. Licenses may be free, for a symbolic, modest or a larger fee, depending on the market value of the IPRs and the strategy of the procurer and may be exclusive,[40] partially exclusive or nonexclusive.

However, the contracting authority should keep in mind that when the innovation has potential applications on the private market, the private actor is in a better position than the government to commercialise the novel product, to decide in which jurisdictions patents should be applied for, or to enforce the patents in case of infringement. Moreover, the supplier should be incentivized to invest in the commercialization of the novel product without concerns that licenses are also made available to its competitors. As a consequence, the supplier should at a minimum obtain an exclusive license (when ownership is retained by the procurer). When IP ownership is granted to the supplier, the procurer should at a minimum have the right to use the IP (on exclusive or non-exclusive terms) in order to ensure continuity of its internal operations as well as the possibility to grant a license to another firm when practical application of the invention is not fulfilled or not done to the agreed extent (either through commercialization, internal implementation or licensing).[41]

The Commission does not provide detailed recommendations on the implementation of the IPR strategy. For example, the Commission's guidance does not deal with the impossibility of a supplier to grant a license to the contracting authority on the 'background' IPR resting on the underlying existing technology,[42] the need to request the PCP participant to disclose all background IPR he may be aware

---

38 Commission 2007b, 8.

39 Ecorys 2011, 64.

40 An exclusive license to use the IP means that the licensee is the sole beneficiary of the licensed rights to exploit and commercialise the IP.

41 Rambøll Management 2008.

42 It could be envisaged that the PCP participant is prevented by pre-PCP agreements to transfer or grant a license on the background IPR. In such case, the contracting authority may need to include obligations for eventual sub-contracting.

of[43] or to require licensing of background IPR to third parties when the invention cannot be practiced without such license etc.

Moreover, as mentioned before, the Commission does not seem to have had in mind the division of other IP rights than patent rights. When copyrighted products (such as a software) are the result of the PCP, the following sharing of risks and benefits could be envisaged: the PCP-participant may retain the moral right to be indicated as the author of the expression of his/her ideas, while the contracting authority obtains permission (equivalent to a royalty-free license) to reproduce and re-distribute the copyrighted expression of ideas (it could be a book, a study or software etc.) within and/or outside its organisation.

Scenario's for sharing benefits through license-contract design will directly affect the incentives perceived by both procurers and R&D providers involved. Research into design for IP licensing must remain outside the scope of this book.

Inspiration on public guidance for dealing contractually with benefit sharing through IPR could be found in the Bayh-Dole Act, however. The Bayh-Dole Act was adopted in 1980 in the US, at a time when the US government owned 28.000 patents, but licensed less than 5% to businesses. Businesses were in their turn reluctant to invest in the production of innovations which could also be licensed to competitors. The government became aware that public spending on R&D would be far more effective if small businesses would retain ownership on the inventions funded with public money.[44]

The Bayh-Dole Act, which governs since 1980 the division of rights to inventions made by small businesses under government grants, contracts and cooperative agreements, brought about the needed change. It imposes a standard division of IPR that is similar to the Commission's recommendation for PCP: the supplier obtains the ownership and the government a '*nonexclusive, nontransferable, irrevocable, paid-up license to practice or have practiced for or on behalf of the United States the subject invention throughout the world*'. A government agency may deviate from this standard clause (e.g. for national security reasons or due to the location of the business outside the US) upon motivation and subject to appeal possibilities.

The Bayh-Dole Act provides detailed contractual clauses for different IPR strategies as well as contractual enforcement clauses. For example, the supplier needs to disclose the invention to the government agency in order to obtain ownership and is therefore mandated to keep records of the background IPR in order to be able to retain IPR outside the SBIR clauses.[45]

The Commission's guidance neither clarifies whether other benefits than IPR (such as for example profits gained with commercialization of the innovative solution developed during the PCP procedure) may be shared in order to rely on the exception provided by Articles 14 of Directive 2014/24/EU and 32 of Directive 2014/25/EU.

43 PROGR-EAST 2012, 45–6.

44 Sidebottom 2001.

45 DeVecchio 2007.

Prior to the 2014 Framework for State aid for R&D&I, which clarified under which conditions the PCP can be considered not to contain state aid, the Commission implied from the EU state aid rules an obligation for the procurer to request from the PCP participants financial compensation (under market conditions) for the allocation of IP ownership rights.[46] In order to estimate the market value of the ownership rights, the PCP participant should consider the commercialisation opportunities and the associated risks assumed by the company (e.g. the costs for maintaining the IPRs and commercialising the products). The procurer was advised to request either an ex-ante compensation (price reduction on the price for performing the R&D during the PCP) or an ex-post compensation (royalties on sales/profits made by the PCP participant with the commercialisation of the results generated during the PCP e.g. from selling products or licensing out IPR).[47] Although this guidance was provided with the idea to ensure compliance with the EU state aid rules, the compensation mechanisms also ensured compliance with the benefit sharing condition of the Procurement Directives.

Thus, although the 2014 Framework for R&D&I simplified the conditions for proving that the contract was awarded under market conditions, a public procurer still needs to make sure that benefits are shared in order to rely on the exemption from the Procurement Directives.

5.3.2 Compliance with the TFEU Fundamental Principles

The PCP Communication was based on the premise that although PCP falls outside the scope of application of the Procurement Directives, the TFEU principles of equal treatment, non-discrimination and transparency remain applicable. In this context, the Commission adopted a pro-competitive approach and interpreted the TFEU principles to imply an obligation to organize a fully-fledged competitive award.[48]

Accordingly, a PCP call should be published EU-wide and sufficient information should be provided (on design of the competition, eligibility, sharing of risks and benefits etc.) to allow the objective comparison of the received proposals. All the requirements/criteria applied throughout the PCP procedure need to be '*understandable, quantifiable and verifiable*'.[49]

The initial functional and performance requirements, as well as the award criteria and risk-benefit sharing arrangements are not subject to change or negotiation during the PCP procedure.[50] However, the Commission considers that there is

46 Commission 2016.

47 Ibid.

48 Commission 2007a.

49 Commission 2007a, 10–1.

50 Commission 2007b, 3–4, 10.

some flexibility to progressively specify the tender specifications (technical/scientific minimum requirements) with each PCP phase.[51]

Section 5.4 investigates whether the approach embraced by the European Commission in the PCP Communication is in line with the currently available EU case-law on the applicability of the TFEU to contracts falling outside the scope of application of the Procurement Directives. It concludes on the degree of procedural flexibility in conducting a PCP, compared to a procurement procedure governed by the Procurement Directives.

5.3.3 Compliance with the EU State Aid Rules

At the time when PCP was contemplated, the 2006 Framework outlined the principles for scrutinizing State aid for research and development and innovation.[52] According to the 2006 Framework, procurement of R&D did not involve state aid, if the contract was awarded according to market conditions. A tender procedure conducted in accordance with the applicable Procurement Directives constituted a presumption that the purchase was market conform.[53] The 2006 Framework did not mention the procurement of R&D services that fell outside the scope of application of the Procurement Directives.

In the absence of specific guidance in the State aid rules, the PCP Communication recommended the procurer to pay a market price, which ought to reflect the market value of the risks assumed by the participating company (such as costs for maintaining the IPR and commercializing the developed products/services) and of the benefits received by the participating company (such as the IPRs and the corresponding commercialization opportunities). This would normally mean that less than the total cost of the R&D should be paid by the procurer.[54]

In later guidance, the Commission advised the procurer to define prior to the PCP call, the maximum price he was willing to pay. According to the Commission, the maximum price needed to be calculated by deducting from the total cost of R&D[55] plus a reasonable profit margin, the market 'present' value of the commercialization opportunities left to the participating company (this value will need to reflect also the risks assumed by the participating company, such as

[51] Commission 2007b, 9.

[52] Commission 2006.

[53] Commission 2006 para 2.1.

[54] The risk-benefit sharing should try to balance two aspects: on the one hand, the procurement must be interesting enough for relevant suppliers from a financial point of view; on the other hand, the procurer should not carry all financial, technical or operational risks. See Rambøll Management 2008.

[55] This is made of all the costs incurred by the company—for example the market value of the salaries of researchers/developers in a certain sector and the costs of R&D material required to perform the work. Commission 2016, question no 8.

the cost carried by the company for maintaining the IPRs and commercializing the products).[56] Bidding companies would be invited to compete by offering an equal or lower price.

For obvious reasons, it is extremely difficult to value to the commercialization opportunities of products which have not yet been developed and the European Commission did not recommend a specific calculation method.

It recommended though a more accessible alternative, namely to ask bidding companies (1) to show how they calculated the price reduction offered in return for the IPR benefits (this calculation should be accompanied by a business case) and (2) to include a financial expert in the PCP tender evaluation committee to assess whether the business-case and associated price reduction were in line with normal market conditions in that sector.[57]

In 2014, a new Framework for Research and Development and Innovation ('2014 Framework')[58] was adopted. It included reference to PCP and explained under which specific conditions PCP would not entail State aid. According to the 2014 Framework, the payment of a market price can be presumed, when all of the following conditions are fulfilled:

(a) the selection procedure is open, transparent and non-discriminatory, and is based on objective selection and award criteria specified in advance of the bidding procedure;
(b) the envisaged contractual arrangements describing all rights and obligations of the parties, including with regard to IPR, are made available to all interested bidders in advance of the bidding procedure;
(c) the procurement does not give any of the participant providers any preferential treatment in the supply of commercial volumes of the final products or services to a public purchaser in the Member State concerned; and
(d) one of the following conditions is fulfilled:

- all results which do not give rise to IPR may be widely disseminated, for example through publication, teaching or contribution to standardisation

[56] Commission 2007b, 9.

[57] Commission 2016 question nr 8: 'one way used by patent traders to calculate the price reduction for IPR ownership rights uses the so-called *present value method*. It is normal practice that companies make a business case, and thus estimate the potential market over the years to come, when deciding to start investing in a new development or not. The price reduction on the PCP bid towards the procurer can be calculated as a portion of the 'present' value of projected profits for the company (the 'present' value is the value discounted back in time to the day of the bid), that is proportional to the investment/risks taken by the government (PCP price paid to the company) compared to the total investments required to turn the R&D efforts into a commercially viable product (this includes the projected investment/risks that will be carried by the company e.g. costs of maintaining IPR projection, further production, marketing and commercialisation investments). Companies can extract these values from the business case they prepare at the moment they make their PCP offer'.

[58] Commission 2014.

bodies in a way that allows other undertakings to reproduce them, and any IPR are fully allocated to the public purchaser, or

- any service provider to which results giving rise to IPR are allocated is required to grant the public purchaser unlimited access to those results free of charge, and to grant access to third parties, for example by way of non-exclusive licenses, under market conditions.'[59]

When the procurer deviates from any of the above mentioned conditions,[60] he will need to follow the State aid rules. In Chap. 7, Sect. 7.4, I will outline the applicable rules as defined by the GBER and Framework for State aid for R&D&I.

5.3.4 Compliance with the GPA

The procurer is not allowed to purchase the innovation developed during the PCP directly, from one of the PCP participants. The procurer is mandated to offer the possibility to companies that may have developed suitable solutions outside the scope of the PCP, to compete for the contract. To this end, the procurer is mandated to organize a separate commercial procurement procedure in compliance with the Procurement Directives.[61] This approach is in line with the pro-competitive approach adopted by the Commission, who believes that seeking maximum competition will lead to the best outcome (e.g. in terms of best value for public money, best technological solution etc.).

According to PCP Staff Working Document this approach is a consequence of previous choices made by the EU within the framework of the World Trade Organisation ('WTO') Government Procurement Agreement ('GPA'). Separating the R&D procurement from the procurement of the developed innovation will allow the contracting authority to require participating businesses to perform a significant portion of their PCP activities in the European Economic Area or a country having concluded a Stabilisation and Association Agreement with the EU.[62]

This would enhance job creation and growth in the EU and partnering countries. The PCP Staff Working Document further praises this approach for its potential to identify superior innovations developed outside the framework of the PCP as well as to put competitive pressure on the offered prices.[63] The commercial procurement will however need to grant access to suppliers from the GPA partners,

[59] Commission 2014, Sect. 2.3.

[60] Deviation from the first 2 conditions will amount though to a breach of the procurement principles.

[61] Commission 2007a, 4.

[62] Commission 2007b, 10.

[63] Commission 2007b, 9–10.

(whenever the contract is covered by the GPA) and from other countries that have signed and international agreement with the EU.[64]

5.3.5 Summarizing Remarks

I analysed in this section the PCP features that are a consequence of legal requirements, as interpreted by the European Commission in the PCP Communication. I concluded that the European Commission missed the opportunity to clarify the concept of R&D and to define clear mechanisms to deal with the exploitation of emerging IPRs.

I also concluded that procurers may deviate from the following recommendations:

- the market price criterion. Procurers may choose to fulfill the conditions defined in the 2014 Framework for State aid for R&D&I (that came to simplify the proof that PCP took place under market conditions). Procurers may even deviate from the 2014 Framework conditions, provided that an alternative approach to compliance with the applicable EU State aid rules is followed (e.g. calculation of the market conditions accompanied by notification in accordance with Article 108(3) TFEU).[65]
- the division of risks and benefits recommended by the Commission.

A procurer may not deviate from the following obligations:

- to maintain unchanged the pre-established division of risks and benefits throughout the PCP;
- to apply the same award criteria and tender specifications throughout the PCP; the procurer may though gradually specify the award criteria and tender specifications. For example, the procurer may define award sub-criteria.
- to open the PCP award to competition from EU companies.
- to deploy a separate commercial procurement in compliance with the applicable Procurement Directive, whenever he decides to purchase a solution to the public need addressed through the PCP.

The PCP Communication and the accompanying PCP Staff Working Document define an obligation to conduct a fully-fledged competitive procedure for the award of the PCP contracts, with limited procedural flexibility following the award. In the following section, I will test the Commission's interpretation of the obligations deriving from the fundamental public procurement principles (non-discrimination, equal treatment and transparency) against the available jurisprudence from the EU courts.

---

[64] Commission 2007b, 10. See Recital (17) Directive 2014/24/EU and recital (27) Directive 2014/25/EU.

[65] Commission 2014, para 34.

5.4 Procedural Flexibility in the Deployment of PCP

As already mentioned in Sect. 5.3.2, the PCP Communication holds that PCPs conducted in collaboration between contracting authorities from different Member States need to comply with the TFEU fundamental principles of equal treatment, non-discrimination and transparency. The Commission derives from these principle extensive procedural obligations.

When the PCP Communication was published, the Court of Justice of the European Union (CJEU) had decided in a series of cases on the applicability of the TFEU and had explained the extent of the applicable TFEU obligations for contracts which are (partially) excluded from the scope of the Procurement Directives (such as services concessions, IIB services and contracts under the threshold of the Procurement Directives). The CJEU has, however, not yet judged in matters of PCP contracts.

Despite inconsistencies and controversies in the interpretation provided by the European judges (as I will illustrate below), the case-law suggests that the CJEU adopts the same approach to the whole range of contracts that (partially) fall outside the application of the Procurement Directives, irrespective of contract type (whether concession, II B service or contracts whose value is under the thresholds) and of contract value.[66] This allows me to assume that the CJEU will adopt the very same line of reasoning when considering PCP contracts.

This section analyses the case-law of the CJEU and concludes on the circumstances that determine the applicability of the TFEU to PCPs. This section also deals with the extent of the obligations flowing from the applicability of the TFEU principles as compared to procedures falling within the Procurement Directives. Based on this analysis, this section will clarify the degree of procedural flexibility a PCP offers.

To achieve this, the following subsections outline the Court's different interpretations of the Treaty's applicability outside the scope of the Procurement Directives (depending on the existence of cross-border interest or irrespective thereof) and of the obligations deriving from the application of the Treaty. The discussion in Sect. 5.4.1 covers case-law up to the *Germany v Commission* case, which was decided in May 2010. Based on case-law from the *Germany v Commission* case onwards, Sect. 5.4.2 presents the resolution of the dispute on the concrete obligations flowing from the applicable Treaty provisions and principles. Section 5.4.3 draws conclusions.

5.4.1 Rebuttable Presumption of Cross-Border Interest and Applicability of Treaty Principles

The CJEU has pronounced several decisions on the applicability of the TFEU principles to contracts (partially) falling outside the Procurement Directives.

[66] CJEU, *Germany v Commission*, Judgment, T-258/06 [2010] ECR II-2027 paras 83–84.

I consider these decisions to show inconsistencies. Firstly, the decisions are inconsistent regarding the question whether the TFEU is automatically applicable to contracts excluded from the Procurement Directives or whether it is only applicable when a contract presents cross-border interest (when companies from other Member States are/may be interested in obtaining the contract). Secondly, the decisions are inconsistent regarding the application of the equal treatment principle as independent principle (even in purely internal situations), or only in cases of discrimination on grounds of nationality. Thirdly, the decisions are inconsistent concerning the obligation to organize a competitive award in all cases, or only when the contract is relevant for the Internal Market.

These inconsistencies are illustrated below.

RISAN Case

In the RISAN case of 1999,[67] regarding a service concession awarded on a non-competitive basis, the Court hastily dismissed the question of the referring Italian judge regarding the applicability of the free movement rights established by the Treaty. The European judge underlined that the complainant was an Italian company and that the whole situation in question was purely internal to one Member State. This did not justify the application of the TFEU provisions on the freedom of movement for persons or on the freedom to provide services.[68]

Telaustria Case

In the Telaustria case of 2000,[69] the European judge changed course. It decided that, despite the explicit exemption of service concessions from the Procurement Directives, the TFEU remains directly applicable to such contracts.[70] The Court adopted this approach despite the fact that all the parties involved in the case belonged to the same Member State (Italy).[71] The Court seemed to establish a non-rebuttable presumption that *any* service concession contract is potentially of interest to companies from other Member States.

The Court singled out the non-discrimination principle on the ground of nationality as the key principle that needs to be complied with outside the scope of application of the Procurement Directives.[72] The Court considered that the principle of

---

[67] CJEU, *RI.SAN. Srl v Commune di Ischia and Others,* Judgment, C-108/98, [1999] ECR I-5238.

[68] Ibid., paras 21–53.

[69] CJEU, *Telaustria,* Judgment, C-324/98 [2000] ECR I-10745. In this case, Telekom Austria, a contracting authority endowed by the Austrian legislation with operating a telecommunication service had awarded a contract for the production and publication of lists of telephone subscribers to a private undertaking, without competition.

[70] *Telaustria*, above n 69, para 60.

[71] In the area of the four fundamental freedoms, EU case-law states that the EU law (including the Treaty) is not applicable if the elements of a case are confined to the borders of one Member State and there is no factor connecting the case to any of the situations envisaged by [EU] law. In other words, a cross-border element is the necessary condition to justify the application of EU law. See for example, CJEU, *Mathot,* Judgment, C-98/86 [1987] ECR 809; and CJEU, *Oosthoek,* Judgment, C-286/81 [1982] ECR 4575; CJEU, *Bekaert,* Judgment, C-204/87 [1988] ECR 2029.

[72] *Telaustria*, above n 69, para 60.

non-discrimination '*implies, in particular, an obligation of transparency in order to enable the contracting authority to satisfy itself that the principle has been complied with*'.[73] In other words, only by advertising the contract, the contracting authority could prove that the non-discrimination principle was not breached.[74] The approach of the Court to import the transparency obligation into the TFEU, after it had been considered as a necessary consequence of the non-discrimination principle within the scope of the Procurement Directives, was criticized in the literature. Arrowsmith and Kunzlik concluded that the Court derived positive obligations from the non-discrimination principle, although this principle had been defined within the context of the Treaty as implying only negative obligations.[75]

The Court was also criticized for giving the same interpretation to the obligation of transparency as within the scope of the Procurement Directives and for suggesting an obligation to organize a competitive award procedure.[76] According to the Court the contracting authority should ensure '*for the benefit of any potential tenderer, a degree of advertising sufficient to enable the services market to be opened up to competition and the impartiality of procurement procedures to be reviewed*'.[77]

Coname Case

In the Coname case,[78] the third case concerning a strictly national situation in the context of a non-competitive award of a service concession,[79] the Court nuanced the position taken in Telaustria towards the applicability of the TFEU and towards the interpretation of the transparency obligations.

The Court introduced the possibility to rebut the presumption that a contract excluded from the scope of application of the Procurement Directives automatically falls under the scope of the TFEU. In this case, the Court decided that the TFEU will not be applicable, when it can be proven that undertakings from other Member States would not be interested in the contract. In such cases, the impact on the fundamental freedoms of the TFEU would be too uncertain and indirect to justify the applicability of the TFEU.[80]

---

[73] Ibid., para 61.

[74] Ibid., paras 61–62.

[75] The free movement provisions of the TFEU prohibit unjustified discrimination. Arrowsmith and Kunzlik 2009.

[76] Hordijk et al. 2011, 151; Arrowsmith and Kunzlik 2009, 82–3.

[77] *Telaustria*, above n 69 para 62.

[78] CJEU, *Coname,* Judgment, C-231/03 [2005] ECR I-7287. In this case, the company Coname has been entrusted for one year the maintenance, operation and monitoring of the methane gas network by the municipality Cingia de' Botti. When the municipality subsequently directly awarded the same contract to Padania, Coname complained that the contract had to be tendered in compliance with the Treaty.

[79] All parties to the case were Italian.

[80] *Coname*, above n 78, para 20.

However, the presumption of applicability can only be rebutted when special circumstances such as the '*very limited economic value*' of the contract can be brought as proof.[81] The Court did not explain when a contract has very limited economic value (for example, whether only the monetary value of the contract should be considered or whether additional circumstances may also be relevant). However, the position adopted by the Court seems to imply that there are only restrictive possibilities to rebut the presumption that companies from other Member States may be interested in the contract.[82] Moreover, the Court did not spell out whether lack of interest means that a competitive tendering does not need to be organised, but (considering cost-related arguments) this would be the logical conclusion.

The Court subsequently pointed out which TFEU obligations specifically apply, in case a certain cross-border interest could not on forehand be excluded. The Court referred again to the non-discrimination principle, that would be breached in the absence of transparency.[83] The Court took a step back compared to the Telaustria case and stated that the transparency principle does *not* entail an obligation to organize a procurement procedure, but only obliges contracting authorities to allow access to appropriate information regarding the contract before it is awarded, '*so that, if an undertaking from another Member State had so wished, it would have been able to express its interest in obtaining the contract*'. This suggests that the contracting authority gets a second chance to conclude that the contract is not of interest to the Internal Market and can be awarded without consideration of the Treaty principles. It could be concluded that when no foreign company expresses interest following the advertisement, the contracting authority would be allowed to disregard the Treaty obligations.[84]

On the other hand, the Court did not clarify which concrete obligations rest on a contracting authority if an undertaking from another Member State would express its interest in the contract. If no procurement procedure needs to be organized, it could be concluded that the contracting authority should be able to award the contract by inviting the undertaking of its choice as well as the interested foreign undertakings to submit an offer.[85] This conclusion has however categorically been rejected by the Court in the subsequent case-law. Applicable national legislation may also exclude this possibility.

Parking Brixen Case

The Parking Brixen case[86] came next, the fourth case in a row concerning service concessions. It confirmed the inconsistent approach of the European judges to the

---

[81] Ibid., paras 17–20.

[82] Hordijk 2011, 154.

[83] *Coname*, above n 78, para 19.

[84] Advocaat-Generaal Keus, *P1 Holding B.V. v Gemeente Maastricht en Q-Park Exploitatie BV*, Conclusion, HR 18 januari 2013, LJN: BY0543.

[85] Hordijk et al. 2011, 155.

[86] CJEU, *Parking Brixen*, Judgment, C-458/03 [2005] ECR I-8612.

possibility to rebut the presumption that a contract (partially) excluded from the Procurement Directives is of interest to companies from other Member States. In this case, the Court ignored the Coname judgment and suggested that service concession contracts should always be awarded in compliance with the TFEU. The Court explicitly stated: '*Notwithstanding the fact that public service concession contracts are, as Community law stands at present, excluded from the scope of Directive 92/50 [former public procurement directive, added by the author], the public authorities concluding them are, none the less, bound to comply with the fundamental rules of the EC Treaty (…).*'[87]

When confronted by the defendant party with the argument that a cross-border element was missing, as all the parties involved in the main proceedings resided in one Member State (Italy again), the Court stated that in the absence of advertising and opening to competition, it is not possible to prove that undertakings of other Member States would not be interested to provide the same services.[88]

Regarding the applicable Treaty obligations, the Court went even a step further than in the Telaustria case. It stated that the equal treatment principle applies as an independent principle, even in the absence of discrimination on grounds of nationality.[89] The Court used the following reasoning: equal treatment is a general principle of EU law and Articles 43 and 49 of the old Treaty as well as the non-discrimination principle on the basis of nationality set out in Article 12 TEC are expressions of the equal treatment principle.

This marks a change compared to the previous Coname case, where the Court left the door open to the interpretation that after publicizing the contract, a contracting authority may conclude that the contract had not attracted the attention of foreign companies and consequently the non-competitive award would not amount to discrimination on the basis of nationality. The conclusion in Parking Brixen—that the equal treatment principle applies irrespective of discrimination on the basis of nationality—provided the Court with a solid basis to scrutinize procurement decisions taken in 'purely internal' situations, when all the parties belonged to the same awarding Member State, and potentially no undertakings from other Member States were interested in the contract.

The Court clearly stated that '*a complete lack of any call for competition in the case of the award of a public service concession such as that at issue in the main proceedings does not comply with the requirements of Articles 43 EC and 49 EC any more than with the principles of equal treatment, non-discrimination and transparency*'.[90]

---

[87] Ibid., paras 46–49.

[88] Ibid., paras 54–55.

[89] Ibid., para 48.

[90] Ibid., paras 49–50.

The interpretation of the Court was disputed in literature.[91] Some authors criticized the tendency of the Court to import obligations into the Treaty which had previously been created within the context of the secondary procurement legislation.[92] Arrowsmith[93] has pointed out that the application of the equal treatment principle[94] would open the door to judicial scrutiny of non-discriminatory procurement decisions under the Treaty, which would conflict with the interpretation of the Court in Keck[95] as well as with the principles of legal certainty, subsidiarity and proportionality.

ANAV Case

The Parking Brixen approach to public services concessions was confirmed in the ANAV case.[96] It looked like the Court had made up its mind on the fact that public service concessions imply a non-rebuttable presumption of potential cross-border interest, that the equal treatment principle is an independent principle applicable irrespective of the existence of discrimination on the ground of nationality and that a contracting authority should always organize a competitive award procedure.[97]

An Post Case

And yet, in the An Post case,[98] which concerned the non-transparent award of a IIB service, the Court returned to the Coname interpretation regarding the applicability of the TFEU and made no reference to the Parking Brixen case. The Court considered that the TFEU is not applicable unless a '*certain cross-border interest*' in the contract is present.[99] The Court underlined that there was a legislative assumption that IIB service contracts are not, in light of their specific nature, of

91 Manunza 2006; Hordijk et al. 2011, 158; Krugner 2003; the contrary view is argued by Tridimas 2006.

92 Arrowsmith and Kunzlik 2009, 85.

93 Arrowsmith and Kunzlik 2009, 87.

94 The equal treatment principle has been defined in the *Fabricom* case as requiring that comparable situations must not be treated differently and that different situations must not be treated in the same way unless such treatment is objectively justified'. See CJEU, *Fabricom v Etat belge,* Judgment, C-21/03 [2005] E.C.R. I-1559 para 27.

95 In the Keck case, the Court decided that under Article 28 TEC, only measures relating to the characteristics of the products in question would be covered when non-discriminatory, while 'selling arrangements' such as rules on opening hours of retail outlets will only become subject of scrutiny if discriminatory. CJEU, *Criminal proceedings against Bernard Keck and Daniel Mithouard,* Judgment, Joined cases C-267/91 and C-268/91 ECR I-06097.

96 CJEU, *ANAV v Commune di Bari and AMTAB Servizion SpA,* Judgment, C-410/04 [2006] ECR I-3303 paras 18–23.

97 Ibid., paras 18–20.

98 CJEU, *Commission v Ireland,* Judgment, C-507/03 [2007] ECR I-9777 (An Post case).

99 Ibid., para 29.

cross-border interest.[100] The Court decided that the Commission could not just rely on an assumption that a IIB service contract necessarily is of certain cross-border interest.[101] A mere statement by the Commission that a complaint was made to it in relation to the contract in question was not considered by the Court to be sufficient proof.[102]

The Court did not deal with the applicability of the equal treatment principle. It only decided that, when cross-border interest exists, lack of transparency would amount to a difference in treatment in the disadvantage of interested undertakings from other Member States.[103]

APERMC Case

In the subsequent APERMC case the Court bounced back to the Parking Brixen approach, this time in the context of a public service contract with a value below the threshold. The case did not make any reference to the An Post case.[104] The Court concluded that the Treaty is automatically applicable and that '*the principle of equal treatment of tenderers is also to be applied [...] even in the absence of discrimination on grounds of nationality*'.[105]

Commission v Italy Case

In the Commission v Italy case,[106] the following case regarding a non-competitive award of a contract with a value below the threshold, the Court chose the An Post line of argumentation again and dismissed the APERMC approach. The Court decided that a Member State is not mandated to adopt legislation regarding compliance with the TFEU for the award of contracts under the threshold, but a case-by-case evaluation of the relevance of the contract for the Internal Market should be made, in order to conclude whether the TFEU fundamental principles are applicable.[107] The Court reiterated that in case of a certain cross-border interest, the absence of transparency will lead to '*a difference in treatment to the detriment of undertakings which might be interested in the contract but which are located in other Member States*'.[108]

Moreover, the Court expressly stated that articles 43 and 49 TEC '*do not lay down a general obligation of equal treatment but contain (...) a prohibition on*

[100] Ibid., para 25.

[101] Ibid., para 33.

[102] Ibid., paras 29, 32–34. The Commission brought as an argument the fact that it had received a complaint from an undertaking from another Member State.

[103] Ibid., para 30.

[104] CJEU, *Asociation Profesional de Empresas de Reparto y Manipulado de Correspondencia,* Judgment, C-220/06 [2007] ECR I-12175 (APERMC case), paras 70–75.

[105] Ibid., paras 71–74.

[106] CJEU, *Commission v Italy,* Judgment, Case C-412/04 [2008] ECR I-619.

[107] Ibid., paras 65–68.

[108] Ibid., para 66.

discrimination on the basis of nationality'.[109] The Commission had failed to demonstrate the existence of such discrimination.

SECAP Cases

The subsequent SECAP cases[110] dealt with the discriminatory nature of a national legislation imposing the automatic exclusion of abnormally low tenders in contracts with a value below the threshold, without granting the opportunity to tenderers to prove that their offer is genuine and viable. Tenders were qualified as abnormally low according to a pre-set mathematical formula.[111]

The Court underlined that the fundamental rules and general principles of the Treaty apply only when the contracts in question are potentially of certain cross-border interest.[112] The Court stated that the application of the formula to contracts excluded from the scope of the Procurement Directives, but nevertheless presenting a cross-border interest, amounted to indirect discrimination, since it created disadvantages for undertakings from other Member State that may be able to offer a genuine and viable solution at a much lower prices as a result of concrete competitive advantages.[113]

In the SECAP cases, the Court also provided examples of circumstances which should be taken into account when deciding whether cross-border interest is present or not: the monetary value of the contract in question, in conjunction with its place of execution and its technical complexity.[114] The Court made clear that a cross-border interest is absent when the economic interest at stake in the contract in question is very modest. However, even low-value contracts may be of certain cross-border interest when the execution of the contract is situated in a place that is likely to attract foreign companies (for example in the vicinity of borders with other Member States).[115] The Court clarified that it is the duty of the contracting authority to assess whether a contract whose value is below the threshold is of cross-border interest.[116]

Regarding the applicability of the equal treatment principle, the Court followed the same approach as in the An Post and Commission v Italy cases. It decided that not allowing the tenderers to prove that their bids are genuine and viable breaches the non-discrimination principle when cross-border interest is present.[117]

---

[109] Ibid., paras 106.

[110] CJEU, *SECAP SpA and Santorso Soc. Coop. Arl. Comune di Torino*, Judgment, Joined Cases C-147/06 and C-148/06 [2008] ECR I-3565 (SECAP cases).

[111] Ibid., paras 23–24.

[112] Ibid., para 21.

[113] Ibid., para 26.

[114] Ibid., para 24.

[115] Ibid., paras 29–31.

[116] Ibid., para 30.

[117] Ibid., paras 25–26.

ASM Brescia Case
In the ASM Brescia case, the Court ruled on yet another preliminary question from the Italian judge regarding the legality of an early termination of a concession contract for the distribution of natural gas, which had been awarded without a competitive tendering procedure.[118]

The Court followed the same line of reasoning as in the An Post case. It pointed out that public authorities are bound to comply with the fundamental rules of the Treaty, when awarding a service concession contract. The Court assumed that the respective concession presented a certain cross-border interest, based on the criteria identified by the national judge, such as the place and the economic interest at stake.[119] Accordingly, the lack of any transparency, amounts to a discriminatory measure against undertakings located in other Member States, who might be interested in the concession.[120]

Serrantoni Case
In 2009 the Court judged on the conformance with the fundamental rules of the Treaty, of an Italian law that provided for the automatic exclusion of both permanent consortia of firms and member companies, whenever they submitted competing tenders in the context of the same procedure.[121] The tendering procedure at issue regarded a works contract with a value under the threshold. The Court stated that the fundamental rules of the Treaty are applicable whenever the contract in question is of certain cross-border interest.[122] In this case, a competitive procedure had been organized. As a consequence, the Court further focused on the proportionality of the national rule and on its discriminatory effect.

Wall Case
In the following Wall case,[123] the question arose whether change of a subcontractor in a service concession contract requires reopening the contract to competition. In this case, the existence of a cross-border interest was not disputed and the contract had been awarded in competition. The Court embraced the view that the principle of equal treatment applies[124] and interpreted it by reference to case-law regarding contracts falling within the scope of application of the Procurement Directives.[125]

---

[118] CJEU, *ASM Brescia SpA v Commune di Rodengo Saiano,* Judgment, C-347/06 [2008] ECR I-05641 (ASM Brescia case).

[119] Ibid., para 62.

[120] Ibid., paras 57–59.

[121] CJEU, *Serrantoni Srl, Consorzio stabile edili Scrl v Comune di Milano*, Judgment, C-376/08 [2009] ECR I-12169 (Serrantoni case).

[122] Ibid., paras 22–24.

[123] CJEU, *Wall AG v Stadt Frankfurt am Main,* Judgment, C-91/08 [2010] ECR I-0000 (Wall case) para 37.

[124] Ibid., para 37.

[125] Ibid.

Conclusions

I conclude from the above case-law that there are two diverging approaches regarding the applicability of the TFEU principles to contracts (partially) excluded from the Procurement Directives. It is unclear whether the reasons for these inconsistencies lie in the principled opinions of the different European judges or other circumstances peculiar to the facts of the case.

According to the approach established in the Parking Brixen case, the potential interest of companies from other Member States in contracts falling outside the Procurement Directives cannot on forehand be excluded. Moreover, the equal treatment principle is a general principle that applies independent from an obligation to establish a link with the Internal Market and entails an obligation to advertise and to organize a competitive award procedure.

According to the approach established in the Coname and An Post cases, a case-by-case evaluation should be made whether companies from other Member States may be interested in the respective contract. The potential interest of companies from other Member States in the contract depends not only on its monetary value, but also on its technical complexity and/or on the place of execution of the contract. When no cross-border interest is present, the respective contract may be awarded without consideration of the TFEU.[126] When potential cross-border is present, an award in the absence of transparency breaches the non-discrimination principle. Transparency entails an obligation to advertise the contract. When following advertisement no foreign company expresses interest in obtaining the contract, the contracting authority may still conclude that no competitive award procedure in line with the Treaty principles needs to be set in motion.

5.4.2 Germany v Commission Case—Resolution of the Disputes?

Germany v Commission Case

In 2006, the European Commission decided to intervene in the dispute by codifying the EU case law in its *Interpretative Communication on the Community law applicable to contract awards not or not fully subject to the provisions of the Public Procurement Directives* ('2006 Communication').[127] The 2006 Communication does not mention R&D service contracts excluded from the scope of the Procurement Directives, as these had not yet been dealt with in case-law.

---

[126] However, national legislation may still oblige procurers to allow (national) competition.

[127] Commission 2006b.

The 2006 Communication follows the case-law up to just before the An Post case[128] on important points discussed in the previous sections of this chapter:

- Firstly, it embraces a rebuttable assumption that a contract falling outside the Procurement Directives presents cross-border interest and lays the burden of counterproof on the contracting authority.
- Secondly, it adopts the view that when a cross-border interest cannot be excluded, a contracting authority needs to organize a competitive award procedure. The Communication outlines the obligation to publish a call for competition, which should contain the essential information related to the contract as well as the award procedure.

The 2006 Communication does not follow the Coname approach regarding the second possibility to rebut the TFEU applicability if foreign companies do not express interest following the advertisement of the contract. It seems to have chosen a middle way between the Coname and the Parking Brixen approaches.

The Commission also details the procedural steps that would comply with the TFEU principle. Summarized, the following obligations flow from the TFEU principles, according to the Commission:

1. Prior assessment of the cross-border interest in the respective public contract;

In case of a positive conclusion regarding the existence of cross-border interest:

2. Prior publication of an advertisement of the public contract through a sufficiently wide coverage medium, including a description of the award procedure[129];
3. Non-discriminatory description of the subject-matter of the contract.[130] Concretely this obligation entails that '*the description of the characteristics required of a product or service should not refer to a specific make or source, or a particular process, or to trade marks, patents, types or a specific origin or production unless such reference is justified by the subject-matter of the contract and accompanied by the words 'or equivalent'*.[131]
4. Use of non-discriminatory selection criteria.[132]
5. Recognition of equivalent diplomas, certificates and other evidence of formal qualifications from other member States—flows out of the principle of mutual recognition.[133]

[128] The Communication dates from before the An Post case.

[129] CFI, *Federal Republic of Germany v European Commission,* Judgment, T-258/06 [2010] ECR II-02027 (Germany v Commission case) para 79.

[130] Ibid., paras 113–115.

[131] Commission 2006b, 7.

[132] *Germany v Commission*, above n 129, para 128.

[133] Ibid., paras 119–120.

6. Time-limits for expressions of interest and submission of offers should allow sufficient time to undertakings from other Member States to formulate meaningful offers.[134]
7. The award needs to take place according to the prior laid down rules and avoid de facto unjustified advantages to a specific tenderer (for example by providing the same amount of information). This is considered particularly important in negotiated procedures.
8. The negotiated procedure without prior announcement of the contract, is allowed under the same conditions as provided within the Procurement Directives for the same procedure, but not limited to these situations.[135] This ensures that the prior publication obligations is not imposed where the Procurement Directives expressly allow for a derogation.[136] Additional grounds for the application of direct negotiations may be based on exemptions from the applicability of the TFEU, such as 106(2) TFEU or one of the justificatory grounds expressly provided for in the Treaty applies (for example, public policy or public health, under Articles 46 EC and 55 EC, or official authority, under Articles 45 EC and 55 EC), or on overriding reason relating to the general interest,[137] or on an 'in-house' exception.[138]

Germany disputed the 2006 Communication before the Court of First Instance ('CFI'), for allegedly creating new obligations for the procurement of contracts expressly excluded by the legislator from the scope of application of the Procurement Directives. The case concerns in particular the extent of the obligations the Commission interprets from the applicable Treaty principles.

In May 2010, the CFI considered the case and concluded that the 2006 Communication does not create new obligations for contracting authorities/entities.[139] Following this confirmation of the Commission's 2006 Communication, it could be that a steady course is adopted in the case-law on these issues, according to which a contract falling (partially) outside the scope of the Procurement

[134] Ibid., paras 122–123.

[135] Ibid., paras 138–143.

[136] Ibid., para 141.

[137] CJEU, *R Industrias Químicas del Vallés v Commission,* Judgment, T-158/03 [2003] ECR II-3041 para 35.

[138] *Coname*, above n 78, paras 23–26.

[139] *Germany v Commission*, above n 129.

Directives needs to be awarded in competition whenever the assumption that foreign companies are not interested in the contract cannot be rebutted.

Sporting Exchange and Engelmann Cases

In the same year, the Court answered a preliminary question regarding the right of a Member State to grant a license to a single operator in the field of games of chance, without competitive tendering.[140]

In line with the Coname and Wall cases, the Court stated that the obligation of transparency applies to public authorities who award service concession contracts, whenever the service concession may be of interest to economic operators from other Member States.[141]

Later during that year, the Court gave a similar ruling in the Engelmann case.[142]

Commission v Ireland Case

A few months later, the Court judged on another case regarding a contract falling partially outside the scope of application of the Procurement Directives. However, in this case, the existence of a cross-border interest was not disputed.[143] As a consequence the Court did not have the chance to confirm the approach embraced by the previously mentioned Commission's Communication.

The CJEU showed though the same tendency as in previous case-law, to interpret the Treaty principle in line with case-law relating to contracts fully covered by the Procurement Directives. The case regarded a complaint of the European Commission against Ireland concerning the procurement of II B services. Ireland had allocated the award criteria weights after the deadline for the submission of bids and amended these weights after a first investigation of the submitted bids.[144]

The Court decided, that the obligation to publicize the weights of the award criteria before the deadline for the submission of bids does not follow from the principle of equal treatment or from the transparency principle. The Advocate-General had noticed in this context that the same outcome had been reached by the Court in the context of a procurement falling under the scope of the Procurement Directives. The Court had judged that assigning scores to the award sub-criteria after the deadline for submission of bids but before the opening of the bids was allowed.[145]

---

140 CJEU, *Sporting Exchange Ltd v Minister van Justitie,* Judgment, C-2013/08 [2010] ECR I-4735 (Sporting Exchange case).

141 Ibid., para 40.

142 CJEU, *Criminal proceedings against Ernst Engelmann,* Judgment, C-64/08 [2010] ECR I-08219.

143 Ireland had voluntarily advertised the contract and the conditions for a competitive award procedure.

144 CJEU, *Commission v Ireland,* Judgment, C-226/09 [2010] ECR I-11807 (*Commission v Ireland*).

145 CJEU, *ATI EAC Srl e Viaggi di Maio Snc, EAC Srl and Viaggi di Maio Snc v ACTV Venezia SpA, Provincia di Venezia and Comune di Venezia,* Judgment, C-331/04 [2005] ECR I-10109 (ATI EAC case).

Of importance to the decision in the discussed case was that the award criteria did not lend themselves to multiple interpretations and could thus not be used to disadvantage bidders from other Member States.[146] Moreover, the award criteria had not been published in the order of relevance and knowledge of the scores before the deadline for submission would not have substantially influenced the formulation of the bids.[147]

Changing the scores of the award criteria after the opening of the bids, on the other side, breaches the equal treatment and transparency principles.[148] It is not necessary to demonstrate the discriminatory effect of the change or show that damages derived thereof.[149]

Belgacom Case

In the Belgacom case, the Court considered preliminary questions from the Belgian judge, regarding the right of public authorities to award a service concession contract (in this case, an exclusive right to operate television cable networks and to provide related services) without competition.

The Court reiterated the by now established approach, that service concessions should be awarded in compliance with the fundamental rules of the TFEU, when there is a certain cross-border interest.[150] In the case at issue, the referring national judge had already expressed the view that undertakings from other Member States would have manifested interest in the concession, had they been aware of it.

The Court clarified that the existence of a certain cross-border interest did not depend on an actual complaint from a foreign supplier (who in the absence of transparency is not enabled to file such complaint) and breach of the Treaty rules may be alleged by an economic operator from the same Member State.[151] The award of the concession with a certain cross-border interest in the absence of any transparency, to a national undertaking, would amount thus to indirect discrimination on grounds of nationality.[152]

Ancona Case

In the Ancona case,[153] the Court ruled on the legality of the award of a service concession related to infrastructure works in the local port areas, without competition.[154] The Court provided clarity on the concrete obligations entailed by the

---

146 *Commission v Ireland*, above n 144, para 45.

147 AG Mengozzi, *Commission v Ireland*, Opinion, C-226/09 [2010] ECR I-11807.

148 *Commission v Ireland*, above n 144, para 62.

149 *Commission v Ireland*, above n 144, paras 63–64.

150 CJEU, *Belgacom NV v Integan*, Judgment, C-221/12 [2013] ECR 2013-00000 (Belgacom case) para 28.

151 Ibid., paras 31–32.

152 Ibid., para 37.

153 CJEU, *Comune di Ancona v Regione Marche*, Judgment, C-388/12 [2013] ECR 2013-00000 (*Ancona*).

154 In this case, the Comune di Ancona had awarded the management of a slipway in the local port, without a public tendering procedure.

principle of transparency and set a low threshold for ruling on the existence of cross-border interest.

The Court's reasoning can be summarized as follows: the award of a service concession contract with certain cross-border interest, in the absence of any transparency would operate in the detriment of undertakings located in other Member States and would amount to indirect discrimination on grounds of nationality. Whenever the public authority decides to disregard the transparency principle, it should invoke objective facts to justify its decision. The Court subsequently dismissed the arguments invoked by the Ancona municipality, that the concession did not generate substantial net revenues or an undue advantage for the operating undertaking. The Court ruled that the concession may still be of interest to economic operators form other Member States, who plan to establish themselves on the market of the Member State where the concession is being awarded.[155]

According to the Court, the transparency principle does not necessarily entail an obligation to call for tenders. However, the upcoming award should be advertised in such a way as to give economic operators from other Member States the possibility to express their interest in the concession.[156] This leaves room for the interpretation that the procurer may award the concession without open competition, in the absence of manifested interest from an economic operator from another Member State.

5.4.3 Conclusions

In this section I analyzed the case-law of the CJEU on the applicability of the TFEU obligations to contracts (partially) excluded from the scope of the Procurement Directives. I also analyzed the extent of the concrete obligations deriving from the TFEU. This analysis was meant to check the Commission's interpretation of the obligations deriving from the TFEU fundamental principles in the context of a PCP procedure. It was also meant to conclude on the degree of procedural flexibility a contracting authority has when awarding an R&D service contract that falls outside the scope of the Procurement Directive. Although CJEU has not decided on matters related to PCP yet, I considered that its interpretation in other cases excluded from the scope of application of the Procurement Directives is relevant for PCP.

CJEU's case-law before the *Germany v Commission* case shows inconsistencies in interpreting the applicability of the TFEU to contracts (partially) excluded from the scope of the Procurement Directives. The Court is also inconsistent in interpreting which concrete obligations derive from the fundamental principles of the Treaty.

155 Ancona, above n 153, paras 49–51.

156 Ibid., para 52.

Following the Germany v Commission case, the Court has streamlined its interpretation. A public procurer may disregard the fundamental principles of TFEU (and particularly the principle of transparency) when awarding a contract that (partially) falls outside the scope of the Procurement Directives only when the contract does not present a certain cross-border interest. This is the case when companies from other Member States do not have an economic interest in the contract, for example, due to the low monetary value, distance from the border, technical characteristics etc. In practice, the European judge sets the bar for proving lack of cross-border interest very high.

This implies that the procurement of R&D services when risks and benefits are shared may present a certain cross-border interest or not, depending on the circumstances of the case. However, the PCP as defined in the PCP Communication is meant to address problems that are common to more than one Member State and are therefore of important economic value. They would, as a consequence, most probably attract the interest of companies from different Member States. From a conceptual perspective, PCP is meant to stimulate the creation of innovative solutions to important public needs. As a consequence, public procurers should be interested in attracting the most capable competitors, and should therefore advertise the contract as widely as possible.

Regarding the concrete obligations flowing from the TFEU, in case of cross-border interest, the case-law remains partially inconclusive. The Commission's 2006 Communication, which was confirmed in *Germany v Commission* case, assumes that a competitive award procedure should be conducted following advertisement through sufficiently wide-coverage means.

Most recent case-law, however, states that the transparency principle does not necessarily entail the obligation to call for tenders. This seems to imply that the public procurer may choose not to organize a competitive award when the advertisement of the contract did not reveal any interest from undertakings from other Member States.

When following the Commission's approach as outlined in its 2006 Communication, the following additional flexibility is available to the public procurer as compared to the provisions of the Procurement Directives:

1. The procurer may choose to carry out negotiations with the providers, similar to the competitive procedure with negotiations as provided by the 2014 Procurement Directives, without the need to follow the time-limits prescribed therein. However, it is important to remind that the European Commission recommends procurers to engage prior to the PCP, in an extensive preparatory phase, which includes a market consultation.[157] The open dialogues is meant to check the state-of-the-art industry development and to confirm the need to procure R&D services in order to fulfil the public need(s).[158] In practice, the mar-

[157] Module 2, Eafip initiative, available at http://eafip.eu/toolkit/module-2/. Accessed 4 July 2016.

[158] Commission 2007a; Horizon 2020 (2016) Annex E.

ket consultation should yield sufficient information to make the need for negotiations redundant.
2. Different time-limits for expressions of interest or submission of bids than prescribed by the Procurement Directives could be applied.
3. Scores could be assigned to the award criteria after the deadline for the submission of bids, but should be assigned before the opening of the bids.
4. The exclusion and selection criteria may entail other requirements than those enumerated within the Directive.

Due to the applicability of the equal treatment principle to contracts outside the scope of application of the Procurement Directives, there is limited room for changing the technical specifications during the subsequent PCP Phases. Arguably, functional and performance criteria could be gradually specified.

5.5 The Concept of R&D Services in PCP

5.5.1 Introduction

As already explained, PCP is one approach to the procurement of R&D services contracts that are exempted from the application of the Procurement Directives. In order to legitimately rely on this exemption, the overall value of the R&D services throughout the 3 PCP phases should exceed the value of other activities (above 50 % of the total contract value).

It is essential for a procurer to understand what R&D is, and how it can check whether the PCP contract is an R&D services contract. Based on the scarce guidance provided by the PCP Communication, the public procurer may encounter difficulties in deciding which activities qualify as R&D services and which activities are related to the R&D project, but do not qualify themselves as R&D services, or even as other R&D activities. Particularly in Phase 3, the public procurer may encounter difficulties in distinguishing between R&D services and other innovative activities that do not qualify as R&D.

The guidance provided under the PCP Communication on these aspects is scarce. The PCP Communication broadly enumerated the R&D activities that form the object of each PCP Phase. Moreover, neither the PCP Communication, nor the Procurement Directives contain definitions of the concept of 'R&D service'.

For additional guidance, public procurers may refer to the OECD publication, the Frascati Manual (or 'Manual').[159] Although it was developed for the purpose of measuring R&D investments in national contexts, its interpretation of the R&D concept is to a large extent relevant to PCP. The Manual provides an extensive analysis of the different types of R&D activities, concrete examples and guidance on the borderline between R&D and other innovative, but non-R&D activities.

159 OECD 2002.

There is no reference made to the Frascati Manual in the PCP Communication. However, at the time of its drafting the Manual was officially endorsed by the European Commission. The Manual is also expressly mentioned as a source of inspiration for the definition of different categories of R&D activities in the area of State aid for R&D and innovation.[160] Moreover, definitions of R&D in line with the Frascati Manual can be found in the Defence Directive.[161] This allows me to assume that it constitutes a legitimate source of additional guidance on the concept of R&D.

Besides the Frascati Manual, the Procurement Directives, the Defense Directive and guidance documents developed by the European Commission in the area of State aid may form a source of complementary guidance.

Based on the analysis of the above mentioned documents, this section aims to provide additional clarity on the meaning of 'R&D services'. In addition, it aims to point out the remaining conceptual difficulties and gaps in the available guidance on this concept. To this end, Sect. 5.2 describes the concept of R&D, as defined in the Frascati Manual. It outlines the generic criteria for identifying R&D activities, as well as specific criteria for identifying R&D in the area of software development and in service innovations.

Section 5.3 outlines the EU guidance on the concept of R&D. It distinguishes between R&D services, on the one side, and R&D works and R&D supplies, on the other side, based on the definition of various types of public contracts in the Procurement Directives. It also presents the description of R&D in the area of defense procurement and state aid. Section 5.4 summarizes conclusions on the comprehensiveness of the existing guidance for PCP and on the remaining gaps.

5.5.2 The Frascati Manual on R&D

R&D Definition and Categories

In the latest version of the Frascati Manual, R&D is defined as '*creative work undertaken on a systematic basis in order to increase the stock of knowledge, including knowledge of man, culture and society, and the use of this stock of knowledge to devise new applications*'.[162]

The Manual distinguishes between three categories of R&D: basic research, applied research and experimental development. The Frascati Manual provides the following definitions for each of these categories.[163]

---

160 Commission 2014 para 75.

161 Recital (13) of Directive 2009/81/EC.

162 OECD 2002, 30.

163 OECD 2002, 64.

Basic research is '*experimental or theoretical work undertaken primarily to acquire new knowledge of the underlying foundation of phenomena and observable facts, without any particular application or use in view*'.

Applied research is '*also original investigation undertaken in order to acquire new knowledge. It is, however, directed primarily towards a specific practical aim or objective*'.

Experimental development is '*systematic work, drawing on existing knowledge gained from research and/or practical experience, which is directed to producing new materials, products or devices, to installing new processes, systems and services, or to improving substantially those already produced or installed*'.

The PCP Communication states that PCP is not meant for '*curiosity driven research*', but should target R&D with certain applications in sight.[164] This leads me to the conclusion that PCP focuses on applied research and experimental development activities, as defined by the Frascati Manual, and not on basic research. In practice, the 2 stages are not clearly separated. New knowledge may be created even during the construction of the prototype in PCP Phase 2 and during its testing in PCP Phase 3. For the public procurer, it is important that the value of the knowledge creation activities (corresponding to the 'applied research') outweighs the value of the 'experimental development' work throughout all 3 PCP Phases.

Borderline Between R&D and Other Innovative Non-R&D Activities

In order to make sure that the PCP contract is meeting the 'above 50 % R&D services' threshold, it is also relevant for the public procurer to distinguish between development activities in Phase 3 and other activities, that are innovation, but do not qualify as R&D services or even R&D works or supplies.

The Frascati Manual recognizes the difficulties in locating the cut-off point between R&D and the innovative non-R&D activities particularly when the innovative non-R&D activities have a scientific and technological basis and are '*very closely linked to R&D both through flows of information and in terms of operations, institutions and personnel*'.[165] The difficulty is also increased when the costs of preparing for production are higher than the costs of the R&D itself.[166] R&D is often carried out at different phases of the innovation process up to the implementation stage. This is due to the fact that R&D is not only '*the original source of inventive ideas but also as a means of problem solving which can be called upon at any point up to implementation*'.[167]

The Frascati Manual distinguishes between innovative activities that can never be qualified as R&D, but may occasionally entangle 'feedback' R&D, and

[164] Commission 2007a, 4.

[165] OECD 2002, para 65.

[166] OECD 2002, para 24.

[167] OECD 2002, para 21.

innovative activities that may be qualified as R&D or non-R&D depending on whether they are '*carried out solely or primarily for the purpose of an R&D project*'.[168]

Innovative activities which can never qualify as R&D are, for example: '*acquisition of technology (embodied and disembodied), tooling up and industrial engineering,(…) other capital acquisition (…) and marketing for new or improved products*',[169] pre-production, production and distribution, business services, market research.[170]

Innovative activities which may qualify as R&D or non-R&D are, for example: scientific and technical information services (such as the provision of library or computer services),[171] management, administration and clerical activities,[172] general purpose data collection, testing and standardization, feasibility studies, specialized health care, personal education of academic staff, patent and license work, policy-related studies, industrial design.[173]

Within this context, particular difficulties are identified by the Frascati Manual in finding the cut-off line between experimental development which is R&D and pre-production development which is not R&D. According to the Manual, technical demonstrations, which are intended '*to make further technical improvements on the product or process*' constitute R&D activities.[174] The successful testing of the original prototype marks the end of the experimental development stage. Only when the testing does not yield the expected results and changes to the prototype are brought, the repeated test will continue to constitute R&D.[175]

A user demonstration which involves that the innovation is '*operated at or near full scale in a realistic environment*' for purposes of supporting policy or promoting the innovation does not constitute R&D. The pre-production planning or getting a production or control system working well, after the product, process or approach has been set, does not constitute R&D either.[176]

168 OECD 2002, para 69.

169 OECD 2002, paras 21–22, 79.

170 OECD 2002, paras 82–83.

171 Namely collecting, coding, recording, classifying, disseminating, translating analyzing, evaluating when performed by scientific and technical personnel or by bibliographic services, patent services, scientific conference and scientific and technical information, extension and advisory service. See OECD 2002, para 70.

172 OECD 2002, para 132.

173 OECD 2002, paras 71–77, 110.

174 OECD 2002, Annex 10 and paras 8–9.

175 OECD 2002, para 115.

176 OECD 2002, para 111.

The initial manufacturing stage may, according to the Frascati Manual, constitute R&D if it '*implies further design and engineering*'.[177]

Generic Criteria to Identify R&D

For situations of uncertainty on whether an activity is R&D or not, the Manual defines generic criteria. These criteria may be applied whenever it is not clear whether an activity is R&D or not. The most important criterion is the '*presence of an appreciable element of novelty and the resolution of scientific and/or technological uncertainty, e.g. when the solution to a problem is not readily apparent to someone familiar with the basic stock of common knowledge and techniques for the area concerned*'.[178]

Other supplementary criteria which are listed by the Frascati Manual as indicators of R&D include: the scope of the project to seek previously undiscovered phenomena, structures or relationships, the application of knowledge or techniques in a new way within the project, the significant chance that the project will result in new (extended or deeper) understanding of phenomena, relationships or manipulative principles of interest to more than one organization, the potential patentability of the results, the involvement of academic staff in the project.[179] The Frascati Manual makes clear that in some blurry situations, the distinction between experimental development and pre-production development '*requires engineering judgement as to when the element of novelty ceases and the work changes to routine development*'.[180]

R&D in Software Development

The Frascati Manual contains specific guidance on identifying R&D in software development. Because PCP was initially envisaged as a suitable instrument to leverage private R&D efforts in the ICT sector, and because innovative ICT solutions are still promoted by EU policy-makers as crucial for the global competitiveness of the European economy, it is important to be able to identify when software development can be qualified as R&D.

The Frascati Manual is concise on this matter. The main conditions to qualify software development as R&D are the following:

- the completion of the development must be dependent on a scientific and/or technological advance (advance in the area of computer software); AND
- the aim of the project must be the systematic resolution of a scientific and/or technological uncertainty.

[177] OECD 2002, para 120.

[178] OECD 2002, para 2.3.1. The components of this definition of R&D match to a large extent with those of patentability according to the European Patent Convention, Articles 52–56. However, purely 'scientific' advances would rarely meet the patentability test, whereas according to the Frascati Manual, they fall within the concept of R&D. See Apostol and Mair 2012.

[179] OECD 2002, para 2.3.2.

[180] OECD 2002, Annex 10 and para 39.

These conditions practically reiterate the generic criteria for identification of R&D. The Manual further specifies that an upgrade, addition or change to an existing program or system will, according to the Frascati Manual qualify as R&D when '*it embodies scientific and/or technological advances that result in an increase in the stock of knowledge*'.[181]

R&D Which Leads to Services Innovation

The 2007 PCP Communication and the accompanying PCP Staff Working Document are not clear on whether PCP is a suitable instrument for the development of innovative services which are not built around an innovative technology. On the one hand, the policy documents talk about the role of PCP to assure the development of technological solutions to meet challenging societal needs.[182] On the other hand, the same policy documents indicate that the result of a PCP can be either an innovative product or service.[183]

The same lack of clarity is evident in the Frascati Manual. Initially, the basic definitions in the Frascati Manual were developed for the manufacturing industry and research in the natural sciences and engineering. Subsequently, these were extended to service activities.

The Frascati Manual acknowledges the remaining difficulties in identifying R&D in services. According to the Manual, these difficulties are mainly due to the fact that R&D in services is not specialised, but covers several areas: '*technology-related R&D, R&D in the social sciences and humanities, including R&D relating to the knowledge of behaviour and organisations*'.[184] When software-related, R&D in services will be present even when the software is not by itself innovative, '*but innovates by virtue of the functions that it performs*'.[185]

The Frascati Manual proposes the use of the same above mentioned generic criteria to identify R&D in services.[186] The following examples of R&D activities in the services sector are given: socio-economic research, insurance and financial mathematics (in the banking and insurance industry), IT systems development for the back office and delivery, service scripts development for the front desk personnel, ICT research and development, logistics simulation, management research, marketing research, environmental research, consumer behaviour, nutritional research, demographics research, religion-oriented research, medical research, law etc.[187]

Analysts have expressed the concern that the reality of service development activities is not fully reflected into the current R&D definition of the Frascati

---

[181] OECD 2002, paras 135–138.

[182] Commission 2007a, 4, 9, 10; Commission 2007b, 2–3, 10–1.

[183] Commission 2007a, 2–3, 8; Commission 2007b, 3–4, 8.

[184] OECD 2002, para 147.

[185] OECD 2002, para 147.

[186] OECD 2002, para 149.

[187] CREST Working Group 2008, 12.

Manual. However, to the knowledge of the author, very few practical solutions have so far been brought up.[188] This led to the conclusion in Chap. 3, that PCP is only to a very limited extent relevant to stimulating the development of innovative services.

5.5.3 EU Guidance on the Concept of R&D

The Concept of R&D Services in the Procurement Directives

In order to qualify for the exemption of Article 14 of the 2014 Public Sector Directive or Article 32 of the 2014 Utilities Directive, the contract should qualify as an R&D service contract and not as an R&D supplies or an R&D works contract. The latter two types of contracts are not exempted from the application of the Procurement Directives.[189] It is therefore important for the public procurer to understand the difference between these categories of R&D. But R&D services contracts, R&D works contracts and R&D supplies contracts are not defined in the Procurement Directives. The Procurement Directives contain though definitions of public services contracts, works contracts and public supplies contracts. Below I will analyse these definitions and I will draw conclusions on the meaning of R&D supplies, R&D works and R&D services.

'Public works contracts' are defined in the Procurement Directives as '*public contracts having as their object one of the following*:

a. *the execution, or both the design and execution, of works related to one of the activities within the meaning of Annex II [for Directive 2014/24/EU] or Annex I [for Directive 2014/25/EU];*
b. *the execution, or both the design and execution, of a work;*
c. *the realisation by whatever means of a work corresponding to the requirements specified by the contracting entity exercising a decisive influence on the type or design of the work.*'[190]

Annex I mentioned above provides examples of activities in a construction or civil engineering project, such as demolition, drilling, boring, architectural activities, assembly of pipelines etc. Moreover, 'work' is defined in the Procurement Directives as '*the outcome of building or civil engineering works taken as a whole which is sufficient of itself to fulfil an economic or technical function*'.[191]

---

[188] CREST Working Group 2008, 31. For a discussion on the economic theories on how innovative services emerge, see Chap. 3, Sect. 3.6.

[189] But R&D supplies may be procured by negotiations without publication of a contract notice. See Article 32(3)(a) Directive 2014/24/EU. And under Directive 2014/25/EU, both R&D supplies and R&D work contracts may be procured by negotiations without prior call for competition [see Article 50(b)].

[190] Article 2(1)(6) Directive 2014/24/EU and Article 2(2) Directive 2014/25/EU.

[191] Article 2(1)(7) Directive 2014/24/EU; Article 2(3) Directive 2014/25/EU.

'Public supply contracts' are defined in the Procurement Directives as '*public contracts having as their object the purchase, lease, rental or hire-purchase, with or without option to buy, of products*'.[192]

Based on the above definitions, I can conclude that R&D works entail the delivery of the physical outcome of building or civil engineering activities. This could, for example, cover the building of a testing installation. R&D supplies, on the other side, refer to the delivery of physical products, such as a prototype.

'Public service contracts' are defined in the Procurement Directives[193] as other activities than the delivery of R&D works or R&D supplies. The list of services in annexes to both the Procurement Directives shows that service contracts cover the delivery of intangible results, such as knowledge.[194]

A public contract is qualified as an R&D service contract if the total value of the services over all the R&D phases exceeds the value of R&D products (such as prototypes), R&D works and other costs covered by the contract.[195]

I can thus conclude that an R&D service contract entails a large share of knowledge creation. As a consequence, whenever the public procurer decides to keep the prototype that is being developed during the PCP Phase 2 or the first products developed under the PCP Phase 3, he needs to make sure the value of the prototype/first products it(them)self(ves) does not outweigh the value of the knowledge creative activities (or R&D services). When the value of the prototype or of the building/installation of the test object (prototype) is larger than the value of the R&D services, the contract will not qualify for a PCP procedure.

Area of Defence Procurement

The Defence Directive[196] adopts almost literally the R&D definitions provided by the Frascati Manual. This confirms that the guidance provided by the Organisation for Economic Co-operation and Development (OECD) on the R&D concept constitutes the leading authority on the interpretation of this concept in the area of public procurement.

The Defence Directive also attempts to clarify the borderline between R&D and non-R&D activities. In line with the Frascati Manual, it clarifies that technological demonstrators (i.e. devices demonstrating the performance of a new concept or a new technology in a relevant or representative environment) fall within the concept of experimental development. A less clear overview is given of activities that fall outside the R&D concept: '*the making and qualification of pre-production prototypes, tools and industrial engineering, industrial design or manufacture*'.[197]

---

192 Article 2(1)(8) Directive 2014/24/EU; Article 2(4) Directive 2014/25/EU.

193 Article 2(1)(9) Directive 2014/24/EU; Article 2(5)(d) Directive 2014/25/EU.

194 Annex XIV Directive 2014/24/EU; Annex XVII Directive 2024/25/EU.

195 See Footnotes 5 and 6 Commission 2007a.

196 Directive 2009/81/EC.

197 Recital (13) Directive 2009/81.

Area of State Aid

The 2014 Framework for State aid for R&D&I (or 'Framework'), European Commission's guidance on the conditions for declaring R&D national subsidies compatible with the internal market, expressly mentions the Frascati Manual as one source of inspiration for the classification of various R&D activities.[198]

The Framework defines three categories of R&D activities: fundamental research, industrial research and experimental development which largely correspond to the Manual's definitions of basic research, industrial research and experimental development.[199] The Framework clarifies that industrial research and experimental development constitute applied research. These 2 categories are thus relevant for PCP.

The Framework pays more attention than the Frascati Manual to drawing a clear line between different categories of R&D activities. The Frascati Manual is less preoccupied with defining the cut-off line between the different R&D categories and is more interested in distinguishing between R&D and non-R&D activities.

Distinguishing between different categories of R&D activities is important in the area of State aid, due to the fact that maximum percentages of the R&D costs per R&D category may be subsidized by a public authority. The closer the R&D activity finds itself to commercialization, the more distortive the subsidy is considered for the good functioning of the Internal market and as a consequence, the less significant the subsidy may be.[200]

The Framework clarifies that the aim of industrial research is to acquire new knowledge and skills needed to develop new, or significantly improved products, processes or services. The creation of components of complex systems falls under industrial research, as well as the construction of prototypes in a laboratory and the construction of pilot environments.[201]

Experimental development, on the other side, covers the creation of new or improved products, processes or services, based on knowledge previously acquired (e.g. during previous industrial research). Typical activities during experimental development include: '*prototyping, demonstrating, piloting, testing and validation of new or improved products, processes or services in environments representative of real life operating conditions where the primary objective is to make further technical improvements on products, processes or services that are not substantially set*'.[202]

---

[198] Commission 2014, para 75.

[199] Commission 2014, Article 1.3(e), (m) and (q).

[200] 100 % of the costs for fundamental research may be funded by Member States, up to 80 % of the applied research activities and up to 60 % of the experimental development activities. See Commission 2014, Annex II.

[201] Commission 2014, Article 1.3(q).

[202] Commission 2014, Article 1.3(j).

The aim of the R&D activities at the experimental development stage should not be to produce something for commercial use. However, commercially usable prototypes or pilots fall under experimental development, where it '*is necessarily the final commercial product and where it is too expensive to produce for it to be used only for demonstration and validation purposes*'.[203] In the context of a PCP, there is no limitation on the subsequent commercial use of the prototype/tested product by the public procurer that awarded the PCP contract, besides the fact the requirement that the PCP contract remains a R&D service contracts. If the cost of keeping the tested product (for use in the operational activities of the public procurer) outweighs the cost of the R&D services, the contract cannot be qualified as a PCP and will fall under the Procurement Directives (if above the applicable threshold).

Besides drawing a strict line between the different categories of R&D activities, the Framework defines the R&D costs which qualify for a subsidy.[204] These include personnel costs, costs of instruments and equipment, costs of buildings and land, costs of contractual research, overhead, operating costs related to the project at issue etc. The PCP guidance does not detail the concept of eligible R&D costs under a PCP contract. Arguably, any of these costs are eligible under a PCP contract, as long as the value of the R&D services outweighs the other costs. Based on the definition of R&D services above, I can conclude that researchers costs correspond, in any case, to the creation of new knowledge.

Finally, the Framework does not define R&D activities that lead to innovation in the services sector. It only defines process and organizational *innovative* activities that qualify as eligible costs. The maximum aid intensities are lower than for traditional R&D activities (15 % of the cost of the project for large enterprises, 50 % for medium and small enterprises).[205]

5.5.4 Conclusions

By limiting PCP to R&D services contracts, the EU legislator and the EU policy-maker sought to provide public funding to those knowledge-creating activities, which promise significant benefits, but do not easily attract the necessary private investments. The EU sought to ensure that public funding is not wasted on funding trivial innovative activities performed by national champions. A correct interpretation of the concept of R&D services is thus important in order to ensure that PCP achieves its objectives as innovation policy instrument. However, the PCP Communication does not provide a clear definition of R&D services or clear guidelines on the types of activities that qualify as R&D services.

---

203 Idem.

204 Commission 2014, Annex I.

205 Annex II Commission 2014.

Although the Frascati Manual has not officially been acknowledged as the authoritative guidance on the interpretation of the R&D concept in the context of a PCP, it provides useful complementary guidance. The Frascati Manual has already been embraced by the European Commission in the area of defence procurement and State aid.

In this section I outlined the most important guidance that may be relevant for the interpretation of the R&D services concept in the context of a PCP procedure, based on the analysis of the Frascati Manual, the definition of various categories of public contract in the Procurement Directives and the description of R&D activities in the Defense Procurement Directive and in the 2014 Framework for State aid for R&D&I.

I can conclude that knowledge creation activities (corresponding to 'industrial research' as defined in the 2014 Framework for State aid for R&D&I) should outweigh in cost other activities in a PCP contract.

Whenever in doubt whether an activity represents R&D, a public procurer may use the generic criteria provided by the Frascati Manual:

- '*presence of an appreciable element of novelty*'; and
- '*the resolution of scientific and/or technological uncertainty*'.

In other words, the solution to a problem should not be readily apparent to '*someone familiar with the basic stock of common knowledge and techniques for the area concerned*'. The Manual admits though the sometimes distinction between R&D and non-R&D activities requires '*engineering judgment as to when the element of novelty ceases and the work changes to routine development*'.

Clarity on the concept of R&D as part of the innovation process in services sectors is more difficult to find.

The Frascati Manual acknowledges the difficulties in defining R&D in services. These difficulties are due to the unspecialized nature of the R&D activities in services. The Frascati Manual proposes the use of the same above mentioned generic criteria to identify R&D in services. The 2014 Framework for State aid for R&D&I, on the other side, does not define R&D in services, but only refers to organisational and process *innovative* activities.

5.6 Distinction from Other Innovation Policy Tools

Other (procurement) tools for stimulating private R&D investments are available. Some of these tools have a design that comes close to PCP. Questions may arise whether these tools are able to perform the same functions and in which ways they differ from PCP.

This section outlines the main differences between the PCP instrument and the instruments which may come close to the working of PCP. These instruments are: (1) functional/performance specifications; (2) competitive dialogue; (3) R&D subsidies; and (4) Forward Commitment Procurement (FCP).

5.6.1 PCP and Functional and/or Performance Specifications

The Procurement Directives allow procurers to formulate their technical specifications in terms of performance levels and/or functions.[206] Why not then, simply formulate ambitious functional and/or performance requirements, that would drive tenderers to innovate, instead of engaging in a PCP.

The answer is simple. If commercially available products cannot comply with the required functions and/or performance levels and the timeline for the purchase is too short to allow for further improvements, the procurement will fail. In such a case, the contracting authority has three options: (1) wait until the market develops by itself the desired product; or (2) initiate a new procurement with less ambitious requirements; or (3) engage in a PCP, in order to accelerate the development of the desired solution.

When innovative products are available, but are not yet commercialized (for example products which have just completed phase 3 of the PCP), ambitious performance and functional specifications (combined with qualitative award criteria) may lead to their purchase. Through such a use of performance and functional specifications, contracting authorities act as leading customers and stimulate, according to some economists, private actors to invest in future innovation efforts.[207] However, this is a different role compared to PCP. PCP is intended to steer private R&D efforts and investments at an earlier stage in the innovation process, towards socially beneficial solutions which would otherwise not be developed or would be developed at a much slower pace.

From an efficiency point of view, it is recommendable that a contracting authority learns about the available solutions in the market and about the stage of development of innovative products before deciding on the level of required performance and/or functions.

Of course, performance and functional specifications may also be used and are even recommended in the context of a PCP, in order to enable suppliers to propose the most suitable solution.[208] In conclusion, formulating functional and/or performance specifications is not in conflict with PCP, it will often be a part of it and will reinforce its functioning.

5.6.2 Competitive Dialogue

Competitive dialogue is a flexible procedure introduced in 2004, with the aim to allow the procuring authority, under certain circumstances, to interact with the

[206] See Articles 42(3)(a) Directive 2014/24/EU and 60(3)(a) Directive 2014/25/EU.

[207] Georgiou 2007.

[208] Commission 2007b, 10.

bidding firms. Initially, competitive dialogue could only be used in complex projects, such as infrastructure/IT projects wherein legal and financial make-up were uncertain.[209] The applicability grounds have been relaxed in the 2014 Procurement Directives.[210] Under the 2014 Public Sector Directive competitive dialogue may be used when the contract includes innovative solutions.

Arguably, competitive dialogue may be used for the purchase of R&D services, but the procedure has not been expressly designed for this type of project. At the end of the dialogue, the unique features of the best solution will be inevitably communicated to the other candidates, when they are invited to submit their final tenders on the basis of this solution. In this case, the participant who proposed that solution is not even sure that he will be the winning bidder.[211]

Compared with the competitive dialogue, PCP has been specifically designed to gradually reduce technological uncertainties and maintain competition throughout the process (by parallel development trajectories).

5.6.3 R&D Subsidies

A distinction between PCP and R&D subsidies is less clear-cut. The European Commission did not follow the US SBIR approach to differentiate between procurement-based PCP and subsidy-based PCP, depending on whether the PCP is developing innovations for the direct benefit and use by a public authority, or for broader public objectives. In the current context, PCP can be applied in both situations, while being labelled as 'procurement' and as a 'demand-side' instrument in its entirety.

The European Commission chose to adopt a muddled approach: PCP is always a demand-side instrument in respect of the purchased R&D services; and PCP may entail an element of State aid or not, depending on whether a market price had been paid for the PCP contract. The second part of the argument was replaced in 2014 with a set of simple criteria that create a presumption of market conformity.[212]

The Commission's understanding of demand-side instruments is dissonant with the approach adopted in the policy- research field. An accepted definition of demand-side innovation policy is: '*all public action to induce innovation and/or speed up the diffusion of innovation through increasing the demand for innovation, defining new functional requirements for products and services and/or improving user involvement in innovation production (user-driven innovation)*'.[213]

---

209 See Articles 1(11)(c) and 29 of Directive 2004/18/EC.

210 Article 26(4) Directive 2014/24/EU and Article 44(3) Directive 2014/25/EU.

211 Commission 2011, 46.

212 Commission 2014, para 33.

213 Edler 2013a, b, 2.

According to this definition, PCP does not qualify as a pure demand-side instrument, as it entails the generation of innovation and not its purchase.[214] Basically, when the public end-user is not involved and commitments for purchase are not clearly articulated, there is no use of demand in the context of the PCP.

Particularly when PCP is aiming to achieve broader public objectives, there is no substantive difference from a regular supply-side R&D subsidy,[215] expect perhaps the possibility to fund under the PCP a higher percentage of the contract costs than accepted by the Commission in the case of R&D subsidies.[216] This has encouraged so far innovation policy agencies in several EU Member States to deploy PCP(-like) schemes, with little involvement of the public end-users (the demand-side).[217]

This muddled approach reflects the Commission's intention to use its broad competences in the State aid area to deter uncompetitive behavior by public procurers through PCPs. The Commission's approach is however not conducive of an effective PCP deployment. Public procurers, who may act as demanding customers of innovations, are left without crucial guidance on how to effectively deploy PCPs, while at the same time being deterred by the risk of breaching State aid rules.

In conclusion, the Commission has not defined clear economic prerequisites for effective deployment of PCP, as opposed to R&D subsidies. Based on my analysis in Chap. 3, I can concluded that PCP as demand-side/procurement-based instrument, is effective in achieving its goals, only when:

- it is employed for the development of innovations for the direct benefit and use by the public procurer;
- the procurer is willing to get closely involved (e.g. supply detailed information on the need; test the prototypes at its premises, close communication with suppliers etc.)
- the procurer is willing to subsequently purchase the innovation.

R&D subsidies are suitable instruments to fund the development of innovations for the achievement of broader public objectives.

Supply-side R&D subsidies and demand-side PCP may also be deployed in a complementary way. Supply-side R&D subsidies may be use to fund basic research and demand-side PCP may be used to pull the most valuable solutions into the commercialisation phase.

---

214 Edler 2013a, b, 7. Edquist and Zabala-Iturriagagoitia 2013, 13, 18.

215 Policy researchers define also demand-side subsidies. These are though monetary funds offered to private or public customers to lower their cost of purchasing the innovation, not offered to the supplier. See Edler 2015 slide 26. Edler 2013a, b, 9.

216 Such as defined in Commission 2014.

217 This is discussed in Chap. 6.

5.6.4 Forward Commitment Procurement

Another instrument which is sometimes advertised as an efficient and suitable instrument to leverage private R&D investments and bring desirable innovations to the market is Forward Commitment Procurement (FCP).

FCP is a procurement approach used in the UK, which involves alerting the private market to the future procurement needs of a contracting authority and allowing the private market a certain period of time to develop a solution at an agreed price and at an agreed level of performance. FCP was inspired from the automotive industry, where companies actively engage with their supply chains to provide information on future requirements and procurements in order to stimulate investment in innovation.[218]

FCP can be defined as '*a commitment to purchase at a point in the future, a product that may not yet exist commercially, against a specification that current products do not meet, on a scale sufficient to make it worthwhile for suppliers to tool up and manufacture*'.

FCP was initially meant to stimulate the leap to commercialization of environmental innovations, as it was observed that an unaided market rarely provides the incentives needed for environmental innovation. FCP was proposed, based on the analysis of how over 100 companies in the environmental sector innovate and of which difficulties they encounter. FCP was considered suitable for environmental innovations which found themselves at the demonstration and scaling-up stage.[219]

FCP is now used in other sectors (such as sustainability and health care) to provide a first market to innovative products. FCP is considered an effective public instrument for situations in which the private actor does not have sufficient information on the size and nature of the future markets, in order to invest in the innovation process.[220]

Through the FCP approach, contracting authorities can articulate credible demand and provide important information about the nature and scale of the demand. This may provide the necessary incentive to unlock private investment in such innovations.[221] Moreover, FCP is profiled as a low risk enterprise from the part of the contracting authorities, which are risk averse when it comes to new products with no track record. Through FCP, the contracting authority alleviates the private investment risks, without actually investing in its development.[222]

---

218 EIAG 2006.

219 EIAG 2006, 4.

220 BIS 2012.

221 EIAG 2006.

222 See http://www.bis.gov.uk/policies/innovation/procurement/forward-commitment. Accessed 11 March 2011.

In conclusion, FCP could be used in combination with PCP, when the private market fails to innovate not only due to missing information on the nature and extent of demand, but also due to difficulties in accessing private R&D funding. It is wise to use only FCP, when the desired solution involves incremental improvements and when it will suffice to signal the intention to buy the developed solution to determine the private supplier to invest in the development of the respective product. PCP is most suitable when the private actor is not ready to invest or does not have the potential to invest in the solution.

5.7 Conclusions

In this chapter I concluded that the purpose of PCP is threefold: (1) to improve public services; (2) to generate solutions to important societal problems; and (3) to enhance innovation and commercialisation capabilities of EU businesses.

I also outlined the features of the PCP procedure as drafted by the Commission in its 2007 Communication and I established that important guidance on IPR sharing and on the interpretation of the concept of R&D is missing. In the absence of express competences to coordinate the practical implementation of a EU-wide PCP program, the Commission adopted a cautious approach, and focused on the legal rules in order to prevent non-competitive, market distortive implementations by national agencies. It paid less attention to defining practical guidance for an effective implementation.

I subsequently concluded that Commission's recommendations to conduct a fully-fledged competitive procedure finds support in the EU case-law concerning contracts (partially) exempted from the Procurement Directives. PCP offers thus a limited degree of procedural flexibility as compared to the provisions of the Procurement Directives. This may bring a procuring authority to the conclusion that voluntary application of the Procurement Directives is beneficial: while not entailing much additional burden, it allows the purchase of the resulting innovation within the framework of the same procedure. However, this is not a viable option when the procuring authority desires to use PCP strategically to enhance the innovative capabilities of EU businesses and limits participation to EU R&D providers (see discussion in Chap. 7, Sect. 7.3.2).

Finally, this chapter outlined the conceptual differences between PCP and other innovation procurement instruments, such as functional and/or performance specifications, competitive dialogue, R&D subsidies and Forward Commitment Procurement. It particularly underlined the current confusion between PCP as demand-side instrument and R&D subsidies. It concluded that the EU policy-maker missed the opportunity to clarify objective grounds for choosing for a PCP instead of other innovation policy instruments.

References

Apostol R, Mair C (2012) The pre-commercial procurement of FLOSS: quirks, conflicts and legal complexities. Paper presented at the UNDERPINN Conference, Manchester (22–23 March 2012)

Arrowsmith S, Kunzlik P (2009) Social and environmental policies in EC procurement law—new directives and new directions. Cambridge University Press, Cambridge

Commission (2006) Interpretative communication on the community law applicable to contract awards not or not fully subject to the provisions of the Public Procurement Directives 2006/C 179/02

Commission (2007a) Pre-commercial procurement: driving innovation to ensure sustainable high quality public services in Europe. COM 799 final

Commission (2007b) Guide on dealing with innovative solutions in public procurement—10 elements of good practice. SEC 280

Commission (2011) Green paper on the modernisation of EU public procurement policy—towards a more efficient European Procurement Market. COM 15 final

Commission (2014) Framework for state aid for research and development and innovation (2014/C 198/01)

Commission (2016) Frequently asked questions about PCP and PPI, https://ec.europa.eu/digital-single-market/news/frequently-asked-questions-about-pcp-and-ppi. Accessed 15 June 2016

CREST Working Group (2008) R&D in services—review and case studies http://ec.europa.eu/invest-in-research/pdf/download_en/service_rd080129.pdf. Accessed 2 Feb 2013

Department for Business Innovation and Skills (BIS) (2012) Forward commitment procurement know how programme, http://www.google.nl/url?sa=t&rct=j&q=&esrc=s&frm=1&source=web&cd=6&ved=0CGQQFjAF&url=http%3A%2F%2Fbis.gov.uk%2Fassets%2Fbiscore%2Finnovation%2Fdocs%2Ff%2Ffcp-introduction-concepts-background.ppt&ei=UcYLUdrdJcSk4AS8xIHIAQ&usg=AFQjCNHfxMdZGSl3GL1UU0SPQf6_rhIkdg&sig2=sQHlqhb8SilETMpo9pa3KQ. Accessed 2 Feb 2013

DeVecchio WJ (2007) Patent rights under government contracts. 07-7 Briefing Papers 1

Directive 2009/81/EC of the European Parliament and of the Council of 13 July 2009 on the coordination of procedures for the award of certain works contracts, supply contracts and service contracts by contracting authorities or entities in the fields of defence and security, and amending Directives 2004/17/EC and 2004/18/EC [2009] OJ L216/76

Ecorys (2011) Study on pre-commercial procurement in the field of security, http://ec.europa.eu/enterprise/policies/security/files/doc/pcp_sec_finalreport_en.pdf. Accessed 29 Jan 2013

Edler J (2013a) Innovation policy—concept, application, critique. In: 13th European Innovation Summit http://joint-institute.eu/files/2013/10/Edler-JIIP-Sep30-final2.pdf. Accessed 4 Mar 2014

Edler J (2013b) Review of policy measures to stimulate private demand for innovation. Concepts and effects. NESTA Working Paper No 13/13 https://www.nesta.org.uk/sites/default/files/review_of_policy_measures_to_stimulate_private_demand_for_innovation._concepts_and_effects.pdf. Accessed 29 Jul 2016

Edler J (2015) Demand side policies for innovation. State of the art presentation in the workshop: demand side policies and public procurement for innovation (Unicamp, Campinas) http://www.ige.unicamp.br/spec/wp-content/uploads/sites/15/2015/05/Edler-key-lecture-demand3.pdf. Accessed 29 Jul 2016

Edquist C, Hommen L (2000) Public technology procurement and innovation theory. In: Edquist et al (eds) Public technology procurement and innovation. Kluwer

Edquist C, Zabala-Iturriagagoitia JM (2013) Pre-commercial procurement: a demand or supply policy instrument in relation to innovation? CIRCLE Paper Series, Paper No 2012/11

Environmental innovations Advisory Group (EIAG) (2006) Environmental innovation: bridging the gap between environmental necessity and economic opportunity, http://www.berr.gov.uk/files/file34987.pdf. Accessed 24 Dec 2013

Expert Group Report (2010) Risk management in the procurement of innovation, concepts and empirical evidence in the European Union, http://ec.europa.eu/invest-in-research/pdf/download_en/risk_management.pdf. Accessed 20 Aug 2012

Georgiou L (2007) Demanding innovation lead markets, public procurement and innovation. London NESTA

Hordijk EP, van der Bend GW, van Nouhuys JF (2011) Aanbestedingsrecht—handboek van het Europese en het Nederlandse aanbestedingsrecht, 4th edn. Sdu Uitgevers

Horizon 2020 (2016) Work Programme 2016–2017. http://ec.europa.eu/research/participants/data/ref/h2020/other/wp/2016-2017/annexes/h2020-wp1617-annex-ga_en.pdf. Accessed 27 Jul 2016

Krugner M (2003) The principles of equal treatment and transparency and the Commission interpretative communication on concessions, 12 PPLR 181

Manunza ER (2006) Alle aanbestedingen zijn interstatelijk. In: Manunza E, Senden L (eds) De EU: de interstatelijkheid voorbij? Blaeu, Willem Jansz, Amsterdam

OECD (2002) Proposed standard practice for surveys on research and experimental development. OECD Publications Service

Rambøll Management (2008) Opportunities for public technology procurement in the ICT-related sectors in Europe. ftp://ftp.cordis.europa.eu/pub/fp7/ict/docs/pcp/pcp-final-ramboll-report-js2_en.pdf. Accessed 29 Jan 2013

Sidebottom DM (2001) Updating the Bayh-Dole Act: keeping the federal government on the cutting edge. 30 Pub Cont LJ 225

Tridimas T (2006) The general principles of EU law, 2nd edn. Oxford University Press

Wilkinson et al (2005) Public procurement for research and innovation. Expert Group Report—developing procurement practices favourable to R&D and innovation (Wilkinson Report). http://ec.europa.eu/invest-in-research/pdf/download_en/edited_report_18112005_on_public_procurement_for_research_and_innovation.pdf. Accessed 26 Jan 2013

Chapter 6
The Realities of Public R&D Procurement Implementation in the EU—Trials and Tribulations

Contents

6.1 Introduction

By 2011, there were no known examples of PCP procedures in the form proposed by the European Commission in its 2007 PCP Communication.[1] By that time, only national initiatives inspired by the US SBIR were being piloted in three Member

[1] Commission 2011.

R. Apostol, *Trials and Tribulations in the Implementation of Pre-Commercial Procurement in Europe*, DOI 10.1007/978-94-6265-156-2_6

States: the UK, the Netherlands and Belgium. These initiatives were all implemented by centralised innovation agencies and resembled subsidies—more than public contracts. These programmes involved no or only sporadic interaction with the end-customer and did not attract EU-wide competition.

The European Commission became aware that contracting authorities with operational needs that positioned them as potential end-customers of innovation needed additional incentives to engage in PCPs. To this end, the European Commission fosters since 2009 collaborations and exchanges of best practices between EU contracting authorities, by funding the set-up of networks. In addition, since 2011, the European Commission funds all of the organisational costs, and part of the contractual costs, of concrete cross-border collaborative PCPs.

This chapter outlines the general state of implementation of PCP(-like) initiatives in the EU. Based on available reviews and studies, it describes the state of implementation of PCPs throughout the EU by 2011 and summarizes the barriers to widespread implementation, felt by EU contracting authorities (Sect. 6.2).

This chapter subsequently describes the set-up and practical implementation of the most established PCP/SBIR(-like) initiatives in the Netherlands, in the UK and in Belgium (Sects. 6.3–6.5).[2] In this context, It compares the features of the three national initiatives with their US source of inspiration. It subsequently establishes whether or not the national initiatives incorporate the prerequisites for an effective implementation of a PCP, as identified in Chap. 3.

Finally, this chapter outlines the efforts of the European Commission to create better PCP practices within the EU (Sect. 6.6) and draws conclusions on the remaining barriers to a wide and effective implementation (Sect. 6.7).

6.2 PCP's '*State of Play*' in the EU

Already during the preparation of the PCP Communication, the European Commission investigated whether there were known practices in the EU, in line with the envisaged PCP procedure. An early report of 2007 indicated there were no known PCP procedures being tested in the EU.[3] Based on interviews with contracting authorities and suppliers involved in innovation-oriented procurements coming close to PCP, the report pointed out several barriers to the up-take of PCP procedures. These are: lack of technical knowledge of the contracting authority, organisational difficulties in cross-border projects, difficulty to agree on shared demand requirements, difficulty to argument the benefits for supplier to participate in a PCP when subsequent commercialisation is not guaranteed.

[2] Although other national initiatives, particularly in the Nordic countries (Norway, Finland, Sweden, Denmark and Iceland) and in Austria and Germany have been deployed, the analysis of these programs remains outside the scope of this book. Bos 2011 slide 14.

[3] Rambøll Management 2008.

Three years after the release of the PCP Communication, the European Commission performed another review of the state of implementation of PCP in Europe. The survey revealed no examples of cross-border collaborative PCP procedures, as envisaged by the 2007 PCP Communication. The Commission's efforts had thus not spurred the desired behaviour.

PCP-'like' initiatives had however been set-up in a handful of Member States by national or regional innovation agencies that were driven by national innovation policy motivations rather than concrete procurement needs. Most importantly, these PCP-like initiatives did not promote EU-wide competition. The initiatives in the UK and the Netherlands were the most established, followed by the ones in Belgium, Finland,[4] Sweden,[5] Spain,[6] the Czech Republic[7] and Italy.[8]

The Commission's PCP Survey revealed that EU contracting authorities expected a greater effort on the part of the EU to stimulate the implementation of PCPs (through sharing of practices as well as through funding).[9] The survey further confirmed that concerns on compliance with the EU state aid rules constituted a reason for contracting authorities not to implement PCPs.[10]

Another study performed in 2011[11] confirmed that PCP is growing in popularity in the EU Member States. Based on interviews with contracting authorities, the study concluded that this was partly due to the success of the US scheme (which was replicated in the Netherlands and in the UK), and partly due to the European Commission's efforts to promote this instrument. However, the study confirmed the conclusion of the previous EU review, that individual contracting authorities that had the concrete needs and had the potential to act as end-customers were rarely involved in the available PCP-'like' schemes.[12]

In the same year, an OECD study confirmed that EU contracting authorities tend to favour already proven, low-risk solutions and that they lack knowledge and capabilities as well as incentives to adopt a different attitude.[13]

---

[4] See http://cordis.europa.eu/fp7/ict/pcp/docs/pcp-case-finland-v3.pdf Accessed 8 November 2013.

[5] In Sweden, VINNOVA launched a pilot measure in May 2010 that co-finances the acquisition of R&D services, up to a maximum of 50 % of the total cost. See Widmark 2011.

[6] http://cordis.europa.eu/fp7/ict/pcp/docs/spain_pcp_v3.pdf Accessed 8 November 2013.

[7] In the Czech Republic, a programme called BETA will run during the period 2012–2016 to procure research, experimental development and innovation at the demand of public administration bodies (nine ministries or other state bodies). The first call of the BETA programme was launched in February 2011. Technopolis 2010, 23.

[8] See http://cordis.europa.eu/fp7/ict/pcp/docs/italy-pcp-v4.pdf Accessed 2 February 2013.

[9] Commission 2011, 5.

[10] Ibid. Already in 2003, the same concern that EU State Aid legislative provisions constitute a barrier to the funding of R&D project in advanced development stages was expressed by the Dutch Social Economic Council in an advice to the Dutch government before the introduction of the SBIR-like initiative. Sociaal Economische Raad 2003, 30.

[11] Izsak and Edler 2011, 22–3.

[12] Izsak and Edler 2011, 22–3.

[13] Camerer and van Eijl, 2011, 179.

In conclusion, PCP conducted in collaboration between contracting authorities from different Member States with the aim to find innovative solutions to shared needs, did not occur by 2011.

The reviews and studies analysed in this section identify the following barriers to the uptake of PCP:

- lack of technical knowledge;
- aversion to risk;
- organisational difficulties in cross-border projects;
- difficulty to agree on shared demand requirements;
- difficulty to convince suppliers of the benefits to participate in PCP when subsequent commercialisation is not guaranteed;
- concerns regarding compliance with EU State aid.

In the next sections, I will outline which type of PCP(-like) programs were being implemented in the UK, the Netherlands and Belgium by 2011 and beyond and I will describe the Commission's efforts to spur wider implementation.

6.3 The UK SBRI

6.3.1 Background and Evaluation of SBRI (2001–2008)

In 2001, the UK set up the first European scheme for strengthening the demand-side of its public innovation policy, aiming to emulate SBIR's success in the US.[14] The UK scheme was called the Small Business Research Initiative ('SBRI'). It encouraged public bodies to invest 2.5 % of their external R&D budgets in small and early stage UK technology companies that encountered difficulties in accessing private funding.[15]

Similar to the US SBIR, the SBRI scheme provides for two staged-funding of R&D, for the feasibility study at Phase 1 and for product development at Phase 2. The SBRI scheme covered 100 % of the R&D costs with a maximum of £200 k per project. However, contrary to the US SBIR, a participating company needed to be able to fund itself 65 % of the total costs before any work could start. Grants for multiple projects were excluded.[16]

The SBRI had a very slow start. Until 2005, it had only advertised contracts of around £2 m[17] per year instead of the expected minimum of £100 m.[18]

---

[14] Turville 2007, 129 http://www.hm-treasury.gov.uk/d/sainsbury_review051007.pdf. Accessed 2 February 2013.

[15] Connell 2006, 4.

[16] Connell 2006, 3.

[17] Bound and Puttick 2010, 3, Connell 2006, 5.

[18] Lord Sainsbury's report shows that between 2001 and 2005, 2.5 % of the UK government's R&D budget constituted more than £100 m. See Turville 2007, 120.

In 2005, in an effort to boost the SBRI program, the contribution of 2.5 % of the external R&D budgets of all government departments was made mandatory by legislation. Despite this measure, Lord Sainsbury's report revealed two years later that the attitude change needed to make the SBRI program a success had not occurred.[19] Due to the unclear formulation of the legislation, government departments continued to include into the mandatory 2.5 % contribution, investments in policy development research (besides scientific and technical research). As a consequence, only 1 % of the 200 funded projects placed before 2008 were in line with the definition of R&D as defined by the UK Treasury.[20]

The reluctant attitude of the government departments to participate in the SBRI scheme was attributed to two main reasons.

> *Firstly*, the SBRI scheme was imposed top-down without clarification of its objectives and functioning.[21] The Department of Trade and Industry inappropriately underscored the aim to stimulate the innovativeness of companies, without highlighting the opportunity offered by the SBRI to help achieve each department's public objectives. As a consequence, the individual government departments did not feel incentivized to identify needs for innovative technologies (solutions) and did not initiate SBRI competitions.[22]
>
> *Secondly*, R&D projects did not pass the mandatory value-for-money assessment.[23]

Lord Sainsbury's report provided concrete recommendations to bring the SBRI programme more in line with the US SBIR counterpart. The improved SBRI was launched in 2008 and was followed by two early evaluations in 2010, performed by Nesta and Pro-Inno Europe and a more recent and more comprehensive evaluation in 2015. In the following sections, I will outline these developments.

19 Turville 2007, 135.

20 Bound and Puttick 2010, 7.

21 Technopolis 2010, 32.

22 Technopolis 2010, Ernst andYoung 2011, Connell 2006, 2.

23 See Connell 2006, 35. The value-for-money assessment should be applied to all procurements, before taking a decision to start the procedure. In summary, the value-for-money assessment entails a check on the viability of the project (whether efficiency, accountability or equity arguments oppose the envisaged procurement), desirability (assessment of the relative benefits compared to other routes which may achieve better outcomes) and achievability (analysis of market interest and availability of market solutions, assessment of the capacity of the contracting authority to manage the envisaged process). In addition, the value-for-money assessment entails factors such as an optimum allocation of risks and calculation of whole life costs which cannot always be complied with in pre-commercial procurements. See also: Treasury 2006.

6.3.2 SBRI—Features of the Latest Version (2008 and Later)

(a) Introduction

Lord Sainsbury's 2007 report recommended to bring SBRI more in line with the US SBIR scheme and to attune it to the objectives of the departments involved.[24] Lord Sainsbury submitted concrete proposals to this end. Departments should publicize on a regular basis the technological areas in which SBRI competitions will be subsequently launched. The SBRI competitions should be strictly limited to funding R&D activities and should exclude projects falling within the field of humanities and social sciences. The SBRI awards should be in the form of contracts, not equity loans or grants, in order to ensure that the governmental departments clearly define the objectives of the awarded projects and check whether these have been fulfilled. In this manner, the completion of an SBRI project would become a quality label for SBRI participants to show to future investors and customers.[25]

Regarding the organisational structure of the SBRI scheme, the report suggested to grant a central administrative role to the Innovate UK (at that time called Technology Strategy Board), an agency of the UK's Trade Ministry similar to the Small Business Administration in the US. Innovate UK would be made responsible for publicizing twice a year a list of up-coming SBRI calls and their technological areas. Innovate UK would also be responsible for the administration of the award procedure, while the evaluation of the SBRI proposals would be performed jointly with the awarding department(s).[26] Finally, Lord Sainsbury recommended to decrease the percentage of the extramural R&D funds to be invested in SBRI competitions to 1.5 % and to progressively increase it to 2 and 2.5 % in the subsequent two years.[27]

Based on these recommendations an adapted SBRI program was implemented in April 2009, following an initial pilot in 2008.[28] Since 2008, the program has been increasingly used by government departments.[29] By 2010, 28 SBRI calls had been published and 1030 offers had been received, while a total of 373 contracts had been awarded. 283 of these were Phase 1 contracts and 90 were Phase 2 contracts. The 373 contracts were concluded with 283 suppliers, which indicates that some suppliers won contracts in more than one SBRI competition. The value of the contracts amounted to a total of £24 million. Of that amount, 74 % went to SMEs, the remainder to large companies.[30]

---

[24] Turville 2007, 12.

[25] Turville 2007, 131.

[26] Turville 2007, 131.

[27] Ibid.

[28] Bound and Puttick 2010, 3.

[29] Use has increased in terms of budgets, number of calls, number of applications and number of awards. See MIoIR 2015, 43.

[30] Holland 2009, 10.

Since 2010, a surge in the number of SBRI competitions can be observed. The total number of published calls by August 2012 was close to one hundred.[31]

(b) *Objectives*

The program's objectives are: (1) to spur the development of innovative solutions for policy/operational needs of Government departments; and (2) to support technological development by firms. The program is explicitly open to support for innovative technologies for private users, whenever justified by a public objective.[32]

(c) *Non-mandatory participation*

Between 2008 and 2014, 17 departments in total have participated in the SBRI scheme.[33] Each department defines its innovation challenges in Innovation Procurement Plans. The declared aim is to define the challenges in a manner that attracts sufficient bidders and that leaves room for the most innovative proposals.[34]

Participation in the SBRI and budget set-asides are currently voluntary. Innovate UK regularly organises workshops to encourage the implementation of SBRI competitions by explaining its functioning and benefits for the policy objectives of the different departments. In 2011, £20 m were set aside by the Department of Health for SBRI competitions. Innovate UK reserved in its turn £10 m for co-funding participation by 7 other public bodies such as the Welsh Government, WRAP (working together for a world without waste), NHS London, NHS Midlands and East, the National Centre for the Refinement, Reduction and Replacement of Animals in Health (NC3Rs), the Ministry of Defence and the Department for Environment, Food and Rural Affairs.[35]

As of mid-2014, SBRI spending exceeded £200 million, calculated from 2008.[36] The largest budgets dedicated to SBRI between 2008 and 2014 came from Innovate UK (28 %) Department of Health (DH) and the National Health Service (NHS) (21 %), the Ministry of Defense (20 %) the Department for Energy and Climate Change (DECC) (14 %).

(d) *Decentralised implementation*

In line with the US example, Innovate UK was attributed coordination and support roles similar to those of the US Small Business Administration. Innovate UK

---

[31] See http://www.innovateuk.org/deliveringinnovation/smallbusinessresearchinitiative/competitions.ashx Accessed 4 September 2012.

[32] MIoIR et al. 2015, 24.

[33] MIoIR 2015, 31.

[34] The co-financing is meant to incentivise these departments to employ their own R&D funds in SBRI competitions. Holland 2009, 8.

[35] TSB 2012, 20.

[36] MIoIR et al. 2015, 5.

provides operational support in, for example, defining the SBRI challenge, administering the procurement, finding expert evaluators for SBRI bids, or funding the competition etc.[37]

Innovate UK checks the challenges proposed by the various departments and selects those that are truly suitable to be addressed through an SBRI competition. This non-mandatory advice is in practice followed by the involved departments.[38]

Independent from the SBRI scheme coordinated by Innovate UK, other PCP-like initiatives have been implemented since 2006 by the Department of Health's National Innovation Centre (NHS) and the Energy Technologies Institute (set up in 2006 as a private company by global energy companies and the UK Government). They follow the same approach as Innovate UK, but independently implement the whole SBRI process. Interesting to remark is the requirement that the NHS introduced for applicants from other Member States than UK, namely to present proof that the developed products would (also) be commercialized on the UK market.[39]

(e) *Eligibility criteria*

The UK scheme remains open to small and large businesses. However, since its inception and up to 2011, approximately 41 % of the total SBRI budget went to small firms with fewer than 10 employees, while large firms with more than 250 employees accessed around 30 % of the SBRI budget.[40] Besides small and emerging businesses, academia and charities are eligible for participation, provided they demonstrate access to a route to market for the developed solutions.[41]

It is not clear how compliance with the minimum requirement that only R&D service contracts are eligible for funding through the SBIR is ensured. No market consultation in relation to each SBRI competition is organized. However, the Innovate UK regularly launches Innovation Platforms ('IPs') with the aim to identify the range of technologies that can provide solutions to societal challenges in various areas. These IPs are also used to identify the range of policies and regulatory actions needed to bring the novel technologies to the (global) market. Therefore, thorough market research and economic/business research studies are performed.

The market research engages relevant stakeholders (such as businesses, academics, government agencies) in an effort to identify the available technologies and the relevant ongoing R&D projects (a technology roadmap). The commissioned studies are meant to outline which (combination of) policies and legislations can ensure the large-scale deployment of the novel products and which

---

[37] Technopolis 2010, 32. SBRI Review 2014, 26.

[38] MIoIR et al. 2015, 27.

[39] My research does not separately investigate this initiative, due to the fact that the same approach is followed as the SBRI as well as due to the limited amount of information available. FAQ Department of Health 2012.

[40] MIoIR 2015, 6.

[41] TSB 2011, 2.

changes in the system (for example in the health care system) are required by the new solutions. Moreover, studies may be commissioned to identify the expectations of the end-users and their perception of the novel solutions (for example the openness of end-users to acquire the new skills to use the new technologies; the privacy objections etc.).[42] However, as already mentioned, the IPs do not cover all the areas in which SBRI competitions are organized and do not seem to be directly linked to the SBRI competitions.[43] In addition, the market research is performed at national level.[44]

(f) *Phases*

In line with the US SBIR, the amount of funding per call has been increased to between £50 and £100 k for Phase 1, and between £250 k and £1 m for Phase 2, but deviations from these indicative amounts is possible. The phase length for both Phase 1 (6 months) and Phase 2 (2 years) is also flexible.[45] However, the award of multiple sequential Phase 2 contracts to the same company is not envisaged. This entails that tolerance to early failure is not expressly embedded in the programme and that closer to market projects may be favoured.

Commercialization following the completion of Phase 2 is up to the SBRI finalist company. The government does not guarantee the purchase of the developed novel products.[46] The UK SBRI follows in this respect the PCP guidance and differs from the US SBIR.

(g) *Percentage of funded R&D costs*

Following the US SBIR approach, both Phase 1 and Phase 2 of the SBRI provide 100 % of the feasibility and prototyping costs.[47] As already mentioned in the overview of the NL SBIR, this approach disregarded the PCP guidance.

(h) *IPR arrangements and award criteria*

IPR arrangements are described in very broad terms (the R&D service provider retains the Intellectual property),[48] while generic award criteria on this issue are not published.

---

[42] More information can be found at http://www.innovateuk.org/ourstrategy/innovationplatforms/assistedliving/assisted-living-innovation-platform.ashx Accessed 4 September 2012.

[43] There are currently six innovation platforms: low carbon vehicles—established 2007; assisted living—established 2007; low impact buildings—established 2008; detection and identification of infectious agents—established 2008; sustainable agriculture and food—established 2009; stratified medicine—established 2010. See TSB 2012, 21.

[44] See for example the Assissted Living Roadmap exercise of 8 January 2007: https://connect.innovateuk.org/c/document_library/get_file?p_l_id=145400&folderId=609151&name=DLFE-4588.pdf.

[45] MIoIR et al. 2015, 27.

[46] TSB 2011, 3.

[47] TSB 2011, 4.

[48] TSB 2011, 3.

6.3.3 SBRI Evaluations

2010 Evaluations

Two reports by Pro Inno Europe and Nesta have evaluated the intermediate results of the program, following its re-launch in 2008–2009.[49]

The report by Pro Inno Europe showed that both the participating departments and the participating businesses were positive about the functioning and the results of the new program. Government departments considered that the program enabled them to access innovative ideas and new suppliers. Participating companies pointed out several advantages:

- SBRI offered the opportunity to closely collaborate with potential future customers;
- SBRI provided funding for projects that could not find private investors, while matching funding were not required;
- participation in the SBRI functioned as a certification of quality, enabling future acquisition of venture capital.[50]

The Pro Inno report further listed the main strengths of the scheme: flexibility in the support level provided by Innovate UK during the SBRI competition; short evaluation times and simple procedures; broad involvement of the funding agency with the innovation project compared to subsidies.[51]

The report also mentioned a few downsides: a low number of participating departments; relative high costs of conducting the scheme; the lack of a market consultation that precedes the definition of the SBRI challenge; the support gap at Phase III[52]; the lack of budget continuity (no central budget for SBRI is available, while the R&D budgets of the individual departments may suffer cuts in times of economic downturn).[53]

The Pro Inno report concluded that the SBRI program would benefit from increased political support and from improved knowledge of the benefits and risks of the scheme. Interestingly, the Pro Inno Europe Report pointed out that there was moderate support among stakeholders for addressing shared European needs through the set-up of a similar program by the EU (as funding agency). According to the report, such a program would have the advantage of avoiding the criticism that national public funds are spent without immediate visible results.[54]

The second mid-term assessment, performed at Nesta in 2010, reached similar positive conclusions. Based on interviews with SBRI participants and on the

---

49 Holland 2009, Bound and Puttick 2010.

50 Holland 2009, 10.

51 Holland 2009, 12.

52 The reports recommends SBRI staff to encourage procurers to purchase the results of SBRI projects.

53 Holland 2009, 13.

54 Ibid.

analysis of 10 of the 28 SBRI competitions launched between 2008 and 2010, the report concluded that SBRI provides much needed funding in a challenging financial climate. By acting as 'lead demonstrator', the government strengthens the credibility of participating companies and increases their prospects to access private investments.[55] When deployed on a sufficiently large scale, the program creates and boosts market opportunities for participating firms.[56]

In line with the previous mid-term evaluation, the evaluation performed at Nesta praised the decentralized implementation of the program as well as its procedural flexibility (allowing adaptation of the SBRI to the needs of each participating department)[57] and deplored the lack of support after the firms exit the SBRI program (e.g. subsequent commercial procurement of the developed innovations). It also advocated the need to enable regular impact assessments and to widely expose success stories with other public departments.[58]

Unlike the Pro Inno report, Nesta's Report concluded that voluntary participation supported by (financial) incentives from Innovate UK may potentially be more effective than mandatory participation. According to Nesta, this would reduce the risk that contracting authorities fund SBRI competitions just for the sake of complying with mandatory spending thresholds.

2015 Evaluation

The evaluation performed in 2015 concludes that the SBRI is '*sound in concept and effective in practice*' and recommends its continuation.[59] However, the evaluation report points out that a comprehensive impact assessment is hindered by poor data collection from the involved departments.[60] The first major recommendation is therefore, to create a unified database of participants and projects funded under the program.

Based on responses from surveyed firms (covering SBRI competitions during 2011 and 2012), the evaluation finds evidence that SBRI encourages firms to conceptualize their ideas and to engage in development of innovative solutions that would otherwise not materialize. Over 50 % of the firms indicate they would not have proceeded with the project in the absence of the SBRI award, while 39 % would have reduced the scale or would have delayed the project in the absence of the SBRI award.[61]

---

[55] Bound and Puttick 2010, 15–7.

[56] Bound and Puttick 2010, 15.

[57] Bound and Puttick 2010, 15–7, 20.

[58] Bound and Puttick 2010, 20.

[59] MIoIR et al. 2015, 7–8. See NRC's conclusion regarding the working of the US SBIR in Chap. 4. Arguably, the Brexit does not affect the continuation of the UK SBRI. In practice, continuing trade with the EU on preferential terms (e.g. similar to the signatories of the European Free Trade Agreement), will most probably entail adherence to the EU procurement rules.

[60] MIoIR et al. 2015, 7.

[61] MIoIR et al. 2015, 11.

Firms indicate that the prospect of demand and the opportunity to engage in early-stage discussions with potential customers are key features of the SBRI program.[62] The evaluation also finds evidence of other positive impacts, such as increase in the number of employees and increase in sales.[63] Based on a comparison of SBRI winners with matching firms that did not apply for an SBRI award, the evaluation reports an increase of 12.7 % in sales for the participating firms.

However, the evaluation points out that particularly micro and small firms continue to encounter difficulties in accessing private finance after finalizing the SBRI contract. A solution to this, according to the evaluation report, is to make SBRI beneficiaries aware of any subsequent funding sources upon leaving the SBRI program.[64]

Despite the documented increase in use, a major weakness of the SBRI remains the lack of routine deployment. The evaluation shows that the main difficulty for some of the involved departments is to define suitable challenges and to attribute responsibilities to meet SBRI targets. These difficulties are not present within the NHD/DH and Defense, where SBRI is being strategically used in a systematic way. The evaluation report recommends trainings to develop these capabilities within the involved departments.[65] The evaluation concludes that departments that have been designated targets, use the SBRI program more than department for which a target is not in place. However, the rate of use is still below the targets.[66]

The evaluation report also shows that 65 of the 195 analysed competitions targeted catalytic SBRI, while 130 addressed operational need of the public end-user (direct SBRI calls). Among the implementing Departments the Ministry of Defense deployed by far the most direct SBRI calls (78 of the 130). The report also shows that the direct procurements attracted more applications than catalytic ones.[67] But only 18 % of the total number of successful applications came from non-UK firms.[68]

Certain is that the UK SBRI is being continued and even scaled up. Before the start of the evaluation study, the Government announced that the SBRI would be significantly expended from around £100 m in 2013–2014 to over £200 in 2014–2015. The new targets represent 0.5 % of procurement budgets.[69]

In conclusion, the recent assessment of the UK SBRI, reveals that the program generates positive impacts in terms of company growth and additional private R&D investments, but warns that systematic data collection should be encouraged

62 MIoIR et al. 2015, 8.

63 Ibid., 8–9.

64 MIoIR et al. 2015, 10.

65 MIoIR et al. 2015, 9–10, 74–5.

66 Six departments are assigned targets concerning shares of budget being dedicated to SBRI competitions. MIoIR et al. 2015, 7, 31.

67 MIoIR et al. 2015, 44–6.

68 MIoIR et al. 2015, 48.

69 MIoIR et al. 2015, 63.

in order to facilitate more accurate assessments. The assessment study concludes that the UK SBRI is not being routinely deployed and that trainings and implementation targets have a positive contribution to this end. Finally, the assessment study reveals that a small share of participating companies comes from outside the UK and that approximately 1/3 of the projects are catalytic. Government departments with stringent needs to use the developed innovations (such as NHS and Department of Defense) deploy most of the direct SBRI competitions and attract the more competitors. Their SBRI deployment is also the most systematic.

6.3.4 Projects

In this section, I discuss some characteristics of the SBRI programme, based on a documentary analysis of 27 SBRI calls published on Innovate UK's website between October 2012 and December 2013. I analyse the calls against the following criteria: (1) the existence of a public end-customer, (2) targeting technological innovations, (3) targeting high-risk or uncertain R&D. I have chosen these 3 criteria from the list of criteria in Chap. 3, based on their relevance for the type of information available in the SBRI calls.

My first observation is that most SBRI calls regard the development of innovative solutions for concrete operational needs of the participating public agencies. 19 of the 27 analysed calls were funded by a public agency who could potentially act as end-customer of the targeted innovation. Also interesting to mention is that 13 of these 19 direct PCPs were funded by research agencies of the Department of Defense.

My second observation is that the SBRI program focuses predominantly on technological innovations. 21 of the 27 calls target exclusively the development of technological innovations. In 5 other calls it appears that services innovations are also accepted. Only 1 calls targets exclusively service innovations.

My third observation is that a large share of the calls expressly target high-risk innovations. Thus, 11 of the 13 calls published by Department of Defense stress that submitted proposals should target high-risk R&D and should aim to develop disruptive innovations. Only 2 calls provide indication that late stage technologies are preferred: one requires the delivery of a prototype within one year[70]; another call requires new applications of existing technologies.[71]

[70] See 'Innovation design for future climate resilience in the infrastructure and built environment sectors', available at https://www.innovateuk.org/competition-display-page/-/asset_publisher/RqEt2AKmEBhi/content/innovative-design-for-future-climate-resilience-in-the-infrastructure-and-built-environment-sectors?p_p_auth=KwurO9n8 Accessed 14 January 2014.

[71] See 'land vehicles exercise', available at https://www.innovateuk.org/competition-display-page/-/asset_publisher/RqEt2AKmEBhi/content/land-vehicle-exercise-lvex-2013?p_p_auth=KwurO9n8 Accessed 14 January 2014.

6.3.5 Conclusions

Since 2008, the UK SBRI has been brought more in line with the philosophy and operational make-up of the US SBIR. Hereunder, I summarize whether the UK SBRI presents prerequisites for effectiveness, as identified in Chap. 3.

1. Include a large number of high-risk R&D projects.
   The documentary analysis of the SBRI calls provided indications that only a small share of the competitions, launched by the Department of Defense, target high risk R&D.
2. Target young companies, that experience difficulties in obtaining (sufficient amounts of) private capital
   The UK SBRI program targets both large and small companies. However, statistics show that by 2011, a large share of the total SBRI budget (41%) had been awarded to small firms with fewer than 10 employees. Moreover, the payment of 100% of the R&D costs, while no matching funds are required, provides an additional incentive to small companies to participate in SBRI competitions with their riskiest/most uncertain R&D projects.
3. Budgets are increased in times of economic downturn.
   The targets for investments in UK SBRI competitions have been steadily increased up to over £200 in 2014–2015.
4. Choose topics based on a careful consideration of technological trajectories and market trends.
   It is unclear whether choice of SBRI projects is preceded by a thorough scrutiny of the technologies already available on the market. Innovate UK regularly performs extended analyses of the stage of development of alternative technologies, market structure and end-users' preferences. However, they are not performed in direct relation with the SBRI scheme and are not performed in all areas where SBRI projects are published. This entails the risk that close-to-market technologies are funded instead of early stage R&D.
5. Managers in charge of PCP deployment possess or gain in-depth knowledge of the relevant technological area.
   It is unclear whether SBRI managers possess in-depth technological knowledge. In combination with the lack of a proper market analysis, this may constitute a significant pitfall of the program.
6. Failure is tolerated to a certain extent.
   The UK SBRI does not expressly provide incentives for the project officers to adopt highly experimental and failure tolerant attitudes. Although the amount of funding per Phase is at the same levels as in the US, the possibility to deviate from the maximum values is not provided. Neither is the possibility to award multiple sequential Phase 2 awards to promising projects that have not successfully accomplished the prototyping phase in the first SBRI call.
7. The public purchaser is closely involved.
   Implementation of the SBRI program is decentralized and approaches the US SBIR in this respect. Innovate UK provides different degrees of support, but

SBRI award and contract management is generally performed by the funding agency. Nevertheless, a large share (above 30% of catalytic competitions) of the program does not involve the end-user.

8. The public purchaser is willing to pay the premium price for the early use of the developed innovation and is capable to offer a sufficiently sizeable market for the developed innovation.
   Conform the PCP guidance, the UK SBRI does not ensure purchase of the developed solutions. Although in the UK there is experience with the Forward Commitment Procurement ('FCP', see Chap. 1, Sect. 5.6.4), which can guarantee an end-customer of the developed products, FCP has so far been piloted without any link to SBRI or Innovate UK.[72]
9. Challenge and reward the most innovative companies, instead of shielding inefficient companies from foreign competition.
   Although EU-wide competition is foreseen in the UK SBRI, restricted access to the procurement documentation sheds some doubts regarding compliance with this requirement. In addition, the market scrutiny performed by Innovate UK under the name of Innovation Platforms does not seem to be directly linked to the SBRI competitions and are national in scope. These aspects entail the risk that the SBRI competitions tend to protect national companies from EU and international competition instead of driving them to advance the international state-of-the-art and gain competitive advantages on global markets.
10. Innovative technologies rather than innovative services are targeted.
    Based on the documentary analysis in the previous section, I can conclude that the UK SBRI predominantly targets technological innovation.
11. A continuous scrutiny/measurement of the impact of PCP is performed and lessons learnt are codified in guidance.

    The UK SBRI has regularly been assessed and as a consequence thereof, important changes have been included into the program. However, the latest assessment pointed out that systematic and consistent data collection should be enabled.

In conclusion, the UK SBRI has improved its approach and has scaled up deployment in recent years. However, the program still embed weaknesses, such as insufficient investigation of technological state-of-the-art, insufficient involvement of public end-users, no uptake of the developed innovation, inconsistent data collection.

[72] FCP entails a competitive award under the scope of the Procurement Directives and does not guarantee the purchase of the products developed during the SBRI project. See BIS 2011.

6.4 The Dutch SBIR

6.4.1 Background to Adoption

In the Netherlands, a Small Business Innovation Research (SBIR) program was started in 2004. Initially, the scheme was not considered to be a procurement instrument, but a form of subsidy.[73] SBIR was considered to give more effective support than the existent subsidy schemes, due to its competitive element and due to the envisaged presence of a demanding customer.[74] Later, the legal justification of the scheme became Article 16(f) of Directive 2004/18 and SBIR became a public procurement instrument.[75] Nevertheless, it is still sometimes being labelled as a subsidy on government websites.[76]

Its declared objectives were (1) to identify innovative solutions to societal challenges and (2) to support innovative SMEs.[77] The justification for government intervention through SBIR was found in the difficulties that SMEs encounter when looking for private financing of the first phases of innovative projects. It was also submitted that the private market provided insufficient stimuli for the creation of innovative solutions for societal challenges.[78]

The particular focus on support for SMEs was in line with the rationale of the US SBIR. Following a review by the European Commission though, the Dutch SBIR was modified to allow both small and large companies to participate. In addition, the eligibility condition for the company to reside on the territory of the Netherlands was dropped.[79] Yet, in practice, the scheme proved to be particularly attractive to small and medium sized, mainly Dutch businesses.[80] Statistics show that between 2004 and 2010, less than 10 % of the 252 contracts at phase 1 (Fig. 6.1) and 89 at Phase 2 (Fig. 6.2) were awarded to large companies.[81]

The SBIR scheme was from the beginning divided into two parts: one departmental SBIR run by the NL Agency (Agentschap NL), an innovation agency of the Ministry of Economic Affairs and one run by the Dutch Organisation for Applied Sciences (TNO). The purpose of the second SBIR scheme is primarily to fund

[73] Minister-president 2004.

[74] It was also proposed to complement the SBIR with financial support to private investors of risk capital. Sociaal Economische Raad 2003, 76.

[75] NL Agency 2011.

[76] See for example http://www.answersforbusiness.nl/subsidy/small-business-innovation-research Accessed 20 July 2016.

[77] NL Agency 2011, 3.

[78] Technopolis 2010, 23–4.

[79] Technopolis 2010, 21.

[80] The SBIR scheme is labeled as supportive to Dutch SMEs. NL Agency 2011.

[81] Technopolis 2010, 27.

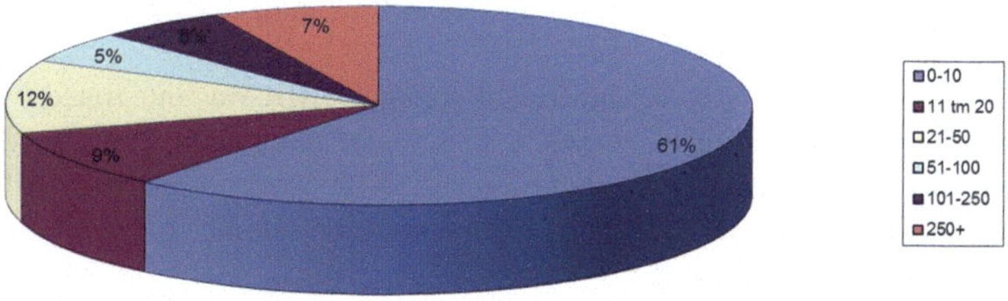

Fig. 6.1 *Source* NL Agency

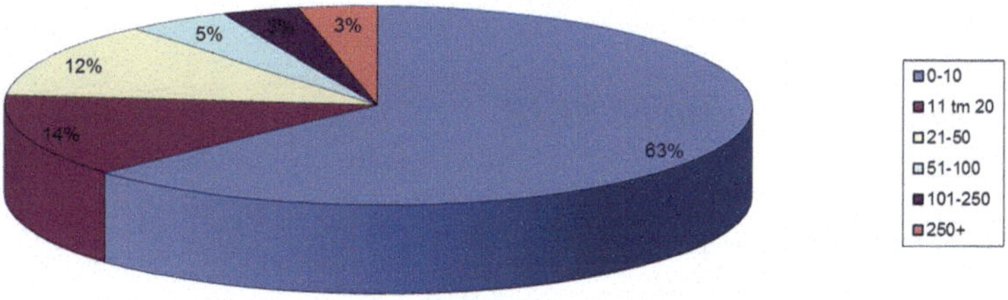

Fig. 6.2 *Source* NL Agency

companies that are willing to commercialise product ideas of TNO.[82] Only the departmental SBIR forms the subject of the analysis in this section as it comes closer to the PCP model.[83]

The departmental SBIR scheme was set-up as a centralised scheme. NL Agency was put in charge of running it for different government departments (ministries). It was not set-up through legislation and there is no official document introducing the SBIR program, besides guidance on how to launch an SBIR competition in accordance with the existing legal framework.[84] This scheme started in 2004 with a first pilot project run by the Ministry of Economic Affairs.[85] In 2005, following the positive assessment of the pilot, SBIR was given green light for broad implementation. At the end of 2008, NL Agency set up an SBIR program office. In the same year, the scheme was taken outside of the Ministry of Economic Affairs and brought under the responsibility of an interdepartmental

[82] Ernst&Young 2011, 14.

[83] Technopolis 2010, 27, 89.

[84] Technopolis 2010, 21.

[85] Minister-president 2004, 4.

entity, named Knowledge and Innovation (Kennis en Innovatie), but continued to be run by NL Agency.

As a consequence of this organizational change, SBIR was integrated by government departments (ministries) into their Societal Innovation Agenda (MIA)[86] budgets. This enables them to regularly launch SBIR competitions.[87] In 2010, six departments were using the SBIR instrument and the number of SBIR calls for proposals was on a rising curve.[88]

In February 2010 the Dutch SBIR scheme was evaluated. Out of the total of 28 projects awarded by then, only the first pilot project (of 2004) was finalised. By that time, the Dutch SBIR had spent €71.5 million.[89]

6.4.2 Features of the Dutch SBIR

(a) *Non-mandatory participation*

Unlike in the US, the implementation of SBIR projects by contracting authorities in the Netherlands is not expressed in legislation. The Societal Innovation Agendas of several Dutch ministries include now references to the SBIR instrument. This provides justification for funding SBIR contracts, but does not mandate them to participate in the SBIR program and to reserve budgets therefore. The evaluation performed by Technopolis in 2010 shows that some ministries had not deployed yet the SBIR instrument.[90]

(b) *Centralised implementation*

The participating ministries are, only marginally involved in the SBIR competition they decide to fund. Unlike in the US SBIR, the funding agencies only dictate the broad topic, while the NL Agency runs the SBIR competition, signs and subsequently monitors the contract execution. NL Agency may also propose a topic to a specific ministry. In both cases, NL Agency provides the ministry extensive support in defining the concrete call requirements.[91] The projects deployed in the first half of 2016 suggest though a closer involvement of public authorities other than

---

[86] Maatschappelijke Innovatie Agenda's.

[87] Technopolis 2010, 42.

[88] Technopolis 2010, 32.

[89] Technopolis 2010, ix.

[90] Technopolis 2010, 30–1.

[91] Technopolis 2010, 34.

ministries, who have concrete operational needs and who can potentially act as early adopters of the developed innovations.

Another difference with the US SBIR constitutes the coordination of the SBIR competition by NL Agency project officers who do not possess in-depth technical expertise on the respective topic.[92]

(c) *Eligibility criteria*

Unlike the US SBIR, but in line with EU prescripts, both large and small companies are allowed to submit offers in NL SBIR calls.[93] Moreover, eligibility is not conditioned as in the US upon ownership or control by EU citizens. Only performance of the R&D within an EU Member State is required. This means that non-EU owned companies may win NL SBIR contracts.

In addition, only proposals for R&D activities are eligible. According to the 2015 SBIR Guide,[94] the following R&D activities may be funded under the SBIR scheme:

- Experimental or theoretical activities which are conducted in order to accumulate new knowledge;
- Planned or critical research which is intended to accumulate new knowledge and capabilities which are necessary for developing new products, processes or services, or to improve substantially existing products, processes or services;
- Acquiring, combining, designing and using existing scientific, technical, business or other relevant knowledge and capabilities for plans, schemes or design of new, modified or improved products, processes or services;
- Making designs, drawings, plans and other documentation, provided that these are not intended for commercial use;
- Developing commercially useful prototypes and pilots, if the prototype is the commercial end-product and the production of such a prototype is too expensive to use it just for demonstration and validation purposes;
- The experimental development and testing of products, processes and services, for so far as these cannot be used or be adjusted for industrial use or for commercial exploitation;
- The production of a limited 0-serie: limited production or supply in order to incorporate the results of field testing and to demonstrate that the product or service is suitable for mass production or supply to acceptable quality standards;

---

[92] None of the 7 employees of the SBIR office of NL Agency has strong technical background. Moreover, they are not full-time engaged in deploying the SBIR programme. See Technopolis 2010, 33.

[93] Also institutes, corporations are currently allowed to participate if they can convincingly demonstrate that they are capable to commercialize the products. Rijksdienst voor Ondernemend Nederland 2015, 5.

[94] Rijksdienst voor Ondernemend Nederland 2015, 5.

The following activities do not, according to the SBIR guide, fall under the concept of R&D:

- Routine or periodical modification of existing products, production lines, manufacturing processes, services and other normal activities, even if these modifications may regard improvements;
- Prototypes whose commercial readiness has already been tested;
- Commercial development such as serial production, delivery intended to achieve commercial viability or to recover R&D costs, integration, customization, incremental modifications and improvements of existing products or processes.

The R&D definitions are generally in line with the Frascati Manual. It is difficult to establish how the R&D definitions work in practice by studying the general description of the NL SBIR awarded projects.[95] There may, however, be serious gaps between the law in the book and the law in action here.

It appears, for instance, that no market consultation or market analysis is undertaken preceding a NL SBIR call. It also appears that no attention is paid to whether the contract can be qualified as an R&D service contract, or otherwise an R&D works (e.g. construction of prototypes) or R&D supplies contract (e.g. prototypes).[96]

As a consequence, it may happen that the desired functionality is available on the market or that the contract involves marginal innovation and cannot qualify as R&D service contract.

(d) *Phases*

Following the US model, the Dutch SBIR scheme provides funding at two stages, namely the feasibility stage, which investigates the viability of the idea, and the development stage, which covers the full R&D effort and the development of a prototype or proof-of-concept/demonstration. Phase 1 is funded with €20,000–€50,000 and may take up to 6 months. Phase 2 is funded with €150,000–€500,000 and may take up to 2 years.[97] It is not expressly allowed to deviate from the maximum amounts or time-limits, but this happens in practice.

The Dutch scheme provides considerably lower amounts of funding than its US counterpart.[98] Moreover, the timeline for Phase 2 is limited compared to both the US SBIR (which does not specify maximum timelines for Phase 2) and to the EU guidance (4–5.5 years for a whole PCP procedure).[99] In addition, the NL SBIR

[95] For a description of 25 SBIR awarded projects see NL Agency 2011.

[96] The R&D service condition was included in the EU procurement legislation in order to discourage funding of innovative products that are very close to commercialization.

[97] Rijksdienst voor Ondernemend Nederland 2015.

[98] The EU PCP does not prescribe specific amounts of funding.

[99] Phase 2 of the NL SBIR covers the activities of both Phase 2 and 3 of a PCP as described in the PCP Communication.

does not explicitly allow multiple sequential Phase 2 awards to the same company. This indicates that tolerance to early failure is not sufficiently embedded in the program.

Subsequent commercialisation (after Phase 2) is not financially supported as part of the Dutch SBIR, but the NL Agency engages in alternative support activities: spreads information on the project, organizes visits from ministries to the project and organizes workshops in which companies present their developed products.[100] Contrary to the US SBIR, and in accordance with the EU rules, the NL SBIR does not allow direct purchase of the developed innovations by the funding agency. Instead, a separate procurement procedure needs to be organized. This has been identified by the Dutch Department of Defence as a disincentive to launching SBIR competitions.[101]

(e) *Percentage of funded R&D costs*

Initially, the NL SBIR followed the US model and funded 100 % of the R&D costs.[102] Following an early check by the European Commission, this requirement was amended. The NL SBIR currently requires bidders to offer a discount for retaining the ownership of the developed innovative product.[103] This was in line with the PCP Communication requirement to ensure that a market price is paid and no State aid is granted. At the same time, this deviated from the practice within the US SBIR program, where 100 % of the R&D costs and a small profit are covered.

In practice though, compliance with the market price requirement within the NL SBIR competitions is not effectively enforced.[104] It is not clear whether the evaluation commission covers suitable expertise to check compliance with this requirement. Moreover, participating companies perceive that they receive 100 % of the R&D costs.[105] This supports the conclusion that the market price criterion is no more than a formality. The NL SBIR hasn't availed itself of the possibility to drop the market price altogether, as allowed by the 2014 Framework for State aid for R&D&I. Further discussion on this issue can be found in Chap. 7.

(f) *IPR arrangements*

The IPR arrangements within the Dutch SBIR for both Phase 1 and 2 are in line with the recommendations made by the European Commission in the PCP Communication, as well as with the US SBIR. IP ownership remains with the SBIR participant, while the government retains a royalty-free license to use the

100 Ibid., 35.

101 Technopolis 2010, 30–1.

102 Corbett 2006 'Juridisch kader voor SBIR' slide 2.

103 Rijksdienst voor Ondernemend Nederland 2015, 5.

104 The guidance for implementation of SBIR does not mention any obligation for the award commission to check whether the reduction indicated in the SBIR bids corresponds to market realities.

105 Technopolis 2010, 89.

results. It also obtains the following rights: to disseminate the results, to make the knowledge public when justified by the public interest, and to mandate the supplier to provide licenses to third parties under reasonable conditions.[106] Unlike in the US, however, the provisions are drafted in very general terms and no enforcing mechanisms are specified.

(g) *Award criteria*

The bids are evaluated against the following general criteria, which may be further specified on a case-by-case basis[107]:

- Impact:
  - Potential of solving the societal problem which is the subject of the NL SBIR call
  - Degree of innovativeness (originality and inventiveness of the proposed solution);
  - Quality of the proposal (is the impact description supported by convincing argument?)
  - Practical value for the users;
  - Value for money (weighing the value of the proposed solution against the bid price);
- Technological feasibility:
  - Is the proposed approach feasible, promising and inventive?
  - Does the party have the suitable capabilities to develop the technology?
  - Quality of the technical bid:
    Clear description of state-of-the-art;
    Clear description of planned R&D activities;
    Suitable approach and means to achieve the proposed results;
    Clear description of the approach.
- Economic perspective:
  - Are there convincing arguments to believe that the product will be commercialised?
  - is the company/consortium capable to bring the product to the market?
  - are steps towards commercialisation clearly described?

The award criteria are improved comparing to the initial SBIR Guide of 2011. 2 award criteria lay a strong accent on the innovativeness and quality of the proposal, while 1 assesses the potential for commercialisation. This enables truly innovative proposals to get access to SBIR contracts. As a downside, one of the award criteria unnecessarily penalizes bidders who focus on the development of the solution and are not interested in commercializing it themselves, but may grant licenses to other parties to this end.

[106] Rijksdienst voor Ondernemend Nederland 2015, 8.

[107] Rijksdienst voor Ondernemend Nederland 2015, 6.

6.4.3 Evaluation

In March 2010, Technopolis performed the first evaluation of the Dutch SBIR scheme, based on the analysis of the SBIR calls, literature, interviews and surveys.[108] The evaluation does not cover an impact assessment, but only input and process aspects. In this section, I summarize its findings.

According to Technopolis, the SBIR program provides the participating departments relatively quickly with multiple innovative solutions.[109] Participating companies are also positive. They consider that the SBIR awards accelerate access to the market by enhancing the trust of public and private clients in their innovative products. They also point out that participation in the SBIR program enables them to get valuable insights into the technical feasibility of the developed product as well as into the competitive strengths of their innovative ideas/solution compared to other ideas/solutions on the market.[110]

In addition, the participating companies indicate that the provision of 100 % funding of the phases[111] were the key reasons to participate in the SBIR competitions.[112] The SBIR awards were considered crucial for stimulating the development of the products, which would otherwise not be funded by the company itself or by external private investors. The participating companies expect that the received SBIR awards will positively impact their turnover and growth.[113]

Surveryede companies are less positive regarding the role of the participating government agencies in purchasing the developed products.[114] They point out that the SBIR competitions do not reflect actual purchasing needs of the involved public departments, and as a consequence, procurers are not involved.[115]

Public departments that seek to satisfy their operational needs through SBIR competition, such as the Dutch Department of Defence, express discontent with the requirement for a separate procurement procedure for the purchase of the developed innovations.[116]

According to the evaluation report, NL Agency planned to address this weakness, by encouraging government agencies to engage in commercial procurements of innovations).[117] Other support measures such as regulation, certification,

---

[108] Ibid.

[109] Technopolis 2010, viii.

[110] Technopolis 2010, 26.

[111] In the evaluation this phrase is understood as meaning that no external funding is required. At Phase 2, the availability of external funds is considered a plus for the award of the contract.

[112] Technopolis 2010, 26.

[113] Technopolis 2010, 41.

[114] Technopolis 2010, 39.

[115] Technopolis 2010, 38.

[116] Technopolis 2010, x, 31.

[117] Technopolis 2010, 27.

standardization or the requirement to pay back the funding of Phase 2 in case of commercial success were also contemplated.[118] The author could not identify information of these initiatives. This suggests that no significant progress has been achieved.

The evaluation subsequently identifies barriers to the deployment of SBIR competitions: the difficulty encountered by public departments when trying to assign R&D funds to SBIR competitions; the inadequate marketing of SBIR as innovation instrument of the Ministry of Economic Affairs; the lack of understanding of this instrument; the lack of incentives to deploy SBIR competitions (such as practical support, mandatory set-asides, enthusiast ambassadors etc.).[119]

Regarding the organizational make-up of the Dutch SBIR, Technopolis concludes that its centralized deployment by the NL Agency presents both advantages and disadvantages. On the one side, experience is gathered and easily spread. On the other side, NL SBIR remains disconnected from the needs and strategic policy agendas of the different participating departments.[120]

Unfortunately, the evaluation does not provide information on the compliance of the SBIR programme with the legal provisions (such as the presence of R&D activities) or on the degree of innovativeness of the selected projects.

Another study concludes that up to 2008, the overall innovation policy implemented by the Dutch government (of which NL SBIR is part of) hasn't triggered significant improvements in the innovative capabilities of Dutch companies. On the contrary, Dutch SMEs have become less innovative between 1998 and 2008, and the percentage of innovative SMEs is considerably lower compared to the EU average.[121] Although this research does not specifically assess the NL SBIR, it suggests though that the NL SBIR, as part of the overall innovation policy, did not achieve a significant positive impact by 2008.

A survey performed by the European Commission in 2010 and a study performed by Izsak and Edler in 2011 confirm that the NL SBIR had been driven by national innovation policy motivations and had not favoured EU-wide competition. In addition, both documents conclude that centralized deployment meant limited involvement of end-users and hindered commercial roll-out of the developed products.[122]

To the knowledge of the author, no impact assessment of the SBIR has been made public in the last 6 years.

In conclusion, the NL SBIR programme has been positively received by participating companies for providing access to needed funding and for providing insights into the technical feasibility of the developed product as well as into the competitive strengths of their envisaged innovations compared to those available

118 Technopolis 2010, xi, 27.

119 Technopolis 2010, 30–1.

120 Technopolis 2010, 38.

121 Stam 2008, 40–1, 340.

122 Commission 2011, 4; Izsak and Edler 2011, 22–3.

on the market. The NL SBIR is mainly criticized for the limited involvement of the end-users and consequently for the lack of support at the commercialisation phase. Participating government agencies with concrete needs (such as the Department of Defence) have criticized the prohibition to purchase the developed innovations without competition.

6.4.4 Projects

This section provides an overview of the main characteristics of NL SBIR funded projects. It is based on a documentary analysis of all 37 SBIR calls for proposals that have been published by NL Agency by January 2014 since its inception, as well as on a documentary analysis of the available summaries of phase 2 projects in 8 of the 37 SBIR competitions. I have analysed these documents against several effectiveness criteria, as identified in Chap. 2: (1) the existence of a public end-customer, (2) targeting technological innovations, (3) targeting high-risk or uncertain R&D. I have chosen these 3 criteria from the list of criteria in Chap. 3, based on their relevance for the type of information available in the SBIR calls.

As I only had access to the calls for proposals, not to the submitted proposals or to the intermediate R&D results, my research is to some extent interpretative. In order to verify some of the conclusions I have conducted individual interviews with two of the NL Agency employees who have been involved in the set-up and implementation of the NL SBIR initiative.[123]

My first and most important observation is that the majority of the NL SBIR calls are catalytic. This means that the NL SBIR competitions do not develop novel solutions for the direct benefit or use by public end-customers. Only 5 of the 37 NL SBIR calls analysed have been conducted for a specific public end-user and another 6 may have both a public and a private end-customer.[124]

My second observation is that the SBIR calls not only cover technical solutions, but also the development of non-technological solutions to societal problems. 21 out of the 37 calls for proposals target service innovations. Such are: the call for new services to ensure longer independent and healthy living for the elderly; the call for solutions to make travelling by train more attractive; the call for solutions to develop and increase landscape quality and to stimulate a sustainable and profitable recreation sector; the call for solutions to reduce the number of kilometers in transporting agricultural products etc.[125] Based on the analysis of the calls, it is

[123] The individual interviews were loosely structured, and consisted exclusively of open-ended questions.

[124] See http://www.agentschapnl.nl/onderwerp/aanbesteden-van-innovaties Accessed 2 February 2013.

[125] See http://www.agentschapnl.nl/onderwerp/aanbesteden-van-innovaties Accessed 2 February 2013.

not possible for me to research and conclude whether the projects were evaluated against the R&D *services* minimum requirements.

My third observation, is that the NL SBIR does not pursue groundbreaking, but merely incremental innovation (e.g. new applications of existing technologies). This observation is based on the analysis of the available descriptions of phase 2 SBIR projects. Illustrative examples are the two Phase 2 projects performed as part of the 2009 SBIR call titled 'Innovatie voor recreatie en ruimte' (Development and conservation of landscape quality together with the development of a sustainable and profitable recreation sector). The first project regards the construction of a forest hut exclusively of sustainable materials, while the second regards placing labels on several prohibition signs in natural habitats and linking them to a webpage that contains the reasons for the adoption of the respective prohibitive measure.[126] Another illustrative example is the outcome of the 2009 SBIR call titled 'Bevorderen en behouden biodiversiteit' (Foster and maintain biodiversity). The innovative solution to avoid destruction of biodiversity when mowing wet grassland, regarded in this case a mowing machine equipped with caterpillars instead of wheels.[127]

Since August 2014, only 8 SBIR competitions have been started, all in the first half of 2016. Another 6 Phase 2 projects were ongoing, meaning that no SBIR projects have been started between August 2014 and April 2016. Arguably, this is partially a consequence of the re-organisation of Agentschap NL at the beginning of 2014, now called Rijksdienst voor Ondernemend Nederland (Netherlands Enterprise Agency or RVO.nl). The SBIRs that have been launched in 2016 are of a lower value than the preceding ones, but involve public end-customers more actively (e.g. these offer testing fields in Phase 2 and assurances to procure the developed solutions).[128]

Despite the positive improvements, the low number of SBIR competitions being launched, shows that SBIR is still not being deployed in a systematic manner by government departments. NL SBIR is not financed from a separate budget, but from the existing R&D budgets of the different governmental departments no(mandatory) targets for dedicated SBIR budgets have been formulated. The implementation of SBIR projects depends on the efforts undertaken by RVO.nl to promote the SBIR scheme. These efforts are not backed by financial means, e.g. to co-finance SBIR competitions, as in the case of Innovate UK.[129] Lacking these incentives, RVO.nl has apparently not identified effective means to convince government departments and/or decentralized public authorities to launch SBIR competitions in a systematic manner.

---

126 See http://www.rvo.nl/subsidies-regelingen/projecten-sbir-innovatie-voor-recreatie-en-ruimte Accessed 15 January 2014.

127 See http://supplymanagementcongress.nl/ Accessed 12 August 2012.

128 See, for example, the SBIRs competition for transport solutions in region Twente, for solutions to reduce discomfort related to public works and for noise reducing solutions along the provincial roads, available at http://www.rvo.nl/subsidies-regelingen/veiligheid-sbir.

129 Technopolis 2010, 43.

6.4.5 Conclusions

The conclusions in this section are mainly based on the analysis of projects initiated up to 2014. The projects initiated in 2016 suggest a change in approach, towards a closer involvement of public end-users with concrete operational needs. It is though not clear whether they reflect a permanent improvement.

By reference to the prerequisites identified in Chapter 2, I draw conclusions concerning the effective implementation of the NL SBIR.

1. Includes a large number of high-risk R&D projects.
   The analysis of the SBIR calls in Sect. 6.4.4 suggests that the NL SBIR program does not target the riskiest/most uncertain R&D projects.
   The analysis in Sect. 6.4.2 also showed that the program does not embed clear safeguards against the risk that close-to-commercialization projects are funded instead of early-stage R&D projects. The Dutch SBIR program does not require an analysis of state-of-the-art in the targeted field. It is also not clear whether compliance with the requirement that 'R&D services' exceeds the value of other activities is checked or enforced.
2. Focus particularly on young companies that experience difficulties in obtaining (sufficient amounts of) private capital.
   The NL SBIR targets both large and small companies, that are in principle equally entitled to participate in SBIR competitions. In practice though, the SBIR contracts prove particularly attractive to small and medium sized firms (as shown in Sect. 6.4.1).
3. Budgets are increased in times of economic downturn.
   The program has not launched any competitions between 2014 and the beginning of 2016, and no targets for dedicated SBIR budgets by procurers have been set.
4. Choose topics based on a careful consideration of technological trajectories and market trends.
   The NL SBIR does not encompass a market analysis or an open consultation of suppliers on the envisaged SBIR topic.
5. Managers in charge of PCP deployment possess or gain in-depth knowledge of the relevant technological area.
   None of the 7 employees of the SBIR office of NL Agency (current RVO.nl) had in 2014 strong technical background and were not full-time engaged in deploying the SBIR program.
6. Failure is tolerated to a certain extent.
   Lower maximum amounts of funding per stage and shorter timelines for the R&D effort are available than within the US SBIR, while no apparent flexibility increase the maximum values. Moreover, the possibility to award multiple, sequential Phase 2 award to the same company for continuing research is not available. This does not incentives the NL SBIR officers to select earlier stage R&D projects that might not deliver immediate results.

Moreover, the program does not appear to benefit of sufficient political support to encourage risk-taking and experimentation. There are no mandatory targets for government agencies to deploy SBIR competitions and RVO.nl does not have any mechanisms to incentivize deployment (e.g. budgets to co-finance competitions, or capabilities to enthusiast public authorities). This puts pressure on RVO.nl to select projects with better prospects of success (e.g. closer to commercialisation) in order to show immediate results.

7. The public purchaser is closely involved.
   The deployment of the Dutch SBIR has been centrally organized by Agency NL (currently RVO.nl), in the name of different ministries. Most often neither Agency NL nor a ministry is the end-user of the developed innovation, and no action is taken to involve end-users into the SBIR project. The projects deployed in 2016 show a closer involvement of public end-users. In 4 of the 8 competitions, they commit to offer a testing site. It is though not clear whether this marks a permanent change in approach or it is only a circumstantial result.
8. The public purchaser is willing to pay the premium price for the early use of the developed innovation and is capable to offer a sufficiently sizeable market for the developed innovation.
   In line with the PCP guidance, the Dutch SBIR does not allow the direct procurement of the innovative outcomes. This is experienced as a disincentive to engage in NL SBIR competitions by public agencies (that want to use NL SBIR competitions to develop innovative solutions for their own operational needs). However, in 1 of the 8 SBIR competitions launched in 2016 the public end-user commits to launching a subsequent procurement.
9. Challenge and reward the most innovative companies, instead of shielding inefficient companies from foreign competition.
   Following alignment with the EU legal rules, the NL SBIR is open to competition from EU companies. In practice though, the requirement of using the Dutch language[130] during the whole SBIR process functions as a powerful de facto barrier to participation by firms from other EU countries. In combination with the absence of a serious investigation of state-of-the-art in the relevant field, this leads to a factual protection of national companies from European and international competition.
10. Innovative technologies rather than innovative services are targeted.
   The documentary analysis in Sect. 6.4.4 showed that the large majority of launched calls targeted the development of innovative services, without any relation to technologies.
11. A continuous scrutiny/measurement of the impact of PCP is performed and lessons learnt are codified in guidance.
   The Dutch SBIR went through an early qualitative assessment. Six years further down the road, no other impact assessment has been performed. Moreover, the only assessment performed in 2010 did not trigger any noticeable changes in guidance or in practice.

[130] Rijksdienst voor Ondernemend Nederland 2015, 4.

In conclusion, the Dutch SBIR program has so far been mainly grounded in an innovation policy mindset which is subsidy-like and national in scope. Partly due to the need to comply with EU rules, partly due to an insufficient understanding of the fundaments of an effective R&D procurement, the Dutch SBIR failed to provide the link with the real needs of public end-users and failed to challenge national companies to advance their innovation capabilities. Instead the program has funded close-to-market solutions without clear prospects of uptake.

The SBIR competitions launched in 2016 suggest an improved approach. In 5 of the 8 competitions, the targeted needs belong to public authorities with concrete operational activities, who can act as end-customers of the developed innovations. However, serious shortcomings in the SBIR approach continue to be upheld: the lack of a prior analysis of state-of-the-art, the continuous use of the Dutch language, the lack of regular evaluation. More importantly, the NL SBIR is still only sporadically used and is not scaling up. Due to limited political commitment, setting budgets aside for SBIR is not mandatory, while RVO.nl does not have co-funding means to encourage public procurers to engage in SBIR.

6.5 The Flemish PoI

6.5.1 Description and Initiation Background

The UK SBRI and the NL SBIR are the first and most established PCP-like initiatives in the EU. In 2006, IWT (Agentschap voor Innovatie door Wetenschap en Technologie, the Flemish innovation agency) followed suit. IWT explored (in the context of a thematic working group of the Innovation Platform on Environmental Issues and Energy) the possibilities to use Procurement of Innovation ('PoI') to strengthen the technological base of the Flemish region, to find cost-efficient solutions to important socio-economic problems or to improve public services.[131] Because explicit discrimination in favour of Flemish businesses is not allowed by EU procurement rules, IWT directed the deployment of PoI towards areas wherein Flemish companies already possess core competencies.[132]

PoI was defined as procurement of products/services *'that do(es) not exist, but that could (probably) be developed within a reasonable period of time, through additional or new innovative work by an organization that commits to also produce, supply, and sell the developed product' (author's translation).*[133]

PoI incompasses thus both PCP and public procurement of innovative solutions (PPI).

---

[131] Veys 2009, 37.

[132] IWT 2008, 3, 5.

[133] IWT 2006, slide 8. Inspired by Edquist and Hommen 2000, 22–3.

IWT pointed out that the following elements were considered crucial for the successful deployment of PoI:

- political support for the PoI;
- dialogue between the contracting authorities and suppliers;
- sharing of risks and benefits;
- use of foresight techniques;
- use of the risk management expertise by the public buyer.[134]

Subsequently, IWT refined the methodology, partially based on the lessons learnt with the framework of the European OMC-PTP project.[135]

The following steps are adopted before the start of a specific competition:

(1) Each ministry defines its political ambitions;
(2) Contracting authorities define master plans under the supervision of the Ministries and in line with their political ambitions. The master plans justify the need for new solutions in relation to the more effective and efficient performance of public tasks. In addition, the master plan signals political commitment for the development of new technologies to the market and encourages other contracting authorities to get involved.[136]
(3) IWT defines a list of requirements for the desired innovations and a list of Key Performance Indicators.[137]
(4) The market is consulted in order to find out whether the desired solutions are commercially available or need to be developed. This is done though a so-called Innovation Platform, established for a period of 6 months.[138] The Innovation Platform is also meant to identify other innovation policy instruments besides or instead of public procurement, which would be (more) suitable to stimulate the development of the desired solution.[139]
(5) The information obtained through the Innovation Platform is processed into an Innovation Matrix: one of the axis will indicate the type of involvement of the government in the procurement of the technology: direct procurement, co-operative or catalytic procurement; the other axis will indicate the stage of development of the required technology: feasibility study, prototype, field tests, commercially available (Fig. 6.3).[140]

---

134 Ibid.

135 The OMC-PTP project was a project funded by the European Commission under FP6 and had the objective to set up pilot programmes involving various forms of procurement of new technology and innovation in the participating countries and provide a platform for exchanges of experiences and feedback. See http://cordis.europa.eu/search/index.cfm?fuseaction=result.document&RS_LANG=EN&RS_RCN=12564029&q Accessed 4 September 2012.

136 IWT 2008, 7.

137 Veys et al. 2009.

138 IWT 2008, 10.

139 Veys et al. 2009, 37.

140 IWT 2008, 4. The Matrix was inspired by Hommen's Matrix. See Hommen and Rolfstam 2006, 112.

	Explorative				Integration/Adaptation	Diffusion
	Feasibility	Concept	Prototype	Pilot		
Direct procurement						
Cooperative procurement						
Catalytic procurement						

Fig. 6.3 The structure of a PoI innovation matrix (*Source* Presentation of Peter Thevissen en Stephan Corvers, Brussels, January 2007)

Lack of explorative trajectories in the Innovation Matrix is considered an indication that insufficient attention has been paid by the government agency to future socio-economic needs.[141] The filled-out Innovation Matrix provides support for the choice of the most suitable procurement instrument.[142] If the technology already exists (e.g. finds itself at the integration/adaptation or diffusion phase on the Matrix) but it is not yet broadly commercialised, commercial procurement should be chosen. When the technology finds itself at an R&D stage (e.g. concept, feasibility, prototype, pilot), PCP should be chosen.[143] The entire approach can be visualised as follows: (Fig. 6.4).

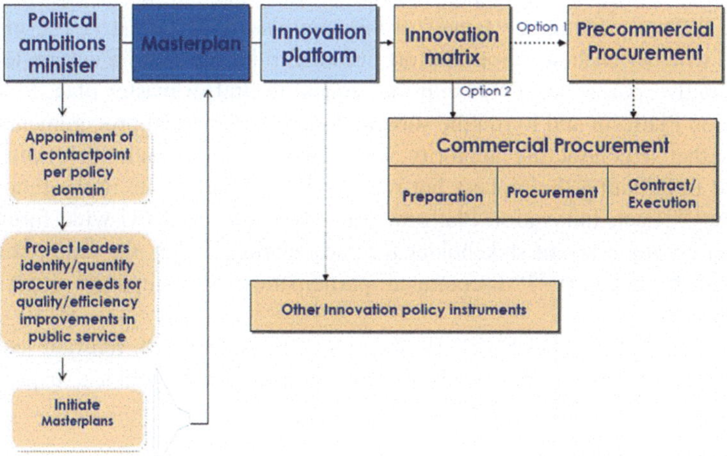

Fig. 6.4 PoI model (*Source* The Flemish model for procurement of innovation, IWT (2008))

141 Concept van Innovatief aanbesteden voor Vlaanderen 11. IWT 2008, 8.

142 IWT 2008, 7.

143 Ibid.

6.5.2 Features of the Flemish PoI

In this section I summarise the PoI in terms of what I consider its defining features:

(a) *Non-mandatory participation*

The policy described in the previous section was approved by the Flemish government in July 2008. Within this context, an Action Plan was drafted that focused specifically on the procurement of R&D. IWT was appointed to pilot pre-commercial procurement calls between 2009 and 2014. IWT received to this end a budget of € 10 million.[144]
The Flemish PoI has past the piloting stage. In the meantime, IWT was incorporated into VLAIO (Agentschap Innoveren en Ondernemen). It appears that the program is being continued. Methodology and organizational improvements are announced However, no new PCP competitions have so far been initiated. It appears that no mandatory budgets have been set. Implementation remains thus voluntary.

(b) *Centralised implementation*

The Flemish PoI has since its inception been centrally driven by IWT. The centralized set-up of the programme bears a strong resemblance to the NL SBIR. IWT has been in charge of organizing Innovation Platforms and of subsequently conducting PCP procedures, on behalf of the commissioning ministry. The ministry decided whether an Innovation Platform needed to be set-up on a certain topic. It subsequently approached IWT with the request to draft a master plan, to run an Innovation Platform and to run the subsequent pre-commercial procurements.[145] It appears that a contracting authority with concrete needs were not necessarily involved in initiating the process but were invited to participate in the Innovation Platform.[146] Each Innovation Platform was advertised on a EU-wide forum and was open to any relevant stakeholder for participation.[147] Yet, the required use of the Flemish language[148] discouraged participation of companies from other Member States.
More in line with the US SBIR, IWT employs personnel with relevant technical expertise depending on the needs of each project. Such technical expertise is

[144] Vermeulen 2011, 115–22.

[145] IWT 2008, 10–1.

[146] IWT 2008, 10.

[147] Chapter 5.1, http://www.innovatiefaanbesteden.be/juridisch Accessed 10 November 2013.

[148] And the long timeline of an Innovation Platform combined with non-reimbursement of participation costs may discourage companies from other Member States from participating. See also: Chapter 5.2, http://www.innovatiefaanbesteden.be/juridisch Accessed 10 November 2013.

particularly used during the Innovation Platforms to determine the degree of technical innovation needed for the development of the desired solutions.[149]

(c) *Eligibility criteria*

The activities that may be eligible for award are not defined. It is therefore not possible for me to conclude whether these are in line with the definition of R&D, as outlined in the Frascati Manual or as used within the US SBIR. IWT has, however, been in charge of supervising compliance with the minimum legal requirements governing PCP throughout the whole process.[150]

(d) *Phases*

The Flemish PCP procedure is divided into 3 phases: feasibility study, prototype and pilot project. For each phase, IWT made the following budgets available: up to 80,000 euro for the feasibility study, up to 500,000 euro for prototyping and between 750,000 euro and 1.5 million euro for the pilot. Each client ministry was allowed to provide additional budgets.[151] These amounts are in line with the US SBIR approach.

No regulatory guidance is provided on the time constraints for the different Phases, and neither is such guidance available on the possibility to fund multiple sequential Phase 2 awards to the same contestant.

Similar to the NL SBIR and the UK SBRI, the Flemish programme does not offer the possibility for a contracting authority to directly purchase the results of the pre-commercial procurement. No alternative support is provided for the commercialization phase. However, IWT required the involved contracting authorities to sign a letter of engagement by which they committed to organize a subsequent commercial purchase.[152] It is not clear in how far this commitment has been honored.

(e) *Sharing arrangements for IPR and R&D costs*

The Flemish program does not define a pre-set approach to IPR sharing. This is decided on a case-by-case basis. Depending on the type of project, the R&D service provider may also be required to transfer to the government a share of the profit made during commercialization.

IWT guidance showed that a market price needed to be paid for the acquired R&D services, reflecting the pre-defined division of IP rights. However, no specific

---

[149] IWT 2008, 9.

[150] Vermeulen 2011.

[151] IWT 2008, 12.

[152] See http://www.innovatiefaanbesteden.be/juridisch Accessed 10 November 2013.

mechanism to ensure compliance with this requirement was provided.[153] The guidance admitted that in some cases state aid may granted, but compliance with EU State aid rules would be decided on a case-by-case basis.[154]

Following the completion of the pilot in 2014, the PoI program would be notified to the European Commission for a compliance check against the EU legal rules.[155] It is unclear whether this has been the case.[156]

6.5.3 Projects

By 2011, the 13 government agencies involved in the PoI had proposed 48 PoI calls, out of which IWT selected 15.[157] By January 2014, IWT had deployed 12 of these 15 projects. I performed a documentary analysis of the information available on the IWT website regarding these 12 projects. A preliminary observation was that 6 of the 12 projects had been either stopped due to lack of funding or had proceeded as a commercial procurement following the conclusion of the innovation platform that desired solutions were already available on the market.

I analysed the remaining 6 projects that were chosen for a PCP trajectory against the same criteria as I used for the Dutch SBIR and UK SBRI: (1) the existence of a public end-customer, (2) technological innovations as target, (3) high-risk or uncertain R&D as target. Based on this analysis, I outline the following observations.

My first observation is that the majority of the PCP calls (4 out of 6) target solutions for a potential public end-customers. However, in 3 of the 4 cases in which a public end-user exists, it is not involved in the project. The PCP is instead deployed by a ministry together with IWT.

My second observation is that the majority of the PCP calls (4 out of 6) target exclusively technological innovation.

My third observation is that the calls do not target high-risk innovations. To illustrate this, I will describe 3 of the 4 technology-oriented PCPs.

The first project within the pilot programme was proposed by the governmental agency of Socio-Cultural Work. The project regards the development of a prototype for an e-book platform, which should provide a permanent and secure inventory of digital editions of Flemish books. This e-book platform is intended for

153 See http://www.innovatiefaanbesteden.be/juridisch Accessed 10 November 2013.

154 Chapter 6, http://www.innovatiefaanbesteden.be/juridisch Accessed 10 November 2013.

155 Ibid.

156 There is no publicly available information concerning this issue.

157 See http://www.innovatiefaanbesteden.be/lopende_projecten Accessed 4 September 2012.

exploitation by editors, book traders, libraries and content collectors etc. The project was financed with € 500,000 by the Ministry of Innovation and Culture.[158]

The innovative element of this project regarded integrating functions of import, inventory, exploitation of text with security issues regarding the content and the need to ensure a full text search facility. The platform envisages in addition '*an archiving function for a future cultural heritage centre and a coding module to produce different formats*'.[159] I find it very difficult to read anything beyond standard and well-established technology in this project.

A second project finds itself at the market scouting stage and presents already difficulties in receiving the needed input from relevant stakeholders regarding the (technological) areas that may be advanced beyond state-of-the-art.[160] The aim of the project is to develop a website that can catalyse the development and commercialization of environmentally-friendly products and services. Although the innovation platform was set-up at the end of 2012, this project has one and a half year later not moved beyond this stage, which suggests that it may be discontinued in the near future.

The third project that supports the conclusion that no high-risk technological innovation is targeted, regards the construction of energy-neutral buildings.[161] This project explores 4 sub-topics[162]: (1) testing the scale-effects on costs, by building 6 (almost) energy-neutral prototype houses with existing technologies; (2) technological solutions for energy-saving windows, doors and walls in monuments, in which the focus is on existing innovations and quick-wins; (3) development of a life-cycle cost ('LCC') method to calculate the cost of a construction project; (4) exploring the potential cost savings resulting from the application of a cooperative investment model ('ESCO-model') in a school renovation.

None of the envisaged sub-projects describes the technological area that should be advanced beyond state-of-the-art. They target application of existing technologies in already planned renovation projects. The third sub-project has already been stopped following the conclusion that no R&D services were involved.[163] Moreover, there is no information on PCPs being started in the other 3 sub-projects.[164]

---

158 See http://www.innovatiefaanbesteden.be/project/vlaams_e-boek_platform_(vep) Accessed 4 February 2013.

159 Vermeulen 2011, 115–22.

160 See http://www.innovatiefaanbesteden.be/project/katalytisch_eco-aankopen Accessed 21 July 2016.

161 See http://www.innovatiefaanbesteden.be/project/energieneutraal_bouwen_zonder_meerkost/documents Accessed 21 July 2016.

162 Robberecht—Verhaert 2012, 20, 24, 28.

163 See http://www.innovatiefaanbesteden.be/project/energieneutraal_bouwen_zonder_meerkost Accessed 15 January 2014.

164 See http://www.innovatiefaanbesteden.be/theme/duurzaam_bouwen Accessed 21 July 2016.

In conclusion, the Flemish PoI scores poorly in deploying PCPs. Of the 3 remaining projects one has not progressed beyond the market consultation phase.[165] This leaves the Flemish PoI with only 2 PCPs initiated since 2008. Phase 1 of these projects started in the second half of 2013. The first one targets the development of an innovative software capable to support the sub-titling of Dutch speaking television programs,[166] while the other one targets innovative technologies for greenhouses. Only of the last one there is scant information that one party was a awarded (probably a Phase 2) contract.[167]

6.5.4 Conclusions

The Flemish PoI scheme has not generated successful results in terms of PCP competitions.[168] Since 2014, no new PCP competitions have been initiated, while IWT has been re-organised as part of another government agency, VLAIO. Although improvements in methodology and incentives for deployment are announced, there was no sign of them by mid-2016.

In this section I summarize the main shortcomings of the program as identified in the current methodology and practice. These shortcomings affect the potential impact of the program, according to the parameters identified in Chap. 3.

1. Include a large number of high-risk R&D projects.
   The documentary analysis of the deployed PCPs showed that none of the projects targeted high-risk projects.
2. Target young companies, that experience difficulties in obtaining (sufficient amounts of) private capital
   This prerequisite could not be assessed, as there is no information available on the companies being awarded PCP contracts.
3. Budgets are increased in times of economic downturn.
   As already mentioned, since 2014, no new PCP competitions have been initiated. It is unclear whether PCP budgets will be made available in 2016.
4. Choose topics based on a careful consideration of technological trajectories and market trends.
   The Flemish program embeds a market consultation, related to each PCP competition (the so-called Innovation Platform). This represents an significant

---

[165] See http://www.innovatiefaanbesteden.be/project/hydrografische_peilingen_in_ondiep_water_over_grote_gebieden Accessed 21 July 2016.

[166] See http://www.innovatiefaanbesteden.be/project/spraak-_en_taaltechnologisch_ondertitelen_in_het_nederlands Accessed 21 July 2016.

[167] See http://www.innovatiefaanbesteden.be/project/op_weg_naar_een_duurzamere_glastuinbouw_in_vlaanderen Accessed 15 January 2014.

[168] This book does not assess the results on the PoI program in employing commercial procurement.

strength of the program, which prevented so far the deployment of wasteful PCPs. The market consultation is advertised through EU-wide means and participation is in theory open to foreign companies. However, the strong national policy interests of the participating funding agencies drives them to insist on the use of the Flemish language in the majority of the competitions. This discourages in practice foreign participation.

5. Managers in charge of PCP deployment possess or gain in-depth knowledge of the relevant technological area.
   Personnel with relevant technical expertise is employed, depending on the needs of each project. Their technical expertise is particularly valuable during the Innovation Platforms. This represents another important strength of the program.
6. Failure is tolerated to a certain extent.
   The Flemish program is divided into three phases (feasibility, prototyping and pilot). The amounts of funding per stage are flexible, but depend on the financial commitments of the commissioning ministries. In addition, similar to the other two national programs analysed in this chapter, no possibility to award multiple Phase 2 contracts is provided. This points out the limited degree of experimentation and tolerance to failure embedded into the Flemish program. And in practice, not a single high-risk innovation project could be found among the 12 projects investigated.
7. The public purchaser is closely involved.
   The Flemish program is centrally run by a national innovation agency that is not an end-user of the developed innovations. The (private or public) end-users are not involved in the PCP procedure, beyond participation in the Innovation Platforms. As a consequence, the program resembles more a supply-side subsidy scheme than a demand-side instrument.
8. The public purchaser is willing to pay the premium price for the early use of the developed innovation and is capable to offer a sufficiently sizeable market for the developed innovation.
   Similar to the Dutch SBIR and the UK SBRI and in line with the PCP guidance, the Flemish program does not allow the direct purchase of the developed innovations by the participating public authorities. Moreover, no additional (financial or operational) support is provided for the commercialization phase. But letters of engagement to purchase solutions with the performance levels and functionalities of those developed through PCP are signed by the involved contracting authorities before launching the competition. The value of these commitments is weakened by the use of catalytic PCPs that do not target solutions for public end-users.
9. Challenge and reward the most innovative companies, instead of shielding inefficient companies from foreign competition.
   The use of the Flemish language in the market consultation and in the ensuing PCP procedures discourages competition from other EU countries. In practice national companies are shielded from foreign competition. This is a waste of

public funds on solutions that already exist elsewhere is not in line with the rationale of PCP as strategic innovation policy instrument.

10. Innovative technologies rather than innovative services are targeted.
The documentary analysis in the previous section showed that 4 of the 6 launched PCP concerned technological innovation. However, 3 of these 4 seemed to refer to standard and well-established technology.
11. A continuous scrutiny/measurement of the impact of PCP is performed and lessons learnt are codified in guidance.
No evaluation of the program has so far been made public.

In conclusion, the Flemish PoI program has achieved poor results in deploying PCP. The Flemish program has been implemented as a pilot, which put pressure on the deploying entity, IWT, to show successful results. As a consequence, the pilot has turned towards closer to market R&D projects, which either did not pass the state-of-the-art test (made possible by the Innovation Platform) or did not deliver significant results. Moreover, the program was deployed by a government agency, whose core task has always been to subsidize local companies as opposed to soliciting advanced technical solutions to stringent public needs. As a consequence, the fundaments of the program are vested in national interests to provide funding to national companies, leading to a muddled program.

The continuation of the program was recently decided on the basis of an opaque political evaluation of the initial piloting phase. It remains to be seen whether the announced improvements in methodology and operation will lead to better results.

6.6 EU Support for PCP

6.6.1 The Rationale Behind European Commission's Intervention

By drafting the PCP, the European Commission expected to stimulate contracting authorities to contribute to the European innovation agenda from the demand-side. Moreover, the European Commission intended to ensure that this demand-side policy instrument supports and exploits the benefits of EU-wide competition and of EU-wide markets.

In contract with these expectations, PCP-like initiatives have exclusively been implemented as national or regional program, and in a very limited number of Member States. Although some of the challenges issued in different programs are functionally related or even almost identical,[169] none of them resulted in trans-

[169] For example, the call for assisted living and protective equipment for military combat in urban environments is practically identical within the Dutch SBIR and the UK SBRI. See www.innovateuk.org/deliveringinnovation/smallbusinessresearchinitiative.ashx Accessed 4 September 2012.

national cooperation and neither did they result in EU-wide competition. Particularly in the Netherlands and Flanders, procedures conducted in the national languages of the funding agencies constitute a strong barrier against participation by companies from other EU Member States.

Moreover, the PCP-like schemes under consideration present features that are not in line with the requirements for an effective demand-side instrument such as identified in Chap. 2.

Cross-border PCPs as envisaged by the 2007 Communication remained by 2011, largely unknown among individual public procurers in most EU Member States.[170] The study preceding the adoption of the PCP Communication, anticipated that public procurers would not be willing to take the (legal, technical and organisational) risks associated with cross-border PCPs. The study acknowledged that cross-border deployment of PCP, in areas of common European interest, would be highly beneficial (e.g. would enable bundling of resources and interoperability), but warned the European Commission that additional incentives were needed to encourage it.[171]

6.6.2 European Commission Incentivizing Actions

Individual public procurers invoke several reasons for not engaging in cross-border PCP procedures. Some of these have been discussed in Sect. 6.2. They cover: lack of technical knowledge; aversion to risk (particularly when PCP-like initiatives are not institutionalized and are not mandated); lack of clarity around the distinction between PCP and regular subsidies and the accompanying concerns regarding compliance with EU State aid rules; the fact that subsequent direct purchase of the developed innovation is not allowed; the complexity of the procedure itself (to find matching partners in other Member States, to define common requirements and to coordinate common procedures etc.).

Since 2009, the Commission adopted measures meant to relieve some of these difficulties. These are outlined below.

Networks of Procurers

Initially, the Commission financed the establishment of networks of procurers under the FP7 and RFEC programs.[172] These networks would enable public procurers to form consortia for cross-border PCPs and would facilitate exchanges of relevant knowledge and expertise. This measure proved ineffective, as it did not generate the expected good practices.

---

[170] Commission 2011.

[171] PCP Expert Group (March 2006) 29.

[172] http://cordis.europa.eu/fp7/ict/pcp/projects_en.html Accessed 4 February 2013.

Funding PCPs

As a consequence, the European Commission decided to fund, under the FP7 program, all of the organizational costs and part of the contractual costs of PCPs conducted by European consortia of public procurers. In 2011, call 7 allocated, for example, 6 million euro for the development of robotic solutions for elderly patients and mobile access to patient health info. Call 8 made in 2012 a budget of 3 million euro available for joint cross-border PCPs in the area of 'Photonic technologies' aimed at improving quality and/or efficiency of public services. Additional funding for PCP networking has also been made available under Call 8 covering any sector of interest.

There are currently 17 ongoing PCPs funded by the European Commission. The first awarded project is SILVER, a collaboration between several European cities to stimulate the development of robotic solutions to support independent living for the elderly. The project started in January 2012 and would be delivered in 45 months. However, by July 2016 Phase 3 was still ongoing.[173] Moreover, by mid-2016, none of the other PCPs was concluded.

The European Commission published some intermediate statistics concerning these PCPs.[174] They appear to score better than average public procurements in Europe in attracting SMEs[175] and cross-border participation.[176] Moreover, nearly 100 % of the R&D is performed in Europe (although the PCPs only require a minimum of 50 %).

The European Commission intends to continue the funding of collaborative PCPs. For example, pre-commercial procurement was introduced as a new funding instrument in Horizon 2020, the new framework programme for EU support to research and innovation for the period 2014–2020. Horizon 2020 will financially support PCPs conducted by consortia of contracting authorities from different Member States. EU institutions or EU funding bodies may also participate in such consortia.[177] For 2014–2015 € 130–140 million were reserved for collaborative PCPs and collaborative procurements of innovation (PPI).[178]

Data Collection, Studies and Impact Assessment

Besides spurring the use of collaborative PCPs, the Commission has also sought to assess the impact of its intervention in the area of R&D procurement.

---

[173] The only solution chosen to perform Phase 3 was being tested in the first half of 2016 at the premises of all 6 partnering procurers. See http://us11.campaign-archive1.com/?u=ae6c44ff2fd9c166d32db739d&id=58941e4ab3&e Accessed 22 July 2016.

[174] See https://ec.europa.eu/digital-single-market/en/news/updated-results-ongoing-pre-commercial-procurements-pcp-projects Accessed 22 July 2016.

[175] Allegedly 71 % of the PCP contracts by March 2015 have been awarded to SMEs. This percentage is more than double the average in public procurements across the EU.

[176] Allegedly, 31 % of the PCP contracts are awarded to undertakings located across-borders. This is 25 times more than the average in public procurements in the EU.

[177] See http://cordis.europa.eu/fp7/ict/pcp/policy_en.html Accessed 5 November 2013.

[178] Bos 2013.

In 2011, the Commission funded a project with the purpose to collect data on Member States expenditure on ICT- and R&D-related procurement and to develop a methodology for regular collection of data in the future. According to the Commission, availability of such data would lead to better informed decision-making concerning public intervention in support of R&D procurement.[179] The project was finalized in 2014. Its final report shows that Member States spend large budgets on ICT-related procurements (€ 50.3 billion in 2011) while non-defense R&D procurement amounts to € 2.6 billion.[180] The study shows that in a time span of 7 years (since the initial estimations made in 2008) there has been no significant increase in the deployment of R&D procurement.[181] This raises doubts regarding the impact of the measures undertaken by the Commission to trigger wide deployment of PCP.

In the same year (2011), the European Commission explored to what extent greater involvement by the EU in the deployment of innovation procurement (covering PCP and PPI (public procurement of innovative solutions)) would be accepted by public authorities. The commissioned study concluded that contracting authorities envisage a coordination role for the EU in cross-border innovation-related procurement, particularly in learning activities and in drafting procurement specifications. However, they prefer to retain the possibility to assess the bids themselves. A mix of topics is preferred, ranging from common-EU policy objectives to concrete needs of individual contracting authorities.[182]

Signals regarding support for a closer involvement of the EU in the deployment of PCPs have also emerged in national studies. EU involvement in stimulating EU-wide competition in PCPs around challenges common to more than one Member State, is seen as an important pre-condition to escape the '*political criticism that national tax money goes to foreign companies*'.[183] However, there has been so far no analysis of the possibility to combine the national and the EU initiatives on PCP-like schemes. This analysis falls outside the scope of this book.

In 2015, another study commissioned by the European Commission surveyed public procurers with the purpose of finding evidence on the positive impacts of PCP.[184] The study coped with serious difficulties in finding cases of PCP throughout Europe (only 8 cases), which casts doubts on the value of its conclusions. Rather based on literature concerning PCP(-like) competitions, than on the performed surveys, the study concludes on potential wide benefits, ranging from increasing quality in public services, to speeding the commercialization of innovations and incentivizing increased R&D investments.

---

179 T33, Spark and Deloitte 2014.

180 T33, Spark and Deloitte 2014.

181 Public expenditure was 47 % of EU-25 GDP, but only 2.5 billion were spent on R&D procurement, approximately 20 times less than in the US (where the spending was of approximately € 50 billion).

182 Rigby et al. 2012.

183 Holland 2009, 14.

184 Bedin et al. 2015.

Most recently (2015-current), the European Commission has launched the *eafip* initiative in a frantic attempt to scale up the deployment of PCP. The initiative has defined step-by-step guidance for the set-up of national/regional policies concerning innovation procurement (covering both PCP and PPI) as well as for the deployment of concrete projects. The guidance pays particular attention to the preparatory stage, including needs identification, market consultation, IPR search etc. Based on the developed methodology, ongoing PCP or PPI projects will receive support/advice from the *eafip* team of experts.[185]

6.7 Conclusions

This chapter analysed the state of implementation of collaborative PCPs as envisaged by the European Commission in its 2007 PCP Communication. It concluded that very few examples of collaborative cross-border PCP projects are available in Europe, while most of them are being funded by the EU. Studies identified the following reasons for the limited appeal of PCP to contracting authorities:

- lack of technical knowledge to define advanced needs;
- contracting authorities' aversion to risk particularly when PCP(-like) initiatives are not institutionalized and are not mandated;
- lack of clarity around the distinction between PCP and regular subsidies and the accompanying concerns regarding compliance with EU State aid rules;
- the prohibition to directly purchase the developed innovation;
- the complexity of a cross-border procedure (to find matching partners in other Member States, to define common requirements and to coordinate common procedures etc.).

This chapter also analysed the PCP(-like) programs launched in three Member States: the Netherlands, the UK and Belgium. The analysis revealed that these programs miss important prerequisites for wide and effective implementation.

Firstly, *participation is voluntary* in all the national PCP(-like) schemes analysed in this chapter. UK SBRI fares better at this, as clear targets for investment in PCPs are in place and they have been doubled for 2014–2015. In Flanders and the Netherlands, however, the implementation of the schemes depends exclusively on the promotion efforts undertaken by the deploying innovation agency. Arguably, this increases the pressure to come up with success stories and consequently closer-to-commercialization projects are preferred. The analysis of the calls for competition revealed that the projects do not target the riskier and the more uncertain R&D projects, which could benefit most from public funding. This risk appears lower in the case of UK.

[185] See www.eafip.eu.

Secondly, of the three national PCP(-like) initiatives, *none allows for the direct purchase of the developed innovation* by public authorities. This is in line with the EU legislation on public procurement, but in contrast to the US SBIR and to the recommendation to encourage early adoption of innovations.

Thirdly, *only the Flemish program embeds a market consultation*, which prevents wasteful spending on technologies that are already available. However, the use of the Flemish language restricts in practice participation to national companies. This weakens the potential of the subsequent PCP to truly enhance the innovative capabilities of the participating firms. The use of the Dutch language in the NL SBIR calls has the same restrictive effect on competition.

Fourthly, the Dutch and Flemish programs are centrally deployed and consequently *involvement of the end-customers is limited.* Most competitions within these two programs, as well as a large share of the UK SBRI competitions target solutions for the private end-customer, which deprives the projects of valuable inputs from end-users and limits the prospects of early adoption of the developed innovation.

Fifthly, the NL SBIR and the Flemish PoI and to a lesser extent the UK SBRI, *award R&D contracts for the development of innovations in services.* According to the conclusions in Chap. 3, innovation in services does not occur as a result of R&D projects, and the drivers of innovation in services are not well understood. This raises the question whether spending of public R&D funds is in this case justified.

Sixthly, the individual Member States that have so far implemented PCP(-like) programs *are motivated by the desire to support national companies.* This desire can be by itself legitimate, yet may lead to muddled programs. When this occurs, they will miss important characteristics that are needed to achieve their aims.

Since 2007, the European Commission has taken action to boost the implementation of PCPs conducted in collaboration by contracting authorities from different Member States. It has not attempted to harmonize the national programs or to sanction improper deployment, as it lacks the necessary competence. Since 2009, the Commission has provided funding for the creation of procurer networks and since 2011 for the organizational and contractual costs of collaborative PCPs. Funding has increased under the funding program Horizon 2020. More recently, the Commission has focused on data collection and assessment studies. These studies indicate that the Commission's efforts have not led to significant increase in the use of R&D procurement. Currently, the Commission is supporting the *eafip* initiative, in an effort to scale-up the deployment of PCPs, by means of improved guidance and practical advice in the deployment of concrete PCPs.

In my opinion, despite the lack of confirmation that the EU initiatives aimed at boosting investments in R&D procurement have had any significant results, the EU continues (and even intensifies) these initiatives—seemingly unaware of the reasons why these initiatives tend to fail in practice.

There is support among public procurers for a more hands-on approach by the European Commission, at least in the definition of specifications, the identification of common European needs and the sharing of knowledge (on the PCP and on the technological trends). Combined with a closer observance of economic prerequisites for an effective deployment of a demand-side PCP, the coordination provided by the Commission could potentially overcome national policy tendencies and risk aversion. This would ensure that public resources are pulled together to bring needed innovations to the market and to create global competitive advantages for EU firms.

In the next Chap. 7, I will focus on 3 of the most important barriers envisaged by individual contracting authorities to the wide implementation of PCP. I will investigate to what extent legal rules are the origin of these barriers and I will explore possible solutions.

References

Bedin S, Decarolis F, Iossa E (2015) Quantifying the impact of Pre-Commercial Procurement (PCP) in Europe based on evidence from the ICT sector (SMART: 2014/0009)

Holland C (2009) Peer Review of Small Business Research Initiative (SBRI) – UK. Report to INNO-Partnering Forum. European Commission Enterprise and Industry, Brussels

IWT (2008) Vlaams Actieplan Innovatief Aanbesteden (2008-2010) http://www.iwt.be/sites/default/files/IA_Vlaams_actieplan.pdf. Accessed 2 Feb 2013

Rigby J, Boekholt P, Semple A, Deuten J, Apostol R, Corvers S, Edler J (2012) Feasibility study on future EU support to public procurement of innovative solutions: Obtaining evidence for a full scheme http://ec.europa.eu/enterprise/policies/innovation/policy/lead-market-initiative/files/meeting-procurement-feb2012/study-eu-support-public-procurement-innovative-solutions_en.pdf

T33, Spark & Deloitte (2014) Quantifying public procurement of R&D of ICT solutions in Europe. https://ec.europa.eu/digital-single-market/en/news/quantifying-amount-public-procurement-ict-and-rd-across-europe. Accessed 22 July 2016

Vermeulen H (2011) Demand-side innovation policies in Flanders. In: Demand-side Innovation Policies (OECD 2011)

Chapter 7
Legal Barriers and Conceptual Pitfalls

Contents

7.1 Introduction

In Chap. 6 I showed that (1) the obligation to conduct a separate competitive award in order to purchase the innovative solution targeted by the PCP competition, and (2) the legal uncertainty regarding compliance with EU State aid rules were identified by contracting authorities as important barriers to the wide implementation of PCP. Contracting authorities (at least in Belgium, Denmark and the Netherlands) expressed even the concern that (3) a PCP finalist[1] might need to be excluded from a subsequent competitive procedure due to the important knowledge benefits gained during the PCP.[2]

[1] A PCP finalist is an undertaking which completed successfully all the PCP stages.

[2] Izsak and Edler 2011, 18.

R. Apostol, *Trials and Tribulations in the Implementation of Pre-Commercial Procurement in Europe*, DOI 10.1007/978-94-6265-156-2_7

Particularly individual contracting authorities, who can act as early adopters of the developed innovations, feel discouraged to use PCP. Stimulating these authorities to act as entrepreneurial risk-taking actors in the innovation market is crucial for achieving the desired policy aims. The above mentioned barriers weaken thus the potential positive impact of PCP as innovation policy instrument.

According to the Commission's PCP guidance, the above mentioned barriers find their origin in WTO and EU legal rules. In this chapter, I clarify the legal rules that underlie the above mentioned barriers. To this end I investigate in Sect. 7.3 to what extent the GPA rules are the source of the first barrier. I also outline the flexibility available in the EU Procurement Directives to purchase the PCP outcomes. In this context the new innovation partnership procedure is scrutinized. In Sect. 7.4, I clarify the State aid rules applicable to R&D procurement with or without aid and I will point out the pitfalls in the Commission's approach. In Sect. 7.5 I analyse whether the applicable procurement rules oblige the public procurer to exclude the PCP finalist(s) from the post-PCP commercial procurement and I clarify how the public procurer can fulfil its obligation to level the playing field.

Based on this analysis, in Sect. 7.6 I draw conclusions on the suitability of the current regulatory framework to advance EU's interests in the area of R&D and innovation and I will point out possible solutions to the problems thus identified.[3]

Before entering the discussion on the above mentioned barriers, I will outline the legal landscape in the EU and I will point out the differences between the EU as a supranational order and a national/federal state (Sect. 7.2 below). This will increase the understanding of the background for some of the choices of the EU legislator and policy-maker regarding the design of the PCP.

7.2 The EU Project

I pointed out in Chap. 4 that there are no EU public institutions as technically advanced and financially endowed as the US Federal agencies that implement the SBIR program. In the EU, diverging national interests have prevented the creation of such institutions. This section shows how the EU was founded and subsequently enlarged and how it differs from a national state.

The basis of the current European Union was laid in the 1951 Treaty of Paris,[4] establishing the European Coal and Steel Community (ECSC) after the Second World War. The aim of the Treaty of Paris was to supervise the steel and coal sectors, which during the war had been used in the production of war munitions. This would prevent a rehearsal of the 1939–1945 catastrophe.[5]

---

[3] Parts of this Chapter are based on a previously published article by the author. See Apostol 2012.

[4] Treaty of Paris 1951.

[5] Chalmers et al. 2010, 10.

This initial economic collaboration was subsequently extended through the Treaties of Rome of 1957 establishing the European Economic Community (EEC) and the European Atomic Energy Community (EURATOM). These treaties were determined by the increased awareness that coordination of the economic activities and policies of the European states would lead not only to an increase in political stability but also to general welfare.[6]

The Treaty of Rome provided the most important tools to achieve economic integration: the obligations for the Member States to refrain from taking action which may impede upon the freedom of movement of goods, workers, services and capital over the borders of the Member States. At the same time, the Treaty of Rome provided the institutional capabilities and the legislative competences to achieve this economic integration.[7]

Through subsequent amendments and accession of new members (28 Member States currently[8]), the European Communities were gradually enlarged. Legislative competence was granted to the EEC in additional sectors (health, safety at work, economic and social cohesion, research and development and environmental protection and cooperation in foreign policy,[9] monetary union and culture, education, health and consumer protection, home affairs,[10] area of freedom, security and justice, immigration, asylum, discrimination based on sex, race or ethnic origin, religion or belief, disability, age or sexual orientation[11]) and simplified voting procedures were introduced.[12]

Initially, the deepening and widening of the EEC was supported by the desire of the Member States to increase their economic leverage in a globalized economy. Later, awareness grew that further economic integration could only be achieved if the political union was strengthened.[13] This led to the adoption of the Treaty of Maastricht in 1991.[14] But the enlargement with new Member States, each with particular structures and values revealed the challenge to reaching a relatively homogenous basis for a further political integration.[15]

The fact that the EU is not comparable with a federal state and is not moving into that direction became obvious in 2004, when the Constitutional Treaty was rejected in two referendums in France and the Netherlands. The negative outcome

---

[6] Treaty of Rome Article 1.

[7] Chalmers et al. 2010, 32.

[8] On 1st of July 2013, the newest member, Croatia, acceded the European Union.

[9] Single European Act.

[10] Treaty of Maastricht.

[11] Treaty of Amsterdam.

[12] The Treaty of Amsterdam extended the qualified majority voting to new fields, thus making the veto an exception. See Chalmers et al. 2006, 43.

[13] Obradovic 1996.

[14] Chalmers et al. 2006, 61.

[15] Zielonka 2001, 513–5.

of the referendums signaled the reticence of the European citizens to accept the message of federative integration of the Constitutional Treaty. The EU was perceived as an undemocratic intruder into areas of national competence.[16] The lack of the elective element and the non-transparent decision-making mechanisms were advanced as potential reasons for the rejection.[17] The Treaty was rebranded Treaty of Lisbon and was adopted in 2007 (and entered into force in 2009).

Despite the drawback of 2004, the European Union remains a unique political union which reached more deeply into the way Member States govern and regulate themselves and their societies than any other international organisation.[18]

The EU has so far achieved important successes, such as an uninterrupted period of 50 years of peace and unprecedented levels of welfare.[19] But the ambitions of the EU have also grown, and presently cover areas such as security and international justice, ensuring environmental protection and curing world poverty, reaching global leadership based on European values of social welfare.[20] The achievement of these aims requires not only to adapt the EU competences to its ambitions but also to wisely use the flexibility offered by the current legal framework.

The reality for the time being is that there are important differences between the EU and a national state: the EU implements and coerces only very few of its policies (competition, monetary policy, and external trade negotiations). But important areas such as taxation and budgetary spending remain within the exclusive competence of Member States.[21]

According to the Treaty on the Functioning of the European Union (TFEU),[22] fostering industry's competitive potential through policies of innovation, research and technological development constitutes a common goal for the Union and the Member States. The competences to take action in this area are shared between the EU and the Member States based on the principle of subsidiarity. The EU is, for example, allowed to carry out research, technological development and demonstration programs, provided that the exercise of that competence does not prevent Member States from carrying out their own programs.[23] The European Parliament and the Council are expressly authorized to adopt specific measures to support the Member States in this area, as long as they do not cover harmonisation of Member

---

[16] Chalmers et al. 2006, 64.

[17] According to Chalmers et al. 2006, 65–7, this may be simply a question of perception, due to the fact that the areas of competences attributed to the EU do not fall within the themes of main concern to voters (health care, education, law and order, social security and taxation), while sufficient checks and balances are already in place.

[18] Moravcsik 2005; Chalmers et al. 2006, 51.

[19] Chalmers et al. 2006, 61.

[20] Chalmers et al. 2006, 69.

[21] Moravcsik 2005, 370.

[22] Alongside the Treaty on European Union, TFEU forms the Treaty of Lisbon.

[23] Article 180-1 TFEU.

States' laws and regulations.[24] The specific competences granted to the European Commission are to promote coordination of Member States' actions in the area of innovation, research and technological development. In particular, the Commission is allowed to formulate guidelines and indicators, to organise exchanges of best practice, and to prepare the necessary elements for periodic monitoring and evaluation.[25]

In conclusion, the EU is more divided by national interests than what one expects a Federal state would be. These national interests are the reason for the limited competences granted so far to the EU in setting-up a centralized PCP program, centrally coordinated and deployed by supranational institutions such as in the US. The EU Member States have favored negative integration (refraining from action that would damage the European Internal market) rather than positive one (deploying common initiatives). The European Commission was appointed the role of guardian of the internal market. In this role, the Commission has created safeguards against distortive behaviors for the Internal market.

In the sections below, I will point out that reopening competition at the commercial phase, was partially meant to function as such a safeguard. In this context, I will Investigate whether the Commission struck the right balance between maintaining needed safeguards and providing the stimuli for wide deployment of PCP.

7.3 The Burden of a New Competitive Award After the PCP

7.3.1 Introduction

The European Commission advanced the following reasons for separating PCP from the subsequent commercial procurement of the developed innovations. The EU had excluded R&D service from the scope of the GPA[26] but not supplies (such as the commercial outcomes of a PCP). This allowed the EU to disregard the national treatment and non-discrimination obligations vis-à-vis GPA parties in the procurement of R&D services.[27] But it did not allow discrimination against GPA parties in the procurement of supplies. The R&D services contracts could thus be restricted to those companies that are willing to locate a relevant portion of their R&D and operational activities related to the PCP contract in the EU or an

[24] Article 173 TFEU.

[25] Article 173(2) TFEU.

[26] Commission 2007b, 10. Unlike the EU, the US has excluded from the scope of the GPA set-asides on behalf of small and minority businesses. See para 1 of General Notes of the US, part of the Appendix I to Government Procurement Agreement.

[27] The GPA does not legally constrain the freedom EU has in regulating the relations between its Member States. The GPA defines the obligations for the EU as a whole to open its public markets to participation of businesses from the other GPA parties.

associated country.[28] This indirectly discriminatory requirement was chosen by the Commission for its potential to generate knowledge spill-overs within the EU as well as jobs and growth.[29] But this meant that the contracting authority would need to reopen competition at the end of the R&D stage and allow GPA parties to bid for the supply contract.

The Commission also clarified that this approach was in line with its own belief that maximum competition fosters innovation.[30]

One may conclude that a procurer is allowed to purchase the outcomes of a PCP whenever the R&D stage is open to participation by GPA companies, without restrictions related to the location of the R&D services. However, when they employ PCP as strategic innovation policy instrument, to enhance the innovation capabilities of EU/national firms, contracting authorities will not be willing to allow access to non-EU participants.

I will therefore investigate whether, in spite of EU's choice to bring all supplies under the scope of the GPA, the text of the agreement allows direct purchase of R&D outcomes (Sect. 7.3.2). I will further analyse whether this flexibility has been transposed into the EU Procurement Directives (Sect. 7.3.3 below). I will particularly scrutinize the newly adopted innovation partnership procedure, that covers the development and purchase of innovative solutions (Sect. 7.3.4 below). This analysis is relevant, due to the fact that the Procurement Directives were drafted in line with the GPA and are applied equally to EU and GPA economic operators in respect of those procurers and contracts covered by Appendix I of the GPA.[31]

Based on this analysis, I will conclude whether the Commission's approach to PCP is suitable to advance EU's interests in the area of R&D and innovation and I will suggest, where necessary, improvements.

7.3.2 The WTO GPA Constrains

7.3.2.1 Short Introduction to the GPA

The international legal framework for public procurement is the GPA. It was initially negotiated during the WTO Uruguay Round in 1994. An amended GPA text was agreed upon in 2012 and entered into force on 6 April 2014. The GPA currently counts 18 parties, amongst which the EU (representing all its 28 Member States) and the US.

---

[28] This includes countries from the European Economic Area and countries having concluded a Stabilisation and Association Agreement with the EU.

[29] Commission 2007b, 10.

[30] Ibid.

[31] Articles 25 Directive 2014/24/EU and 43 Directive 2014/25/EU.

The GPA is a plurilateral agreement, representing the sum of a series of bilaterally negotiated agreements. This means that parties open their public markets to different extents towards each other depending on mutual concessions. These are laid down in Annexes 1–5 and in the General Notes to Appendix I of the GPA. Annexes 1 to 3 list the entities to which the agreement is applicable. Annexes 4 and 5 list the services that are brought under the scope of application of the agreement, while the General Notes contain additional reservations.[32] GPA's procedural rules apply only in respect to those public contracts included in Appendix I.[33]

GPA does not govern the relations between the EU Member States, but the relations between the EU as a whole and the GPA parties. To this extent, the EU could have drafted separate procurement rules to regulate these sets of relations. However, for reasons of simplicity, the EU chose to formulate one set of rules and to require EU contracting authorities to apply them equally to EU and GPA economic operators. The new Procurement Directives limit this obligation to those procurement situations covered by Appendix I of the GPA.[34] As a consequence, the EU Procurement Directives was drafted in compliance with the text of the GPA.

7.3.2.2 Purchase of PCP Outcomes Under the GPA

The EU left R&D services outside the coverage of the 1994 GPA by not listing them in Annex 4 of Appendix I.[35] Most GPA parties have done the same. This was arguably owed to countries' desire to use these contracts strategically, to strengthen their domestic innovative capabilities.

Besides R&D services, the US also chose to reserve the right to set-aside public contracts to US small businesses.[36] This allows the US to directly procure innovative products developed within the SBIR program, without breaching the GPA.

The EU did not make a similar reservation for small businesses. The EU negotiators arguably feared that this would encourage inefficient awards by Member States, based on national policy motivations rather than competitive merits. As shown in Sect. 7.2 above, EU Member States are still divided by diverging national interests, despite their commitment to achieve shared goals by means of a unique supranational union.

---

[32] http://www.wto.org/english/tratop_e/gproc_e/appendices_e.htm#appendixI Accessed 4 February 2013.

[33] See http://www.wto.org/english/tratop_e/gproc_e/gp_gpa_e.htm Accessed 8 July 2016.

[34] Articles 25 Directive 2014/24/EU and 43 Directive 2014/25/EU.

[35] See EU Annex 4 Appendix I GPA, available at http://www.wto.org/english/tratop_e/gproc_e/appendices_e.htm#ec Accessed 8 July 2016.

[36] PCP Expert Group 2006 7. See para 1 US General Notes Appendix I GPA.

Although the EU did not reserve the right to exclude from the scope of the GPA purchases of the outcomes of an R&D contract, Article XIII(1)(f) GPA allows the direct purchase of first products or services resulting from an R&D contract. Hereafter I investigate whether this provision may accommodate the purchase of PCP outcomes.

According to Article XIII(1)(f) GPA, a contracting authority may conduct a limited tendering procedure (which is the equivalent of the negotiated procedure without prior notice of the EU Procurement Directives),[37] in order to purchase '*a prototype or a first product or service that is developed at its request in the course of, and for, a particular contract for research, experiment, study or original development*'.[38]

The direct purchase of the first product or service resulting from an R&D contract is thus allowed under the following conditions:

- the same contracting authority that commissioned the R&D, purchases the resulting first good or service;
- at the moment of purchase, the good or service has not been commercialized yet;
- the contracting authority is the first customer.
- after the execution of this contract, the purchase of the same goods or services by the same contracting authority or by any other contracting authority needs to be conducted in compliance with a competitive procurement (open or selective tendering).

[37] The limited tendering is defined as the procedure where the entity contacts suppliers individually. Arrowsmith 2002.

[38] Article XIII(1) GPA: 'Provided that it does not use this provision for the purpose of avoiding competition among suppliers or in a manner that discriminates against suppliers of any other Party or protects domestic suppliers, a procuring entity may use limited tendering and may choose not to apply Articles VII through IX, X (paras 7 through 11), XI, XII, XIV and XV only under any of the following circumstances: (…) (f) where a procuring entity procures a prototype or a first good or service that is developed at its request in the course of, and for, a particular contract for research, experiment, study or original development. Original development of a first good or service may include limited production or supply in order to incorporate the results of field testing and to demonstrate that the good or service is suitable for production or supply in quantity to acceptable quality standards, but does not include quantity production or supply to establish commercial viability or to recover research and development costs;

Figure 7.1 below visualizes the relevant GPA provision.

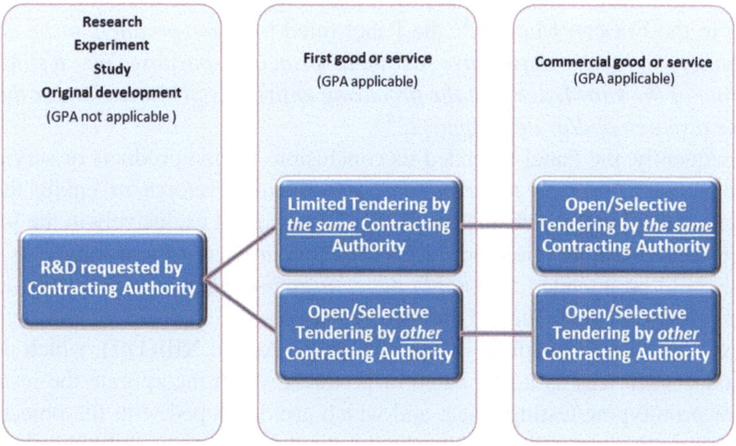

Fig. 7.1 Article XIII(1)(f) GPA

It could be argued that GPA allows the direct purchase of first products or services resulting from a preceding PCP, without inviting suppliers from other GPA parties to compete for the contract award.

Two important questions arise in regard of the GPA ground for purchasing first products/services without competition. Firstly, are 'first products or services', as intended by the GPA, operational products which can be used by the contracting authority in fulfilling its public tasks? Secondly, would favouring domestic businesses during the procurement of the research and development services contract (which is not covered by the GPA) limit the discretion of a GPA party to rely on the limited tendering exception?

Definition of First Products/Services

The Trondheim Panel Report shed light on the interpretation of Article XIII(1)(f) (previously Article XV(1)(e) 1994 GPA).[39] In this case, the United States alleged that the Norwegian Public Roads Administration had wrongfully relied on Article XV(1)(e) to award a contract related to parts of an electronic toll collection system to a Norwegian company. The Norwegian authority argued that the contract regarded the purchase of prototypes developed during a prior research contract.[40]

---

[39] WTO Panel, *Norway—Procurement of Toll Collection Equipment for the City of Trondheim* (13 May 1992, BISD 40S/319).

[40] Ibid. Section 4.7: In examining this issue, the Panel first noted that, while the provision referred to "research, experiment, study or original development", the parties to the dispute had referred only to research and development. Furthermore, although the provision relates to "prototypes or a first product", only prototypes had been referred to. The Panel therefore limited its examination to these aspects.'

First, the Panel clarified that the exception provided by Article XV(1)(e) should be interpreted narrowly and that the Party invoking the provision should bring the proof of conformity.[41] Subsequently, by making reference to the definition of prototypes in the Frascati Manual,[42] the Panel ruled that '*for products to be considered prototypes, they must have as their principal purpose the testing and furthering of the knowledge that the procuring entity was procuring under the contract for research and/or development.*'[43]

Subsequently, the Panel extended its conclusions to first products or services. It underlined that a '*contract for research ... or original development*' entails the purchase of knowledge. Knowledge should not be expressed exclusively in the form of abstract results such as scientific papers. The procurement of a prototype or a first product could be intended to '*enable the contracting authority to learn of, and to test the validity of, the results of the research and/or development in a more practical way*'. This Panel statement is in line with the Article XIII(1)(f), which defines first products/services as a first batch of products which incorporate the results of the prior prototyping/testing stage, and which are developed with the objective to prove their working in real operational environments at certain quality levels.[44]

According to the Panel, the Norwegian authority failed to demonstrate that the purpose of the contract had been the purchase of research and/or development results (in the form of a prototype) rather than a final operational product.[45]

In conclusion, the Trondheim case clarified that a contract qualifies as a research or original development contract and may be awarded through a limited tendering only if the scope of the purchase is to perform testing activities and there is still some uncertainty regarding the potential of the prototype or first product or service to fulfill the operational needs of the contracting authority.

The Panel does not exclude the possibility for the procurer to continue to use the prototype/first product in the conduct of its own affairs whenever the testing/ demonstration was successfully concluded.

In response to my first question, it is thus defendable to conclude that the GPA allows a contracting authority who sponsored the successful demonstration of a first products in a PCP Phase 3, to continue to use its results (in the form of first products or services) in its operational activities, without reopening the award to participation by other GPA economic operators. However, a contracting authority is not allowed to rely on this exemption to order more of the same products, following the successful demonstration.

---

41 Ibid., Section 4.5.

42 Ibid., Section 4.5; OECD 2002;

43 Ibid., Section 4.9.

44 It states: '*Original development of a first product or service may include limited production or supply in order to incorporate the results of field testing and to demonstrate that the product or service is suitable for production or supply in quantity to acceptable quality standards. It does not extend to quantity production or supply to establish commercial viability or to recover research and development costs*'.

45 *Trondheim*, above n 38, Section 4.11.

The GPA ground for the use of limited tendering is relevant whenever the first product/service cannot be retained as part of Phase 3 of the PCP. A public procurer will be able to retain the ownership of the demonstrated product in PCP Phase 3 (first product), only if the value of the first product does not outweigh the value of the knowledge creative activities (R&D services). Otherwise, the public procurer will be breach of the Procurement Directives.

The PCP Requirement to Locate R&D Activities in the EU

The PCP Communication recommends public procurers to require PCP participants to locate the majority of their R&D activities within European Economic Area or within a country having concluded a Stabilisation and Association Agreement with the EU. The Commission explained in the PCP guidance, that this requirement breaches the GPA when the procurer purchases commercial volumes of the innovative products as part of the same PCP. I analyse below whether the Commission's statement is correct. In case of a positive answer, the non-competitive purchase of the first products/services resulting from a PCP would not be possible based on this provision.[46]

Article XIII(1) GPA states that the limited tendering procedure may not be used '*for the purpose of avoiding competition among suppliers or in a manner that discriminates against suppliers of any other Party or protects domestic suppliers*'.

According to Arrowsmith, the introductory provision to Article XIII(1) covers two separate obligations. The first obligation, not to use the limited tendering '*for the purpose of avoiding competition among suppliers*' relates to the reasons for applying the limited tendering.[47] The second obligation, not to use the limited tendering '*in a manner that discriminates against suppliers of any other Parties or protects domestic suppliers*' relates to the way the limited tendering is carried out and not to the reasons for applying it.[48]

According to the first obligation, the use of the limited tendering exception to purchase the first products or services resulting from a PCP, should not be motivated by the desire to protect domestic companies, but by the desire to fulfill an operational need (which cannot be fulfilled by commercially available products).[49] In other words, the purchase needs to correspond to a concrete and real needs of the public procurer.

The prohibition to use limited tendering '*for the purpose of avoiding competition among suppliers*' may entail an additional obligation for a contracting authority to organize informal competitive negotiations, in case there are more than one suppliers who could offer similar solutions. Arrowsmith dismisses this interpretation due

[46] It is worth mentioning that only a GPA party may complain before a GPA Panel against the illegal use of the limited tendering procedure. Moreover, the chances of a challenge by a GPA party are, in practical terms, extremely remote.

[47] Arrowsmith 2003, 282.

[48] Arrowsmith 2003, 282–4.

[49] Arrowsmith 2003, 283 considers, for example, that a wide range of commercial reasons for invoking the limited tendering exceptions should be recognized.

to the legal uncertainty it would create.[50] However, from a practical point of view, whenever the PCP yields more than 1 finalists, it is recommendable to organize informal negotiations with all the finalists.

When the PCP merely yielded one finalist, it is unclear whether the contracting authority should actively investigate the existence of similar solution on the market. The market consultation/research performed at the preparatory stage of a PCP in order to justify the novelty of the R&D services would arguably be a sufficient source of information. In the Trondheim case, the United Stated raised a similar argument. It argued that the contracting authority in question was at least required to consult 'known and eager competitors'.[51] Unfortunately, the Panel did not address this issue.

The second obligation of the introductory provision to Article XIII(1) prohibits the use of the limited tendering '*in a manner that discriminates against suppliers of any other Party or protects domestic suppliers*'. The question arises whether this provision prohibits the PCP requirement to locate R&D activities within the EU.

The definition of the non-discrimination principle in Article III GPA sheds light on the interpretation of the introductory provision of Article XIII(1).[52] The non-discrimination principle entails that suppliers from all parties will be treated no less favourably than domestic suppliers.[53] According to jurisprudence within the GATT, formally identical but de facto (indirect) discriminatory measures are in breach of the non-discrimination principle of the GPA.[54] Against this background, the requirement regarding the location of the R&D activities, although equally applied to both GPA parties and domestic companies, discriminates de facto against companies from GPA state parties, which do not have an establishment in one of the indicated countries.

But this indirectly discriminatory requirement is applied in a procurement excluded from the scope of application of the GPA. If the contracting authority does not impose limitations regarding the place of *production* of the first products, it could be argued that there is no discriminatory use of the limited tendering procedure.

A contrary interpretation would effectively lead to the application of GPA provisions in expressly exempted R&D contracts. In conclusion, it is defendable to argue that the GPA allows a contracting authority to directly purchase the PCP results (namely first products or services) despite the PCP requirement to locate the R&D activities within the European Economic Area or a country having concluded a Stabilisation and Association Agreement with the EU.

---

[50] Arrowsmith 2003, 297.

[51] *Trondheim*, above n 38, Section 3.5.

[52] The limited tendering is subject to compliance with Article III GPA on non-discrimination. Article III.1 GPA provides: 'With respect to all laws, regulations, procedures and practices regarding government procurement covered by this Agreement, each Party shall provide immediately and unconditionally to the products, services and suppliers of other Parties offering products or services of the Parties, treatment no less favourable than: (a) that accorded to domestic products, services and suppliers…'.

[53] Nicholas 2011, 766.

[54] Arrowsmith 2003, 160–1.

This means that the Commission's decision to separate the commercial procurement from PCP may be rooted in its own desire to prevent distortive applications of PCP (such as the national policy-oriented PCP-like initiatives analysed in Chap. 6), rather than legal constraints. Another argument to this end is that the chances of a challenge by a GPA party are, in practical terms, extremely remote. Contorting EU innovation policy to avoid the possibility of such a challenge seems illogical—unless, of course, the contortions are really for an 'internal' EU purpose.

7.3.3 The EU Procurement Directives & the Purchase of PCP Solutions

7.3.3.1 Introduction

This section analyses whether the EU Procurement Directives allow the direct purchase of first products, under similar conditions to the GPA Article XIII(1) (Sect. 7.3.3.2). It also examines whether PCP outcomes may be purchased by negotiated procedure without prior notice based on technical and IPR grounds (Sect. 7.3.3.3)[55] and whether the innovation partnership procedure represents a suitable alternative to PCP (Sect. 7.3.3.4). I will finally conclude whether the 2014 Procurement Directives embed sufficient incentives for contracting authorities to act as early adopters of innovative products or services (Sect. 7.3.3.5).

7.3.3.2 The Purchase of First Products/Services Under the EU Procurement Directives

The 2014 Public Sector Directive allows the purchase of R&D supplies by means of a negotiated procedure without prior publication (which entails direct negotiations with a particular firm).[56] The Directive mentions that the products should be

---

[55] Article 32(2)(b) Directive 2014/24/EU; Article 50(c) Directive 2014/25/EU. The negotiated procedure without prior publication of a contract notice is allowed '*where the works, supplies or services can be supplied only by a particular economic operator for any of the following reasons:*

(i) the aim of the procurement is the creation or acquisition of a unique work of art or artistic performance;

(ii) competition is absent for technical reasons;

(iii) the protection of exclusive rights, including intellectual property rights.

The exceptions set out in points (ii) and (iii) only apply when no reasonable alternative or substitute exists and the absence of competition is not the result of an artificial narrowing down of the parameters of the procurement'.

[56] Article 32(3)(a) Directive 2014/24/EU.

'*manufactured purely for the purpose of research, experimentation, study or development*'.

R&D works contracts may be purchased through a negotiated procedure with prior publication of a contract notice (now called 'competitive procedure with negotiations').[57] This is not expressly mentioned anymore, as the grounds for application of the competitive procedure with negotiations have become more lenient. Accordingly, a contracting authority may choose this procedure when the contract includes design or innovative solutions. R&D works qualify though as such a contract.

The 2014 Utilities Directive contains a general provision allowing direct negotiations for the award of any kind of R&D contracts, whether services, supplies or works.[58]

I can conclude that the Procurement Directives provide the same flexibility as Article XIII(1)(f) GPA. R&D supplies and R&D works cover both prototypes and first products. A contracting authority may thus purchase a first product without competition, only when aiming to demonstrate its working in real environments. The contracting authority may continue to use it in its operational activities after the successful demonstration. However, this exemption ground may not be invoked for the purchase of additional commercial products.

7.3.3.3 The Use of the Negotiated Procedure Without Prior Publication for Technical or IPR Reasons

When wishing to purchase commercial volumes of the PCP results, the contracting authority may turn to the technical and IPR grounds for negotiations without prior publication. 2014 Procurement Directives allow such negotiations when competition is absent for technical reasons or when the protection of exclusive rights (including IPR) is at stake. The same grounds were available to contracting authorities under the previous 2004 Procurement Directives.[59]

The Court of Justice of the European Union (CJEU) has already clarified in case-law, that the scope of application of these provisions is restrictive.[60] In Case C-328/92, in which the European Commission contested the non-competitive purchase of pharmaceutical products by the Spanish government, the European judge clarified that it is not enough that a product is protected by exclusive rights. It must

[57] Article 26(4)(a)(ii) 2014 Directive 2014/24/EU.

[58] Article 50(b) Directive 2014/25/EU.

[59] Articles 31(1)(b) of Directive 2004/18/EC and 40(3)(c) of Directive 2004/17/EC.

[60] CJEU, *Commission v Italy*, Judgment, C-199/85 [1987] ECR I-039 para 14; CJEU, Commission v Italy, Judgment, C-57/94 [1995] ECR I-1249 para 23; CJEU, *Commission v Germany,* Judgment, C-318/94 [1996] ECR I-1949 para 13; CJEU, *Commission v Italy,* Judgment, C-385/02 [2004] ECR I-08121 paras 19–20; CJEU, *Commission v Greece,* Judgment, C-394/02 [2005] ECR I-4713 para 33.

also '*be capable of being manufactured or delivered only by a particular supplier*'. The judge added that this requirement '*is satisfied only in respect of those products and specialties for which there is no competition in the market*'.[61] In other words, the Spanish government could rely on this exception only if it had the following cumulative proof:

- that the owner of the IP of the pharmaceutical products had not granted licenses to other parties for manufacturing and delivering the same IPR protected products; and
- that there were no competing products on the market in respect of functionalities and/or performance levels.

When technical reasons are relied on for derogating from a competitive award, the Court similarly ruled that it must be '*absolutely essential*' that the contract in question be awarded to a particular undertaking, and not to another undertaking.[62] The Court suggested that a contracting authority should prove that the technical difficulties could not be surmounted if the contract were awarded to another undertaking and should rely to this end on a technical report of an independent expert.[63] In other words, the contracting authority should be able to prove that the preferred contractor is the only one on the market who possesses the needed expertise to deal with the respective technical difficulties.[64]

The 2014 rules codify the Court's jurisprudence by requiring that the contracting authority demonstrate that '*no reasonable alternative or substitute exists*' when relying on the technical or exclusive rights grounds.[65]

In addition, the 2014 Procurement Directives require that '*the absence of competition is not the result of an artificial narrowing down of the parameters of the procurement*'.[66] The recitals to the Directives clarify that '*(c)ompetition shall be considered to be artificially narrowed where the design of the procurement is made with the intention of unduly favouring or disadvantaging certain economic operators*'.[67]

The question arises whether this new provisions poses pressure on contracting authority to lower its ambition in terms of required performance and functionality in order to ensure a suitable level of competition.

---

[61] CJEU, *Commission v Spain,* Judgment, C-328/92, [1994] I-01569 para 17.

[62] *Commission v Italy* 1995 paras 24–5; *Commission v Italy* 2004 paras 18, 20 and 21; *Commission v Greece* para 34.

[63] Commission v Italy 1995 para 27.

[64] *Commission v Greece* paras 35–39.

[65] See also recitals (50) Directive 2014/24/EU and (61) reiterate that '*only situations of objective exclusivity can justify the use of the negotiated procedure without publication*' and '*the situation of exclusivity has not been created by the contracting entity itself with a view to the future procurement procedure*'. Moreover, the availability of adequate substitutes should be assessed thoroughly.

[66] Article 32(2)(b)(ii) and (iii) Directive 2014/24/EU and 50(c)(ii) and (iii) Directive 2014/25/EU.

[67] Article 18(1) Directive 2014/24/EU and Article 36(1) Directive 2014/25/EU.

A negative answer is supported by the decision of the CJEU in the Concordia case. In this case, the contracting authority awarded additional points at the evaluation stage to proposals offering vehicles that did not emit more nitrogen oxide than 2 g/k Wh. Competitors complained in this case that only natural gas powered buses could comply with the requirement and there was only one service station in the whole of Finland which could supply natural gas. Moreover, the capacity of the service station was already fully used by one company, which in practice amounted to the practical consequence that only one company could comply with the requirement.[68]

The CJEU performed in this case a test of the legitimacy of the requirement and concluded that integrating environmental protection requirements into Community policies and activities is a Treaty objective and therefore environmental criteria may be used to assess the economically most advantageous proposal.[69]

Establishing the *intention* of the public procurer to unduly favour or disadvantage certain economic operators may seem as a difficult endeavor, that may weaken the effect of this requirement. However, analysts conclude that the European judge does not attribute any particular relevance to the intention of public procurers whenever judging whether they circumvent the provisions of the Procurement Directives.[70]

In conclusion, the public procurer is allowed to set ambitious requirements in line with those used in the previous PCP. When the PCP yields only one finalist, the public procurer may rely on technical reasons to justify a direct purchase from this finalist. This will be possible when the PCP generates groundbreaking solutions, for which there are no reasonable alternatives or substitutes and the PCP finalist acquired unique expertise to deliver the developed solution. The public procurer may not rely on the IPR grounds, as he retains during the PCP a call-back option and/or the right to require suppliers to license IPRs to third parties under FRAND conditions (see Sect. 5.3.1.2 above).

7.3.3.4 Innovation Partnerships

Relation to PCP

In spite of Commission's commitment to maximize competition during and after the PCP, a different approach found its way into the 2014 Procurement Directives. The innovation partnerships allow the set-up of a long-term contractual relation with one or several private undertakings, concerning the development *and* subsequent purchase of an innovative solution, if delivered at the initially agreed

[68] CJEU, *Concordia Bus Finland v Helsingin kaupunki and HKL-Bussiliikenne*, Judgment C-513/99 [2002] ECR I-07213 para 71.

[69] Ibid. para 57.

[70] Sanchez-Graells 2016, 7.

performance levels and costs.[71] The procurer is thus not required to open the commercial purchase to competition at the end of the R&D trajectory. The obstacle of a separate commercial procurement for the purchase of the desired innovative outcome seems to have been eliminated.

Unlike the European Commission, the legislator did not seem worried about breaching the GPA. Whenever the value of the purchased products will exceed the value of the R&D, the Innovation Partnership contract(s) will qualify as supply contracts and will fall under the incidence of the GPA. This means that the procurer will need to allow GPA participation.[72] It is unclear whether the legislator meant to open the partnerships to GPA-wide participation, or whether it deliberately assumed the risk of breaching the GPA, when procurers limit participation to EU firms or require GPA suppliers to locate a significant share of their R&D operations within the EU or within an associated country. The second option is more pertinent, as it is difficult to imagine that EU authorities will be willing to finance R&D trajectories which not only take place outside their national borders, but even outside the EU.

The Procurement Directives provide additional incentives for public procurers to favor Innovation Partnerships over PCPs. Negotiations are allowed in the selection of the partners and no other grounds for use are defined, besides the existence of a need that is not met by commercially available solutions.

The 2014 Procurement Directives state that innovation partnerships are not meant to replace PCP, but to reinforce the means for achieving the innovation goals of the Union. According to the Directives, PCP remains available to contracting authorities who want to procure R&D services that fall outside the scope of the Directives.[73] However, Sect. 5.6 above showed that conducting a PCP outside the scope of the Directives little additional flexibility, particularly in setting time-limits and in gradually specifying (but not changing) the procurement requirements.

This leads me to the conclusion that public procurers would prefer to engage in innovation partnerships rather than in PCPs. Innovation Partnerships do not entail additional procedural burdens compared to PCP, while allowing the direct purchase of the developed innovation. The available EU funding for PCPs under the Horizon 2020 funding program, is perhaps the only reason why public procurers would still consider PCP.

This should be celebrated as good news, as innovation partnerships enable contracting authorities to act as demanding customers and early adopters of desired innovations. Leaving aside the question whether procurers are capable to make

[71] Article 31 Directive 2014/24/EU and Article 49 Directive 2014/25/EU.

[72] See Article 25 Directive 2014/24/EU; Article 43 Directive 2014/25/EU.

[73] Recital (47) Directive 2014/24/EU and recital (57) Directive 2014/25/EU. The legislator clarifies that the Directives aimed to offer additional means to '*facilitate public procurement of innovation and help Member States in achieving the Innovation Union targets*.'

important economic judgments for an effective deployment of an innovation partnership I will further discuss the Commission's approach vis-à-vis innovation partnerships.

Back-Door safeguards

Motivated by the same concerns that Innovation Partnerships will open a Pandora's box of market distortive behaviours, the European Commission decided not to leave this at the whims of public procurers. In its role as guardian of a well-functioning Internal market, the Commission decided to overrule the legislator and to create in the 2014 Framework for State aid for R&D&I a restrictive ground of application. I will describe this below.

The 2014 Framework does not expressly mention Innovation Partnerships, but governs the relation between State aid and procurement of R&D in general. According to the Framework, procurement of R&D services by means of an open or restricted procedure in accordance with the applicable Procurement Directive will benefit of a general presumption of market conditions and absence of aid.[74] An innovation partnership is automatically excluded, as it is awarded based on negotiations.

Subsequently,[75] the 2014 Framework defines several cumulative criteria, which create the presumption of market conditions for R&D procurements that are not conducted in accordance with the open and restricted procedures as prescribed by the Procurement Directives. One of the criteria is the prohibition to give the R&D providers any preference in delivering commercial volumes of the resulting innovation. This is precisely the case of an innovation partnership. In a footnote, the Commission stipulates that this condition is '*without prejudice to procedures that cover both the development and the subsequent purchase of* ***unique or specialized products or services***' [author's emphasis].[76]

Basically, the Framework introduces a far-reaching restriction for the use of innovation partnerships. In other words, the presumption that no State aid was granted only stands in case the products or services developed during the innovation partnerships are 'unique or specialized'. The Framework does not explain these concepts.

Arguably, the Commission will only exempt from the State aid rules innovation partnerships that aim to develop products whose only potential buyer is the contracting authority and that involves all those providers that are capable of developing and supplying the innovation.[77] In this framework, a partnership with just one

[74] Commission 2014a, para 32.

[75] Commission 2014a, para 33.

[76] Commission 2014a, footnote 29 to point 33(c).

[77] Wendland 2015, 47. The author states: 'The market condition presumption only holds in situations where a public purchaser procures products or services that are so unique/specialised that the public purchaser is the only potential buyer and there are no other potential providers on the market outside of the innovation partnership that could be disadvantaged'.

undertaking will be possible in the very rare situation when the procurer is the unique buyer and the undertaking is the unique provider.

In conclusion, in spite of the legislator's will to allow public procurers more flexibility in advancing the national innovation agendas, the Commission significantly restricted the ground for use of innovation partnerships. In the absence of express competences to steer the PCP at EU level (following the model of the US), this is the best approach the Commission has to prevent significant distortions of competition. It is though not the most effective approach.

In the rest of this section, I will describe the innovation partnership procedure and I will point out which aspects concerning the implementation of innovation partnership remain unclear.

Phases

Innovation partnerships may cover the development, as well as the subsequent purchase of the resulting supplies, services or works. The partnership must follow the sequence of steps in the research and innovation process.[78] It is not made clear whether these steps correspond to the R&D phases proposed by the PCP Communication, namely solution exploration, prototyping, field tests or whether they could start at a more fundamental research stage. Moreover, no definition of R&D is provided and no reference to the *Frascati Manual* as guiding authority is made.

The procurer may set intermediate targets (for example, at the end of each R&D phase) to be attained by the undertakings in order to qualify for payment and/or to qualify for the next phase of the partnership. Based on the same targets, the procurer may also decide to terminate the partnership. In order to avail itself of these possibilities, the procurer needs to publish them together with the conditions for their use, in the tendering documentation.[79]

IPR Arrangements

The legislator does not require any specific IPR arrangements in the framework of an innovation partnership. However, the procurer is mandated to describe its choice in the procurement documents.

As a consequence, the procurer may choose to share the IPR with the participating undertaking or to retain the exclusive right to use the outcome of the innovation partnership for its internal operations.

The recitals to the Procurement Directives provides a glimpse of the European legislator's commitment to encourage co-financing by industry and the sharing of the R&D results between the procurer and the participating undertaking.[80] However, the limitation brought by the 2014 Framework for State aid for R&D&I

[78] Article 31(2) Directive 2014/24/EU and Article 49(2) Directive 2014/25/EU.

[79] Article 31(2) Directive 2014/24/EU and Article 49(2) Directive 2014/25/EU.

[80] Recital (35) Directive 2014/24/EU and (42) Directive 2014/25/EU. The European Commission is a committed advocate of minimal intervention at the R&D stage.

concerning the application grounds, lead to the conclusion exclusive development (by which the public procurer retains exclusive rights for the use of the innovation) will be the dominant choice.

The Procedure

Innovation partnerships are concluded according to the procedural rules that govern the competitive procedure with negotiations.[81]

A contracting authority/entity is mandated to start the procedure with an open call by which any interested economic operator in the EU is invited to submit a request to participate within a period of at least 30 days.[82]

The contracting authority/entity will need to describe in sufficiently precise terms the needed solution and will need to formulate minimum requirements which cannot be met by purchasing solutions already available on the market.[83] This prevents the contracting authority from subsequently relaxing these requirements (during the negotiations). This guarantees that in the end a truly innovative solution is developed.

A minimum of 3 undertakings, who were selected on the basis of the qualitative criteria mentioned in the contract notice (such as capacity to perform R&D and to implement innovative solutions), may submit an indicative tender.[84] This initial and all subsequently submitted tenders may be negotiated on any aspect, besides the minimum requirements and the award criteria.[85] During negotiations, candidates should be treated equally. This means that all candidates should receive the same relevant information for the formulation of the tender. Changes in requirements as a result of the negotiations should also be communicated (in writing). However, the contracting authority should not reveal to the other candidates confidential information received during negotiations.

In addition, all candidates should be allowed sufficient time to (re-)submit amended tenders.[86] During the negotiations, the contracting authority/entity may reduce the number of economic operators, based on the award criteria specified in the contract notice.[87]

Purchase of the R&D Results

The new Procurement Directives allow the public partner to directly purchase the supplies, services or works resulting from the R&D trajectory of the Innovation

81 Recital (49) Directive 2014/24/EU and (59) Directive 2014/25/EU.

82 Article 49(1) Directive 2014/25/EU provides for another minimum time-limit of 15 days.

83 Article 31(1) Directive 2014/24/EU and 49(1) Directive 2014/25/EU.

84 Article 65(2) Directive 2014/24/EU and 78(2) Directive 2014/25/EU. The number of invited candidates may be lower, whenever the procurer can demonstrate that there are not enough capable candidates available. The Utilities Directive does not mention a minimum number, but requires that genuine competition is ensured.

85 Articles 31(3) Directive 2014/24/EU and 49(3) Directive 2014/25/EU.

86 Articles 31(4) Directive 2014/24/EU and 49(4) Directive 2014/25/EU.

87 Articles 31(5) Directive 2014/24/EU and 49(5) Directive 2014/25/EU.

Partnership, provided these can be delivered at the initially agreed performance levels and maximum costs.[88]

The Directives impose a proportionality test on the value and duration of the partnership, as well as on the estimated value of the supplies, services or works purchased during the partnership. According to the Directives, the value and duration of the partnership should '*reflect the degree of innovation of the proposed solution and the sequence of the research and innovation activities required for the development of an innovative solution not yet available on the market*'.[89] In other words, the more radical the innovation, the more investment is justified. In addition, '*the estimated value of supplies, services or works purchased shall not be disproportionate in relation to the investment for their development.*'

It is not clear whether this provision refers to the investments made by the contracting authority within the framework of the innovation partnership or whether the investments made previously by the private partner should also be considered. If the second view is accepted, the provision allows significant discretion to contracting authorities to award large value contracts for long durations for the purchase of the R&D results. This holds significant threats for a well-functioning market.

In an earlier version of the Proposals, it was provided that the value and duration of the commercial procurement following the development phase '*shall remain within appropriate limits, taking into account the need to recover the costs, including those incurred in developing an innovative solution, and to achieve an adequate profit*'.[90] Arguably, this provision granted contracting authorities even greater discretion in deciding on the value and duration of a contract for the purchase of the R&D results.

The fact that the old provision was replaced by a proportionality test suggests that the risk of market foreclosure was acknowledged during the negotiations, but there was lack of agreement on a stricter approach. As a consequence, the final text of the new Procurement Directives leaves it to the judiciary to resolve this dispute. The European judges will need to evaluate on a case-by-case basis whether the value of such a contract is proportional in relation to the R&D investments.

The Procurement Directives provide weak safeguards against such negative effects. The requirement to ensure the 'necessary 'market-pull'' and to avoid foreclosing the market did not find their way into the articles of the Directives.[91] The recitals state that engaging several partners could contribute to avoiding negative effects on competition. The warning in the recitals is an acknowledgement of the potential risks to competition. It also provides glimpse of the strenuous negotiations.

---

88 Recital (49) Directive 2014/24/EU and (59) Directive 2014/25/EU.

89 Article 31(7) Directive 2014/24/EU and Article 49(7) Directive 2014/25/EU.

90 Draft of 20.12.2011.

91 Recital (49) Directive 2014/24/EU and (59) Directive 2014/25/EU.

Concluding Remarks

Innovation partnerships represent a powerful innovation policy instrument that can incentivize private undertakings to develop or to speed up the development of important innovations. By eliminating the obligation to conduct a separate commercial procurement, innovation partnerships are also suitable to convince risk-averse procurers to act as demanding customers and early-adopters of innovations.

However, the Procurement Directives do not require the procurers to consider important economic arguments before deciding to deploy innovation partnerships in support of certain innovations. In the absence of a thorough economic assessment, innovation partnerships may worsen the conditions for competition in the Single Market and may eventually stifle or slow down innovation. The negative effects are particularly harmful when the procedure shields one private provider from competitive pressure over long periods of time. More specifically, this lead to reduced R&D investments by competitors (crowding-out effect) or to the market exit of more efficient competitors.

In the absence of express competences to coordinate a similar R&D procurement and aid scheme such as in the US, the European Commission adopted a restrictive approach to safeguarding competition in the Internal market. This is surely not the most effective way to advance EU's innovation agenda.

7.3.4 Conclusions

In conclusion, the EU legislator has translated the flexibility offered by the GPA and allowed the choice for a negotiated procedure without prior publication for the purchase of R&D supplies and works (e.g. a prototype or a first product or service). This means that a public procurer may purchase a first product/services with the purpose of demonstrating its working at expected quality levels in real environments. The public procurer may retain the first product/service for operational use, whenever the demonstration proved successful.

The PCP itself also covers the development of first products at Phase 3. However, this does not entail that the public procurer may retain ownership of these first products and subsequently use them for operational purposes. The requirement that the value of the R&D services is higher that the value of the R&D supplies (prototypes and first products) prevents this scenario in most cases.

Commercial volumes may be purchased by direct negotiations with the PCP finalist,[92] only when the developed innovation performs certain functionalities and achieves certain levels of performance which are not met by other products on the market and the PCP finalist possesses unique expertise to deliver these products. This will be the case when the result of a PCP procedure is a breakthrough innovation, which significantly advances state-of-the-art.

[92] If there are two finalists, a competitive procedure should be organized.

The expressly outlined obligation to demonstrate that no 'reasonable alternative or substitute exists' and that 'the absence of competition is not the result of an artificial narrowing down of the parameters of the procurement' do not restrict the discretion of a contracting authority in defining high levels of performance and advanced functionalities for the desired solutions.

But reliance on these provisions for the direct purchase of a PCP result is not expressly mentioned by the 2014 Procurement Directives. As a consequence, individual contracting authorities may perceive legal risks in pursuing such an approach.

The new Procurement Directives introduce the possibility to award a contract for the development and delivery of innovations, in the form of an innovation partnership. I have analysed in this section whether the new procurement model enables contracting authorities to play their key role in stimulating innovation from the demand side. I concluded that this new procedure fails to strike an adequate balance between European innovation and competition interests. Arguably, the innovation partnership procedure was adopted under the pressure of strengthened national interests. The fact that the Commission felt compelled to limit through the back-door the use of innovation partnerships to 'unique or specialized products', supports this hypothesis.

7.4 Interplay Between PCP and EU State Aid Rules

7.4.1 Introduction

EU public procurers indicated that lack of clarity concerning compliance with the EU State aid rules represent a barrier to the use of PCP. In this section, I outline the recommendations made at that time by the European Commission to ensure compliance with the State aid rule and I criticize them for being inadequate and confusing (Sect. 7.4.2). I subsequently outline the new 2014 Framework for State aid for R&D&I, and I conclude whether it effectively addresses the above mentioned barrier. In this context, I point out the remaining conceptual difficulties (Sect. 7.4.3). Finally, I summarize the conditions for justifying a PCP which involves State aid (Sect. 7.4.4).

7.4.2 The Market Price Criterion—Before 2014

At the time when the PCP Communication was adopted (2007), the EU State aid rules did not expressly mention R&D procurement in general, or PCP in particular. The 2006 Framework for State aid for R&D&I only mentioned that a procurement procedure in accordance with the applicable Procurement Directive created a presumption of market conditions and absence of State aid.[93]

As already explained in Chap. 5, PCP as designed by the European Commission is not conducted in compliance with the Procurement Directives. This means that the presumption did not apply to PCP. The European Commission addressed this gap in the PCP Communication and in subsequent informal guidance.[94]

The PCP Communication explained that EU State aid rules were not applicable when public procurers contract R&D services at a market price, that reflects the division of risks and benefits. By paying a market price, public procurers did not—according to the Commission—provide an unwarranted advantage to a certain economic operator and did not distort competition.[95] In this case, the contract did not require prior notification and prior assessment/approval by the European Commission.

The European Commission outlined two ways of complying with the market price criterion. The first was to determine the maximum price a public procurer was ready to pay for the PCP. This would be achieved by deducting from the total cost of R&D[96] plus a reasonable profit margin, the market present value (MPV) of the commercialization opportunities left to the participating company (this value will need to reflect also the risks assumed by the participating company, in maintaining the IPRs and commercializing the products).[97] Bidding companies would subsequently be invited to compete by offering an equal or lower price. The Communication did not elaborate on the situation when the MPV of the commercialization opportunities may appear higher than the total R&D costs (including reasonable profit margins).[98]

Due to obvious difficulties in estimating the commercialization value of yet-to-be-developed products, the European Commission accepted an alternative compliance test. This consisted of (1) asking bidding companies to offer a reduction in price, in return for the retained IPR benefits, and to submit the underlying calculation; and (2) asking a financial expert to assess whether the offered price

---

93 Commission 2006, para 2.1. The recent Communication SGEI 2012, on the other side, limits the scope to open and restricted procedures. The presumption does not exist for the negotiated procedures. See Commission 2012.

94 Commission 2007b and Commission 2016.

95 Commission 2007b, 8; Commission 2007a.

96 This is made of all the costs incurred by the company—for example the market value of the salaries of researchers/developers in a certain sector and the costs of R&D material required to perform the work. Commission 2016, question no. 8.

97 Commission 2007a, 9.

98 Rigby 2013.

Fig. 7.2 Alternative options for compliance with the 'market price' criterion

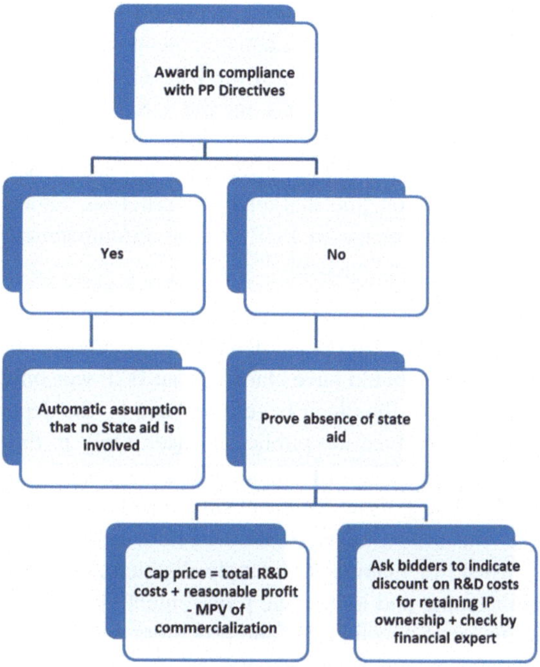

reduction is market conform.[99] Because it is supposed to reflect the prior division of risks and benefits, with ownership of the results going by default to the provider, the market price should in principle be less than 100 % of the R&D costs.

The above options can be visualised as in Fig. 7.2.

Arguably, the European Commission crafted the market price requirement, with the aim to prevent illegal use of PCP, in breach of the State aid rules (which prohibit the payment of 100 % of the costs for applied R&D and require prior notification and prior assessment of the planned aid by the European Commission). As shown in Chap. 6, at the time when the PCP Communication was adopted, two national PCP-like schemes in the UK and the Netherlands covered 100 % of the

[99] Commission 2016, question no. 8: 'one way used by patent traders to calculate the price reduction for IPR ownership rights uses the so-called *present value method*. It is normal practice that companies make a business case, and thus estimate the potential market over the years to come, when deciding to start investing in a new development or not. The price reduction on the PCP bid towards the procurer can be calculated as a portion of the 'present' value of projected profits for the company (the 'present' value is the value discounted back in time to the day of the bid), that is proportional to the investment/risks taken by the government (PCP price paid to the company) compared to the total investments required to turn the R&D efforts into a commercially viable product (this includes the projected investment/risks that will be carried by the company e.g. costs of maintaining IPR projection, further production, marketing and commercialisation investments). Companies can extract these values from the business case they prepare at the moment they make their PCP offer'.

R&D costs. They were being deployed in a subsidy-like fashion, by innovation agencies who did not have concrete needs and could not act as end-customers.

Following the adoption of the PCP Communication and of additional guidance by the European Commission, the UK SBRI continued to cover 100 % of the R&D costs,[100] while the Dutch SBIR, formally embraced the second approach to 'market price', but did not provide for any assessment mechanisms.[101]

In conclusion, the market price criterion, either did not convince risk-averse procurers to engage in PCP, or was circumvented or emptied of a meaningful effect by national agencies.[102]

Criticism

Arguably, the European Commission chose an inefficient approach. The Commission should have clarified that PCP was only allowed for the development of solution for the direct benefit and use by the deploying agencies and only when it closely involved the public end-user. Only in this case, is PCP a procurement, and a demand-side instrument. When the solution is developed for a broader policy objective, it is an R&D subsidy, which differs in no way from those R&D subsidies that are regulated under the Framework for State aid for R&D&I.

Instead of making this simple distinction, the Commission chose to impose a cumbersome and ineffective requirement on both innovation agencies that tried to circumvent State aid rules and procurers with true need and demand of innovation. Commission's approach did not induce procurers to engage in the perils of uncertain and risky R&D procurement.

Instead of requiring a complex calculation, the Commission could recommend that the PCP participants bring matching funds. However, from an economic point of view, requiring matching funds will not stimulate the choice for the most risky R&D projects, that present large costs at early development stages and long-term returns on investment. These projects will not manage to find matching funds, due to private investors' reluctance to invest or due to the high cost of external capital.[103]

The Commission's reasoning ignores thus the fact that PCP should aim to relieve financial restrains for risky but potentially highly beneficial R&D projects that cannot access private funds. A more suitable requirement to comply with the Procurement Directives requirement that benefits are shared, is for procurers to request a share of profits made with commercialisation.

In conclusion, the 'market price' is an inadequate criterion to distinguish between R&D procurement and R&D subsidies. The European Commission

---

[100] TSB 2011, 3.

[101] Companies competing for an SBIR contract were requested to indicate the discount in price they grant for retaining the IPR. However, no control mechanisms are embodied into the award process. SBIR programmabureau van Agency NL 2011, 5.

[102] The Flemish PoI does not set a standard approach regarding the market price criterion.

[103] Hall and Lerner 2010.

missed thus the opportunity to clarify the relation between PCP and State aid and to focus on guiding the procurers with stringent demand to deploy effective PCPs.

7.4.3 The 2014 Framework for State Aid for R&D&I

Since 2014, new State aid rules apply to R&D contracts. The rules expressly mention PCP and define the following cumulative conditions that create a presumption that no State aid is granted[104]:

(a) the selection procedure is open, transparent and non-discriminatory, and is based on objective selection and award criteria specified in advance of the bidding procedure;
(b) the envisaged contractual arrangements describing all rights and obligations of the parties, including with regard to IPR, are made available to all interested bidders in advance of the bidding procedure;
(c) the procurement does not give any of the participant providers any preferential treatment in the supply of commercial volumes of the final products or services to a public purchaser in the Member State concerned; and
(d) one of the following conditions is fulfilled:

- all results which do not give rise to IPR may be widely disseminated, for example through publication, teaching or contribution to standardisation bodies in a way that allows other undertakings to reproduce them, and any IPR are fully allocated to the public purchaser, or
- any service provider to which results giving rise to IPR are allocated is required to grant the public purchaser unlimited access to those results free of charge, and to grant access to third parties, for example by way of non-exclusive licenses, under market conditions.

The new Framework for State aid for R&D&I provides a simplified alternative to the 'market price' criterion. These requirements reflect the features of the PCP. As a consequence, they simplify the task of the procurer and they provide legal certainty.

However, the Framework does not draw a clear conceptual line between R&D procurement and R&D subsidies and does not explain the economic prerequisites for effective PCP deployment. It rather focuses on fair selection of the PCP participants (condition (a) and (b) above), on maximizing competition (condition c) above) and on ensuring knowledge spill-overs.

Nevertheless, the 'end-user' criterion is embedded in the definition of the public contract, as interpreted by the CJEU in the Muller case. According to the Court of Justice of the EU, the key criterion to define a public contract is the direct economic interest of the procurer to gain the ownership of the contract results or the

---

[104] Commission 2014a, para 33.

right to use these results.[105] The fact that the public authority that deploys the PCP should be the end-user/customer is also implied in condition (d) above), according to which IPR or at least a free license to use the developed innovation are granted to the public purchaser.

When PCP deviates from the 2014 Framework conditions, it should be notified and approved by the European Commission prior to its deployment.[106] In practice a public procurer could only deviate from the IPR requirement (condition d), without breaching the Procurement Directives. In the following section, I will describe the applicable obligations in this case.

7.4.4 Applicable Rules to a PCP Subsidy

When the presumption of 'no State aid' is not activated, the contracting authority will need to comply with the EU State aid rules. In 2014, the EU redefined the legislative framework for scrutinizing State aid. The State aid rules are defined in 3 complementary pieces of legislation and guidance: the 2014 General Block Exemption Regulation ('GBER') which defined categories of aid that are exempted from the prior notification obligation, the 2014 Framework for State aid for R&D&I, that explains the conditions for justification of aid that is not exempted under the GBER and the Communication detailing under which conditions State aid to important projects of common European interest will be declared compatible with the Internal market.[107] In this section I describe the content of these rules, as far as relevant to PCP.

In general, the EU State aid rules ensure the achievement of one of the underlying concepts of the European Union, that a market-based economy in which companies are rewarded according to their innovativeness and efficiency is the best way to ensure that consumers get the desired products, at low prices. This eventually leads to increased living standards for all European citizens. Unwarranted support provided by Member States to some national companies may lead to the exclusion from the market or the delayed reward of the most competitive firms, with the related negative consequence (such as higher prices, lower quality goods and less innovation).[108]

[105] CJEU, *Helmut Muller GmbH v Bundesanstalt fur Immobilienaufgaben*, Judgment Case C-451/08, [2010] ECR I-02673 paras 50–51.

[106] Commission 2014a, para 34.

[107] Commission 2014b.

[108] Commission 2005, 3.

Nevertheless, the EU policy makers acknowledge that investment in R&D does not happen at optimal levels and that R&D subsidies may be justified. Because state aid can be distortive and may lead to disincentives for economic operators to invest themselves in R&D if used improperly,[109] the State aid rules define strict economic tests to assess whether the envisaged aid measure is able to achieve its target.

GBER is based on the assumption that certain categories of aid measures have, under certain circumstances, a limited distortive effect on competition and should be exempted from the obligation to notify them to the European Commission for prior assessment and approval. When the R&D aid measure is not exempted under GBER, it will be scrutinized by the European Commission, in line with the provisions of the 2014 Framework for State aid for R&D&I.

According to GBER, aid for R&D projects is exempted, when the following cumulative conditions are fulfilled:

- the aid is only directed towards R&D activities, as defined in the regulation[110];
- only eligible costs are covered, as defined in the regulation[111];
- the aid does not exceed 100 % of the eligible costs for fundamental research; 50 % of the eligible costs for industrial research; 25 % of the eligible costs for experimental development; 50 % of the eligible costs for feasibility studies[112];
- the aid intensity for industrial research and experimental development may be increased up to 80 % of the eligible costs, under certain conditions (e.g. effective collaboration between businesses in two or more Member States, or between businesses and research organisations etc.).[113] For example, an SME

[109] Commission 2014a, para 1.2.: 'When an undertaking receives aid, this generally strengthens its position on the market and reduces the return on investment for other undertakings. When the reduction is significant enough, it is possible that rivals will cut back on their R&D&I activity. In addition, when the aid results in a soft budget constraint for the beneficiary, it may also reduce the incentive to innovate at the level of the beneficiary. Furthermore, the aid can support inefficient undertakings or enable the beneficiary to enhance exclusionary practices or market power.'

[110] Commission 2014b, Article 25(2).

[111] Commission 2014b, Article 25(3).

[112] Commission 2014b, Article 25(5).

[113] Commission 2014b, Article 25(6)–(7).

may receive 80 % of the eligible costs made with industrial research and 60 % of the experimental development costs, when the project is carried out in at least 2 Member States (or in a Member State and a Contracting Party of the EEA Agreement) and in collaboration with at least one other undertaking that does not bear alone more than 70 % of the eligible costs.

- in case of an R&D aid scheme, the budget should not exceed € 150 million.[114] An aid scheme with an annual budget exceeding € 150 million will be temporarily allowed for 6 months, subject to approval by the Commission of a plan to evaluate its working.[115]
- no aid is granted to undertakings that are subject to outstanding recovery of received illegal state aid, based on a previous Commission decision, with the exception of aid to compensate for damages caused by natural disasters.[116]
- no conditions contrary to Union law shall be attached to the aid (such as the requirement for the beneficiary to locate its headquarters in the subsidizing state, or to use nationally produced goods, or the restriction to exploit the results in other Member States etc.).[117]
- the aid shall not exceed[118]:
  - € 40 million per undertaking, per project, when the eligible costs are predominantly dedicated to activities that qualify as fundamental research[119];
  - € 20 million per undertaking, per project, when the eligible costs are predominantly dedicated to activities that qualify as industrial research or, industrial research and fundamental research taken together.
  - € 15 million per undertaking, per project, when the eligible costs are predominantly dedicated to activities that qualify as experimental development.
  - the above mentioned thresholds may be doubled in case of research programmes undertaken jointly by several Member States and involving the participation of the EU.
  - the above mentioned thresholds may be increased by 50 % when the aid is repayable in case of a successful project, with an interest rate equal or higher than the discount rate at the time of the grant.
  - € 7.5 million per feasibility study.

[114] Commission 2014b, Article 1(2)(a).

[115] Commission 2014b, Article 1(2)(a)–(b).

[116] Commission 2014b, Article 1(4)(a)–(b).

[117] Commission 2014b, Article 1(5).

[118] Commission 2014b, Article 4(1)(i).

[119] 'Predominantly' entails that more than half of the eligible activities are fundamental research. See von Wendland 2015.

In addition, the measure is subject to several transparency-related obligations (the eligible costs are well documented,[120] details regarding the R&D subsidy are published on a State aid website, within 6 months from the granting date and remain available for 10 years from the granting date[121]). Member States should also be able to show that the aid has an incentive effect. To this end, it suffices that the request for aid is made by the beneficiary prior to the start of the subsidized activity.[122] Only in case of aid granted to a large company, the Member State needs to show it verified in advance whether the aid triggers an increase in scope, total amount or speed of completion of the project.[123]

When the above conditions are fulfilled, the public authority does not need to notify its intention to grant the aid to the European Commission. The new GBER allows more flexibility compared to its predecessor. One important change is that thresholds for individual aid have been doubled. Another important change is that aid to R&D that finds itself closer to the market is allowed subject to more flexible rules (the repayment of the commercial revenues obtained from the exploitation of a prototype is no longer required and the prototypes developed in laboratory environments are included in the definition of industrial development, which entails that higher percentage of aid may be granted for such activities).[124]

PCP could be exempted under these rules, whether deployed as individual aid or as an aid scheme. The main disadvantage, besides the administrative obligations meant to enable an ex post control, is that the contracting authority will only be able to reimburse part of the eligible costs, with a maximum of 80 % of the industrial research and 60 % of the experimental development costs.

The above described cumulative conditions to benefit of an assumption of compliance with EU State aid rules, can be summarized in the following visual form (see Fig. 7.3).

---

[120] Commission 2014b, Article 7(1).

[121] Commission 2014b, Article 9.

[122] Commission 2014b, Article 6(2).

[123] Commission 2014b, Article 6(3)(b).

[124] Commission 2014b, Article 2(85) and Commission 2014a, point 15(q). See also von Wendland 2015, 27.

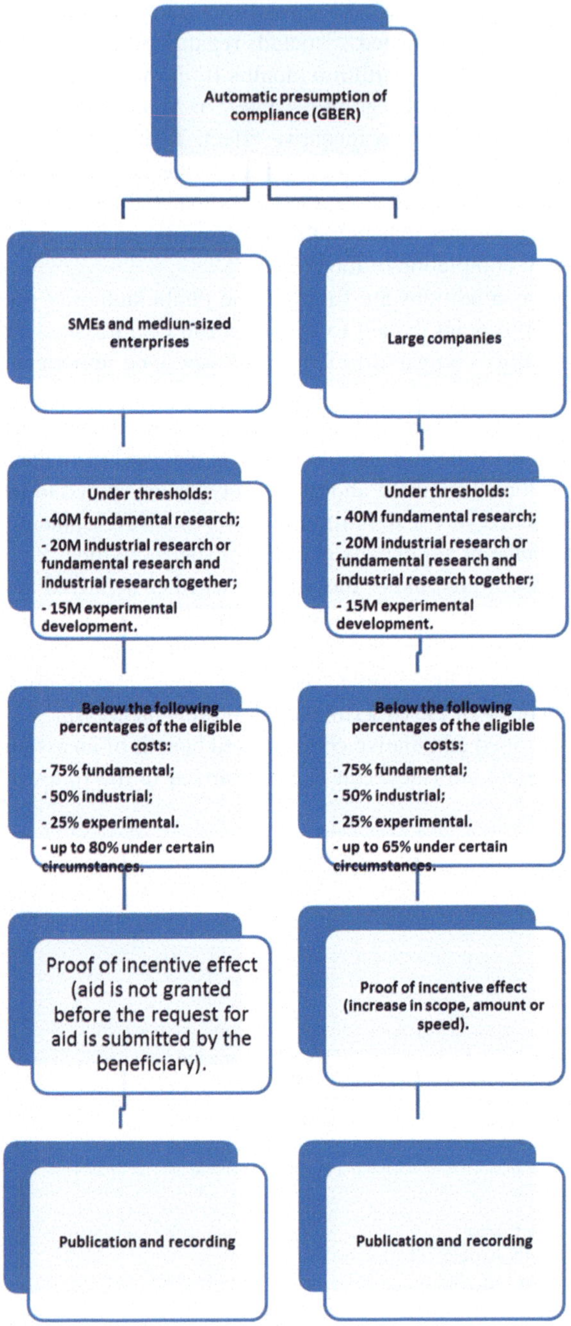

Fig. 7.3 Cumulative conditions to benefit of an assumption of compliance with EU State aid rules

Aid to SMEs or large companies, which are not covered by GBER (such as aids above the value thresholds of 20 million for industrial research and 15 million for experimental development), remains under the scope of the 2014 Framework for State aid for R&D&I and needs to be notified for prior approval to the European Commission.[125] The Framework allows higher intensities of aid for projects of large value. But, such aid will be closely scrutinized by the Commission following the formal notification. The obligation to repay aid in case of commercial revenues generated of the developed prototype has been replaced by an ex ante assessment of the potential future revenues and their deduction from the allowed aid.[126]

Under the 2014 Framework, aid may only be justified if the Commission is satisfied that all of the following criteria are fulfilled:

- the aid aims to increase the level of R&D&I in the Union (e.g. the measure is an integral part of a comprehensive and rigorously justified R&D&I strategy/plan, ex-post impact assessment is envisaged).[127]
- the aid measure is needed to raise the level of R&D, where the market, on its own, fails to deliver (e.g. the Member State should explain how the measure can effectively address the market failures that lead to suboptimal levels of R&D. The 2014 Framework defines 3 types of market failures: positive externalities/knowledge spillovers, imperfect and asymmetric information and coordination and network failures.[128]
- the proposed aid measure is appropriate to achieve its objectives (the Member State demonstrates that there are no less distortive instruments that can address the market failure concerned with the same or better results)[129];
- the aid should incentivize the beneficiary undertaking to extend its activity, or change its approach or location (in any case the activity may not be started before the aid application is submitted by the beneficiary; e.g. show that the project would not be profitable, but would create significant benefits for society)[130];
- the aid should be proportional (not more than needed to induce the desired change in behaviour)[131]; This means, among others, than only certain percentages of the eligible costs of the R&D project may be compensated (100 % for fundamental research, 50 % for industrial research and 25 % for experimental research) with similar possibilities to the GBER to raise the intensities (e.g. up to 80 % of the industrial research costs for SMEs subject to effective collaboration with at least one other undertaking).[132]

[125] Commission 2014a, Section 1.2 para 13.

[126] Commission 2014a, para 87.

[127] Commission 2014a, Section 4.1.

[128] Commission 2014a, Section 4.2 para 49.

[129] Commission 2014a, Section 4.3.

[130] Commission 2014a, Section 4.4.

[131] Commission 2014a, Section 4.5.

[132] Commission 2014a, Annex II.

- the negative effects of the aid on competition and trade are sufficiently limited and do not outweigh the benefits (e.g. the subsidy does not support inefficient undertakings or discourage competitors from investing in R&D, does not increase or maintain market power of certain undertakings in the detriment of consumers etc.).[133]
- all relevant information about the aid measure is available and easily accessible and records are kept for 10 years.[134]

In addition to the above cumulative criteria, the Commission may require that the aid scheme is subject to ex post evaluation by the Member State. This will be the case for aid schemes that present a high distortive potential (presumed in case of large budgets, novel characteristics or significant market, technology or regulatory changes). The draft evaluation plan needs to be submitted at the time of notification. The Commission may decide to limit the aid scheme to a period of four (4) years or less and make the extension subject to re-notification and positive assessment of the performed evaluation (this means that the evaluation needs to be performed while the scheme is still ongoing). The Commission will weigh in the decision to allow extension of the scheme, whether the improvements recommended by the evaluation report are taken into consideration.[135]

This can be visualised as follows (Fig. 7.4).

In a separate Communication, the Commission describes the criteria by which it will assess the compatibility of important projects of common European interest (including R&D projects) with Article 107(3)(b).[136] A project will be considered to be of common European interest based on the following criteria: benefits are not confined to the financing Member States or to the participating undertakings (for example, spillovers for society, improvements to EU's position in R&D&I on the international market through the development of new technologies or creation of new markets), it is rolled-out in collaborative manner by authorities from different Member States, the European Commission is involved in the design and governance of the project, participation is open to any Member State etc.[137] On a case-by-case basis, the Commission will determine the allowed aid intensity. Although co-financing by the beneficiary is encouraged,[138] funding of up to 100 % of the project's eligible costs may be permitted.[139] The Communication also defines specific criteria to be complied with by R&D projects. These favour projects that significantly advance the state-of-the-art in the sector concerned[140] and entail '*a very considerable level of technological or financial risk*'.[141]

133 Commission 2014a, para 4.6.

134 Commission 2014a, Sections 4.7 and 6.

135 Commission 2014a, paras 37, 121 and 123. See also von Wendland 2015, 49–50.

136 Commission 2014c.

137 Commission 2014c, Section 3.2.

138 Commission 2014c, Section 3.2.1 para 18.

139 Commission 2014c, Section 4.1 para 31.

140 Commission 2014c, Section 3.2.3 paras 21–22.

141 Commission 2014c, Section 3.3 para 24.

Fig. 7.4 Assessment of aid not covered by GBER

Once established the common European interest, the Commission applies a necessity and proportionality test as well as an overall balancing test, in order to conclude on the appropriateness of the amount and type of aid.[142]

In conclusion, the new State aid rules for R&D&I have increased the possibility to grant subsidies without prior approval by the European Commission. Up to 60 % and a maximum of € 15 million can be granted to an undertaking for the testing of prototypes in real environments (corresponding to PCP Phase 3) and even up to 80 % and maximum of 20 million reimbursement of eligible industrial research costs for SMEs (corresponding to PCP Phase 2). The standard ceilings for reimbursements can even be exceeded in important projects of common European interest. The European Commission plays the important role of overseeing that aid is appropriate and does not distort competition or harm trade between Member States. The Commission's role is to prevent a wasteful subsidy race between Member States. To this end, it performs a case-by-case assessment.

[142] Commission 2014c, Sections 4.1.

However, the administrative burden of notifying aid and the restriction on the amount of reimbursed costs limit the attractiveness of a PCP with a State aid element.

7.5 The Obligation to Ensure a 'Level Playing Field'

As illustrated in Sect. 7.3.3, a contracting authority will not always be able to conduct direct negotiations for the purchase of a PCP solution in accordance with the current EU Procurement Directives. It will most of the times be required to conduct a separate competitive procurement.

Within the framework of such a competitive procurement, a PCP finalist has significantly improved chances to win the contract, due to the knowledge/IPR acquired during the PCP, and due to the possibility to offer the product at a lower price (as the contracting authority has gained during the PCP the right to freely use the developed product/service).

These circumstances are often considered by contracting authorities (at least in Belgium, Denmark and the Netherlands) as reasons, to exclude the PCP finalist from the later award procedure for the purchase of the developed novel product.[143]

Below I investigate to what extent these concerns are justified. More concretely, I analyze whether the equal treatment principle and the derived obligation to ensure a level playing field allow the public procurer to use in the commercial procurement the same demanding requirements as during the PCP. Additionally, I examine to what extent the contracting authority is mandated to neutralize the advantages possessed by a PCP finalist.

The obligation of a contracting authority to ensure a level playing field for bidders stems out of the principles of equal treatment,[144] and transparency. The principle of equal treatment is meant to '*promote the development of healthy and effective competition between undertakings taking part in a public procurement procedure*'.[145] This principle obliges the contracting authority to afford all tenderers '*equality of opportunity when formulating their tenders, which therefore implies that the tenders of all competitors must be subject to the same conditions*'.[146]

---

143 Izsak and Edler 2011, 18.

144 The equal treatment principle requires that comparable situations must not be treated differently and that different situations must not be treated in the same way unless such treatment is objectively justified. See, for example, CJEU, *Sermide* v *Cassa Conguaglio Zucchero and Others*, Judgment, C-106/83 [1984] ECR 4209 para 28, CJEU, *Spain* v *Council*, Judgment, C-203/86 [1988] ECR 4563 para 25, and CJEU, *SMW Winzersekt v Land Rheinland-Pfalz*, Judgment, C-306/93 [1994] ECR I-5555 para 30.

145 CJEU, *Commission of the European Communities v CAS Succhi di Frutta SpA*, Judgment, C-496/99 [2004] ECR I-3801 paras 110–111.

146 Ibid. para 110; CFI, *Brinks Security Luxembourg v Commission*, Judgment T-437/05 [2009] ECR II-3233 paras 112–115; CFI, *European Network* v *Commission*, Judgment, T-332/03 [2008] ECR II-32 para 125.

Moreover contracting authorities are not allowed to formulate strict technical specifications which *unjustifiably* restrict the access of economic operators to the procurement procedure.[147]

The transparency principle mandates the contracting authority to make relevant information available to all bidders.

Important guidance on the interpretation of these principles has been provided in case-law of the Court of Justice of the EU ('CJEU'). In the Fabricom case,[148] the European judge decided that automatic exclusion of bidders who had previously carried out research, experiments, studies, or development in connection with that procurement was disproportionate and breached the equal treatment principle. According to the Court the firm should be allowed to prove that its involvement in the pre-procurement preparations did not create a risk to competition. The Court did not clarify though whether a contracting authority would be *mandated* to exclude a firm when there is a risk to competition or when the firm involved in the pre-procurement preparations cannot prove there is no risk to competition. But this would be the logical conclusion.

In a subsequent case, the Court of First Instance (CFI) confirmed that the public procurer is not mandated to neutralize *all* the advantages enjoyed by a tenderer as a result of a previous contractual relation,[149] particularly when this is not technically easy and economically acceptable or it infringes the rights of that tenderer (such as IP rights).[150] The Court clarified that the existing contractor and its subcontractors have an '*inherent* de facto *advantage*' whenever they decide to participate in the re-tendering of the contract, which is not the consequence of any conduct on the part of the contracting authority.[151]

However, the public procurer must protect as far as possible the principle of equal treatment and must avoid all consequences which are contrary to its own interests. As a consequence, it should convey all relevant information for the bidder to understand which level of quality and price he needs to offer, unless that

[147] Articles 23(2) Directive 2014/24/EU and 34(2) Directive 2014/24/EU: '*Technical specifications shall afford equal access for tenderers and not have the effect of creating unjustified obstacles to the opening up of public procurement to competition*'.

[148] CJEU, *Fabricom v Belgian State*, Judgment, Joined Cases C-21/03 and C-34/03, 3 March 2005 [2005] I-1559 paras 32–36.

[149] In this case, one company complained that the sitting contractor did not have to follow the 3 months "run in phase" and had an advantage because it did not have to make these costs.

[150] *Concordia*, above n 147, paras 75–76. CFI, *European Dynamics v Commission*, Judgment T-345/03 [2008] ECR II-341 para 73.

[151] Ibid. para 70: 'In that regard, it should be pointed out that the fact that an advantage may be conferred upon an existing contractor by a running-in phase is not the consequence of any conduct on the part of the contracting authority. Unless such a contractor were automatically excluded from any new call for tenders or, indeed, were forbidden from having part of the contract subcontracted to it, it is inevitable that an advantage will be conferred upon the existing contractor or the tenderer connected to that party by virtue of a subcontract, since it is inherent in any situation in which a contracting authority decides to initiate a tendering procedure for the award of a contract which has been performed, up to that point, by a single contractor. That fact constitutes, in effect, an 'inherent de facto advantage.'

information is protected by intellectual property rights or confidentiality.[152] It should also use precise criteria, such as not to favor the incumbent contractor, who based on previously gained knowledge, finds himself in a better position to assess the real needs of the public procurer and to formulate a better offer.[153]

In another case, the CJEU ruled that the principle of equal treatment does not mandate a public procurer to exclude entities that had previously received subsidies, despite their ability to submit lower priced tenders. The CJEU considered that the legislator would have stated such a prohibition explicitly, had it so desired.[154] This clarification of the CJEU is important for the case of PCPs with a State aid element.

Whether a contracting authority is mandated by the equal treatment principle to downgrade its requirements in order to ensure that a large number of potential bidders can submit a compliant offer has also been answered negatively in Sect. 7.3.3.3.[155] Two undertakings would in this case be treated differently only because they are not in identical situations. Such restrictive requirements are justified if they are appropriate to the specific nature of the public task[156] and if they are not formulated with the only objective of favouring one bidder (the PCP finalist).[157] Such requirements could possibly be acceptable even if indirectly discriminatory, but in any case when they are non-discriminatory.[158]

In conclusion, the advantages accumulated by a PCP finalist in terms of knowledge/IPR and costs are inherent advantages and such a bidder does not have to be excluded from participation in the post-PCP procurement procedure. A contracting authority should though make all the necessary information available to the other tenderers, unless it regards information protected by IPR and should define all the requirements clearly.

This is not the same as being mandated to ensure that a large number of bidders comply with the requirements. A contracting authority is allowed to formulate during the commercial procurement the same demanding requirements for the desired product/service as it did in the preceding PCP procedure. The fact that only the

---

[152] Ibid. paras 183–203.

[153] CFI, *Evropaïki Dynamiki v European Investment Bank*, Judgment, T-461/08 [2011] paras 149–150.

[154] CJEU, *Consorzio Nazionale Interuniversitario per le Scienze del Mare (Conisma) v Regione Marche*, Judgment, C-305/08, ECR 2009 I-12129, para 40.

[155] *Concordia*, above n 147, para 86: '*the principle of equal treatment does not preclude the taking into consideration of criteria.... solely because the contracting entities owned transport undertaking is one of the few undertakings able to offer a bus fleet satisfying those criteria*'.

[156] *Brinks Security v Commission*, above n 145, paras 120–121. Based on case CJEU *Evans Medical and Macfarlan Smith*, Judgment, C-324/93 [1995] ECR I-563, the Advocate-General argued in the Concordia case that criteria are not allowed, only if they could not be justified objectively, having regard to the characteristics of the contracts and needs of the CA (para 151).

[157] However, if the winning tenderer also helped in the preparation of the tender, that might be an indication that the award requirements were unduly restricted. CJEU *Ismeri Europa* v *Court of Auditors*, Judgment, C-315/99 [2001] ECR I-5281 para 47.

[158] Arrowsmith and Kunzlik 2009, 63.

PCP-finalist(s) might be able to submit a compliant offer, does not entail a breach of the principles of equal treatment.

7.6 Conclusions

In this chapter I explored the legal rules that underlie three important barriers to the wide and efficient implementation of PCP: (1) the obligation to conduct a separate competitive award in order to purchase the innovative solution targeted by the PCP competition, and (2) the legal uncertainty regarding compliance with EU State aid rules; (3) the perceived obligation to exclude PCP finalists from the subsequent commercial procurement.

I concluded in Sect. 7.3 that GPA allows the purchase of first products/services developed during a PCP, without competition, even when the PCP participants are required to locate a significant share of the R&D activities within the EU or an associated country. This option can be employed whenever the public procurer is not able to retain the first products as part of PCP Phase 3, because the value of the first products exceeds the value of R&D services.[159]

For the purchase of commercial volumes of the PCP solution, the public procurer may rely on the technical grounds offered by the EU Procurement Directives to conduct negotiations without competition. This will be possible when the PCP yielded just 1 finalist, who developed a groundbreaking innovation, for which there are no reasonable alternatives or substitutes available on the market. The requirement that '*no reasonable alternative or substitute exists on the market*' does not constrain the freedom of a contracting authority to define its needs in ambitious terms of functionality and performance.

The newly introduced innovation partnerships seem to have eliminated the first barrier altogether. However, the procedure was adopted under increasing pressure of national interests and fails to strike an adequate balance between European innovation and competition interests. In the absence of a thorough economic assessment, innovation partnerships may worsen the conditions for competition in the Single Market and may eventually stifle or slow down innovation. The partnerships are particularly harmful when they shield one private provider from competitive pressure over long periods of time.

The European Commission, in its role as guardian of the Single market, adopted restrictive application grounds in the 2014 Framework for State aid for R&D&I, with the purpose to restrict the use of innovation partnerships. An innovation partnership will only benefit of a market conformity presumption, when it targets the development and purchase of unique or specialized products and involves all capable providers. On the other side, the 2014 Framework for

159 In this case the contract would qualify as a supply contract. Supply contracts need to be procured in accordance with the Procurement Directives.

State aid for R&D&I, simplifies the use of PCP. It basically creates a presumption of market conformity for PCPs, as defined by the Commission in its 2007 Communication. It appears that the Commission chose PCP over innovation partnerships, as means to advancing EU's innovation policy agenda from the demand-side, seemingly unaware of the lingering pitfalls.

In Sect. 7.4, I argued that the Commission missed the opportunity in the new State aid rules, to clarify that PCP is a procurement and a demand instrument, only when it develops solutions for the direct benefit and use by the deploying procurer and only when it closely involves the public end-user. When the solution is developed for a broader policy objective, it is an R&D subsidy, that should be scrutinized in accordance with the Framework for State aid for R&D&I. I also argued that the end-user/customer is already implied in condition (d) of para 33, according to which IPR or at least a free license to use the developed innovation are granted to the public purchaser. The Commission should though expressly state this, in order to effectively tackle the second barrier addressed in this chapter.

When PCP deviates from the 2014 Framework conditions (e.g. the recommended IPR sharing), it should be notified and approved by the European Commission prior to its deployment. I concluded that the most important difference between a procurement-based PCP and a subsidy-based PCP consists in the funding limitation to less than 100 % of the eligible contract costs as well as in additional administrative burdens.

I finally discussed in Sect. 7.5 the third barrier perceived by some public procurers, namely the obligation to neutralize the inherent advantages of a PCP finalist or even exclude him from a post-PCP commercial procurement. I concluded that the equal treatment principle does not mandate the public procurer to exclude the PCP finalist(s) or to lower the ambitious level of functionality or performance. The equal treatment principle neither mandates him to neutralize an inherent price or technical advantage. It does, however, require the public procurer to provide all relevant information (in precise terms) to all competitors (unless the information is protected by IPR or confidentiality).

References

Agency NL (2011) SBIR handleiding voor ondernemers. http://www.agentschapnl.nl/sites/default/files/bijlagen/SBIR%20handleiding%202011-1.pdf. Accessed 18 Dec 2013

Apostol AR (2012) Pre-commercial procurement in support of innovation: regulatory effectiveness? PPLR 21: 212

Arrowsmith S (2002) Reviewing the GPA: the role and development of the plurilateral agreement after Doha. J Int Econ Law 5: 761

Arrowsmith S (2003) Government procurement in the WTO. Kluwer Law International, vol 16

Arrowsmith S, Kunzlik P (2009) Social and environmental policies in EC procurement law—new directives and new directions. Cambridge University Press, Cambridge

Chalmers D, Hadjiemmanuil C, Monti G, Tomkins A (2006) European Union law: text and materials. Cambridge University Press, Cambridge

Chalmers D, Davies G, Monti G (2010) European Union Law, 2nd edn. Cambridge University Press

Commission (2005) State aid action plan: less and better targeted state aid: a roadmap for state aid reform 2005–2009. Consultation document. COM(2005) 107 final 3
Commission (2006) Community framework for state aid for research and development and innovation. OJ C 323/1
Commission (2007a) Example of a possible approach for procuring R&D services applying risk-benefit sharing at market conditions, i.e. pre-commercial procurement. SEC(2007) 1668
Commission (2007b) Pre-commercial procurement: driving innovation to ensure sustainable high quality public services in Europe. COM 799 final
Commission (2012) Communication on the application of the European Union State aid rules to compensation granted for the provision of services of general economic interest (2012/C 8/02)
Commission (2014a) Framework for state aid for research and development and innovation (2014/C 198/01)
Commission (2014b) Regulation (EU) no 651/2014 of 17 June 2014 declaring certain categories of aid compatible with the Common Market in application of Articles 107 and 108 of the Treaty. OJ 187/2
Commission (2014c) Criteria for the analysis of the compatibility with the internal market of state aid to promote the execution of important projects of common European interest (2014/C 188/02)
Commission (2016) Policy related frequently asked questions on pre-commercial procurement (PCP) and the link with public procurement of innovative solutions (PPI). http://cordis.europa.eu/fp7/ict/pcp/docs/faq-v9.pdf. Accessed 30 Jan 2013
Consolidated version of the Treaty on the Functioning of the European Union 9.5.2008 OJEU C 115/47 (TFEU)
Hall H, Lerner J (2010) The financing of R&D and innovation. In: Hall BH, Rosenberg N (eds) Economics of innovation, vol 1. Elsevier, Amsterdam
Izsak K, Edler J (2011) Trends and challenges in demand-side innovation policies in Europe Thematic Report 2011 under specific contract for the integration of INNO policy trend chart with ERAWATCH (2011–2012). http://ec.europa.eu/enterprise/newsroom/cf/_getdocument.cfm?doc_id=7011. Accessed 2 Feb 2013
Moravcsik A (2005) The European constitutional compromise and the neofunctionalist legacy. J Eur Public Policy 12:349
Nicholas C (2011) Work of UNCITRAL on government procurement: purpose, objectives and complementarity with the work of the WTO 766. In: Arrowsmith S, Anderson RD (eds) The WTO regime on government procurement: challenge and reform. Cambridge University Press, Cambridge
Obradovic D (1996) Policy legitimacy and the European Union. Journal of Common Market Studies 34:208
OECD (2002) Proposed standard practice for surveys on research and experimental development. OECD Publications Service
Rigby J (2013) Impact assessment of pre-commercial procurement. In: Presentation at the OECD workshop on measuring the link between public procurement, R&D and Innovation, 5–6 Dec 2013
Sanchez-Graells A (2016) A deformed principle of competition? The subjective drafting of Article 18(1) of Directive 2014/24. In: Olykke GS, Sanchez-Graells A (eds) Reformation or deformation of the EU public procurement rules in 2014. Edward Elgar Publishing, Cheltenham
Single European Act (SEA) (1986) OJ L169
Treaty of Amsterdam (1997) OJ C340
Treaty of Maastricht on the European Union (1992) OJ C191
Treaty of Rome establishing the European Economic Community (1957) (not published)
TSB (2011) SBRI—government challenges, ideas from businesses, innovative solutions. http://www.innovateuk.org/_assets/sbri_brochure_2011.pdf. Accessed 5 Feb 2013
von Wendland B (2015) New rules for state aid for research, development and innovation: not a revolution but a silent reform. EStAL 1
Zielonka J (2001) How new enlarged borders will reshape the European Union. J Common Market Stud 39

Chapter 8
Concluding Remarks—the Case for EU Coordination of R&D Procurement

This book outlined the trials and tribulations in the implementation of pre-commercial procurement in the European Union up to 2016. PCP was proposed by the European Commission in 2007 as part of a solutions to enhance Europe's competitiveness on the global market and to incentivize the development of solutions to important European problems (such as climate change, ageing, shortage of natural resources etc.). PCP was also advanced as a means to make the public sector more efficient and more performant, in an era of declining economic stability and growth.

Due to its perceived success in bringing innovative technologies to the market and in boosting the competitive advantages of national businesses, the US SBIR program constituted the primary source of emulation. However, the PCP configuration was adapted to the applicable EU laws and realities. As a consequence, PCP embodies major differences from the US SBIR program. The European Commission did not assess the impact of these differences on the effectiveness of PCP.

I concluded in this book that some of these differences do not only discourage PCP deployment,[1] but also weaken its efficacy. I outline below the most important ones.

1. Unlike the US SBIR, PCP was not set-up as a program with clear responsibilities and budgets, under the coordination and supervision of the European Commission.

This is due to the limited competences the European Commission possesses in the area of innovation policy. These competences are mostly limited to defining actions to achieve innovation goals and to monitoring the results, while implementation is left to the Member States. This leaves the European Commission with no direct enforcement mechanisms, besides evidence-based arguments to persuade and leverage peer pressure.

[1] Public procurers invoke lack of expertise in deploying PCP, impossibility to purchase directly the R&D outcomes and the unclear State aid rules As the main barriers to wide implementation.

R. Apostol, *Trials and Tribulations in the Implementation of Pre-Commercial Procurement in Europe*, DOI 10.1007/978-94-6265-156-2_8

Due to these limited competences, the European Commission recommended PCP by means of a Communication, which is not a mandatory instrument. The Communication explained how the applicable legal rules prevent non-competitive and nationally restricted PCP awards, but barely addressed the (economic) conditions for effective implementation.

Assessment studies performed at the request of the European Commission show very few instances of PCP deployment outside those funded under FP7 and Horizon 2020. This shows that legal guidance and co-funding are not sufficient to trigger wide deployment of PCP. At the same time, studies show that the EU is not increasing its overall levels of investment in R&D procurement, which suggests that no alternative R&D procurement initiatives are emerging.

2. Unlike in the US, where public procurers are encouraged and even held accountable if they don't purchase the SBIR results, the PCP excludes direct purchase of resulting innovations.

This feature was indicated by European public procurers as a main barrier to wide deployment of PCP. The Commission justified this choice by the desire to attract international competition, while requiring participating companies to locate a large share of their R&D and operational activities in the EU or an associated country. According to the Commission, this 'location' requirement would only be allowed by the WTO Government Procurement Agreement (GPA) when the resulting innovation is purchased through a separate competitive award that does not discriminate against GPA parties. This is in line with EU's previous choice to exclude only R&D contracts from the scope of the GPA, and not supply contracts.

I concluded in this book that the public procurer may retain the resulting product from PCP Phase 3 for operational use, as long as the contract can still be qualified as an R&D services contract.[2] When this is not the case, I argued that the GPA allows the direct purchase of *first* products or services resulting from a PCP, in spite of the 'location' requirement. The possibility to purchase first products without competition has been translated into the Procurement Directives. However, the public procurer is not allowed to purchase commercial volumes of the desired solution, unless s/he can demonstrate that certain functionalities and certain levels of performance are not met by other products on the market and that the PCP finalist possesses unique expertise to deliver its innovative solution. But reliance on these provisions for the direct purchase of a PCP result is not expressly mentioned by the 2014 Procurement Directives. As a consequence, individual contracting authorities may perceive legal risks in pursuing such an approach.

I also concluded that the Commission's decision to separate the commercial procurement from PCP is rooted in the desire to prevent distortive applications of PCP (such as the national policy-oriented PCP-like initiatives analysed in

[2] This means that the value of the R&D services exceeds the value of the other activities in the contract.

Chap. 6), rather than legal constraints posed by the GPA. In practice, the chances of a challenge by a GPA party are extremely remote. Contorting the EU innovation policy to avoid the possibility of such a challenge seems illogical—unless they are really for the purpose of preventing the deployment of market distortive procurements.

In 2014, the EU legislator seems to have deliberately assumed the risk of breaching the GPA, by allowing the development and subsequent purchase of an innovative solution within the framework of one innovation partnership. The legislator did not clarify whether these partnerships should be open to GPA competition and whether the procurer should require that a large share of the R&D be located within the EU or an associated country. It is though difficult to imagine that national procurers will be willing to finance R&D trajectories which not only take place outside their national borders, but even outside the EU.

Innovation partnerships are more appealing to public procurers than PCPs, as they do not entail additional procedural burdens, while allowing procurers to purchase the R&D outcomes, without reopening competition. This should be welcomed for encouraging public procurer to play the role of demanding customers and early adopters of needed innovations.

However, I argued in this book that the legislator has not created sufficient safeguards to ensure an effective and non-distortive working of this instrument. In the absence of thorough economic assessments, innovation partnerships may worsen the conditions for competition in the Single Market and may eventually stifle or slow down innovation. The negative effects are particularly harmful when the procedure shields one private provider from competitive pressure over long periods of time. More specifically, this may lead to reduced R&D investments by competitors (crowding-out effect) or to the market exit of more efficient competitors.

With similar concerns in mind, the Commission decided to tip the scales in favor of PCP. While clarifying that PCP deployed in line with several conditions mentioned in the PCP Communication will benefit of a presumption of market conformity, the Commission suggested that it will scrutinize for State aid all innovation partnerships, besides those targeting the development of 'unique or specialized products'. I argued in this book, that the Commission will interpret the concept of 'unique or specialized products' restrictively. Arguably, innovation partnerships will only benefit of a presumption of market compliance and will not need to be notified to the Commission, when:

- they target the development of products whose only potential buyer is the procuring authority; and
- they involve all those providers that are capable of developing and supplying the innovation.

The limitation on the use of innovation partnerships was included in a footnote to the Framework for State aid for R&D&I, without express reference to the new procedure. Such an approach creates legal uncertainty and in practice deters procurers from engaging in such partnerships. At the same time, the Commission's efforts to trigger widespread PCP deployment instead are not (yet) paying off.

In conclusion, although the Commission's approach is understandable in the context of a union of national states with diverging interests, it is not conducive of effective R&D procurement practices that can potentially achieve EU's ambitious goals.

3. Unlike the US SBIR, PCP does not introduce a clear demarcation between procurement contracts and State aid (subsidies).

Within the US SBIR the difference between the SBIR contracts and SBIR grants is clear: SBIR contracts address operational needs of public end-users/customers while SBIR grants (the term used in the US for 'subsidies') aim to develop innovations for private end-users.

In the EU, the European Commission chose a muddled approach. The Commission did not define a clear distinction between R&D contracts and R&D subsidies such as in the US, depending on whether the PCP is developing innovations for the direct benefit and use by a public authority, or for broader public objectives. In the current context, PCP can be applied in both situations, while being labelled as 'procurement' and as 'demand-side' instrument in its entirety. I pointed out in this book that unclear conceptualization of PCP is deterring public procurers from engaging in its deployment.

Initially, the Commission defined the 'market price' criterion to limit the ongoing practice of innovation agencies in several Member States, that deployed subsidy-like schemes under the label of R&D procurement. I argued that the 'market price' criterion was inadequate for being easily circumvented by the innovation agencies and for posing an additional burden on those procurers with truly stringent needs. In 2014, the Commission defined several conditions in the Framework for State aid for R&D&I, that cumulatively create a presumption that no state aid is granted during the PCP. However, the Commission missed again the opportunity to clarify the relation between PCP and subsidies and to provide economic guidance on the effective implementation of PCP.

Arguably, this muddled approach was motivated by the Commission's desire to use its broad competences in the area of State aid, to scrutinize potentially harmful R&D procurements. In the absence of competences to define and enforce economic tests in the R&D procurement area, the European Commission imposed restrictions to the use of innovation partnerships and to the direct purchase of PCP results, while not addressing the conditions for wide and effective PCP deployment.

The 17 ongoing PCPs deployed by cross-border consortia of public procurers with EU funding and under the direct supervision of the European Commission (funded under the FP7 and Horizon 2020) are not sufficient to fulfil the policy expectations or to trigger wide PCP deployment. The EU continues (and even intensifies) funding efforts—seemingly unaware of the reasons why its efforts do not generate the expected results in practice.

Public procurers, who may act as demanding customers of innovations, are left without crucial guidance for effectively deployment, while at the same time being deterred by the risk of breaching State aid rules.

This book showed that the Commission's concerns that R&D procurement would be poised by ineffective and potentially harmful practices, are justified. Particularly the Flemish PCPs and the NL SBIR competitions are biased towards support of national companies. They use legitimate mechanisms, such as national language requirements or restricted participation in market consultations preceding the PCP. The national policy aims are by themselves legitimate. However, due to this approach the national initiatives tend to protect national companies from foreign competition. They may thus waste public funds on solutions that already exist elsewhere, instead of driving national companies to advance the international state-of-the-art and gain global competitive advantages. As a consequence, it is doubtful that the national initiatives are capable to achieve their policy objectives.

The strategic deployment of R&D procurement to the benefit of the whole EU economy would therefore, profit from a more hands-on coordination at EU level. Scarce resources could be bundled and channeled towards the development of truly valuable solutions to the challenges faced by the EU in this era. Coordination could among others, be achieved by:

- setting up a Commission service/team dedicated to the coordination of cross-border PCPs;
- identifying common needs in collaboration with public end-users from various Member States;
- checking the feasibility of fulfilling the public needs by the development of innovative solutions within certain timeframes, and establishing state-of-the-art by means of market consultation, patent searches etc.
- checking PCP topics against the technological paths and market trends;
- training public procurers with the purpose to enhance understanding of the rationale and methodology for PCP deployment;
- encouraging public procurers to purchase the PCP results;
- facilitating the communication between public procurers with shared needs.

The Commission has not paid so far much attention to economic considerations that could ensure the achievement of PCP's objectives (incentivize increased private investments in R&D, steer private R&D investments towards socially desirable innovations, improve the competitive position of EU firms in global markets). Based on relevant economic literature, this book identified the following prerequisites:

1. The PCP portfolio includes a large number of high-risk R&D projects, which entail large costs at early development stages and long-term returns on investment;
2. PCP programs focus particularly on young companies that experience difficulties in obtaining (sufficient amounts of) private capital;
3. PCP budgets are increased in times of economic downturn;
4. The selection of PCP projects is based on a careful consideration of technological trajectories and market trends such as to avoid lock-in. This entails that competition is maintained until uncertainty decreases and it becomes clear which innovation is the most valuable.

5. Managers in charge of PCP deployment possess or gain in-depth knowledge of the relevant technological area.
6. Failure is tolerated to a certain extent, in order to encourage PCP managers to choose risky R&D projects, instead of commercially promising (close-to-market) projects. For example, PCP programs should allow multiple sequential awards to the same company and for the same project, to allow the further development of a technology following the first PCP contract.
7. The public end-user is closely involved: provides data regarding their needs, provides input on tested prototypes, even helps with the development of the solutions.
8. The public end-user is willing to pay the premium price for the early use of the developed innovation and is capable to offer a sufficiently sizeable market for the developed innovation;
9. PCP should challenge and reward the most innovative companies, instead of shielding inefficient companies from foreign competition.
10. Innovative technologies rather than innovative services are targeted;
11. Scrutiny/measurement of the impact of PCP is regularly performed and lessons are codified.

The analysis and recommendations in this book must eventually be assessed politically, with the risk in mind that EU initiatives have currently to live in a climate where they can weaken rather than support the intrinsic motivation of Member States to participate in the Union. But this is beyond the scope of this book.

The manufacturer's authorised representative in the EU is Springer Nature Customer Service Centre GmbH, Europaplatz 3, 69115 Heidelberg, Germany. If you have any concerns regarding our products, please contact ProductSafety@springernature.com

Printed and bound by CPI Group (UK) Ltd, Croydon, CR0 4YY

30/09/2026

02225446-0003